Television and Social Change in Rural India

Television and Social Change
in Rural India

Kirk Johnson

Sage Publications
New Delhi * Thousand Oaks * London

First published in 2000 by

Sage Publications India Pvt. Ltd.
M–32 Market, Greater Kailash, Part 1
New Delhi 110 048

Sage Publications Inc.
2455 Teller Road
Thousand Oaks, California 91320

Sage Publications Ltd.
6 Bonhill Street
London EC2A 4PU

Published by Tejeshwar Singh for Sage Publications India Pvt. Ltd., photo-typeset by Line Arts, Pondicherry and printed at Chaman Enterprises, Delhi.

Library of Congress Cataloging-in-Publication Data
Johnson, Kirk, 1967–
    Television and social change in rural India/by Kirk Johnson.
        p. cm. (cloth) (pbk.)
    Includes bibliographical references and index.
    1. Television broadcasting—India. 2. Television—Social aspects—India.
3. India—Social conditions—1947– I. Title.
    HE8700.9.I5 J64   384.55'0954—dc21   2000   99–056221

ISBN: 0–7619–9421–1 (US HB)   81–7036–892–8 (India HB)
        0–7619–9422–X (US PB)   81–7036–893–6 (India PB)

Sage Production Team: Rishi Iyengar, Abantika Chatterji, R.A.M. Brown
and Santosh Rawat.

Dedication

To my beloved wife Sarah

This work would have never been thought out or written but for you. You have always been my source of inspiration, my light, and my love. Thank you for everything.

To my parents, Ray and LaNelma Johnson

Let me express my feelings in the traditional Hindu manner: I place my head at your feet and ask for your blessings.

Contents

List of Tables and Figures

Tables

Figures

Foreword

The recent Indo–Pak conflict in the Kargil sector of the Indian
state of Jammu and Kashmir brought out the powerful role
played by the electronic media in informing and actively involv-
ing a large section of the population throughout the country.
Unlike the earlier wars (of 1962, 1965, and 1971) when the spread
of television was limited in its programming and reach, this time
television channels enabled viewers to see Indian jawans in action
in difficult terrain and the great sacrifices they made. This media
coverage generated an unprecedented wave of sympathy and
support for the defense forces. It demonstrated once again the
power of television as a medium of communication.

Unfortunately, there are hardly any serious studies of the impact of television on Indian society and culture, particularly in
rural areas. The few studies that are available are largely in the
nature of quantitative surveys focusing on specific issues and dealing with the urban population. The present study conducted by
Dr Kirk Johnson is, therefore, a timely effort to fill this gap in our
knowledge. He attempts, first, to understand the dynamics of village life, and then, to explore the role of television in shaping the
social, economic, and political changes in the villages under study.

Dr Johnson is uniquely placed to take up such a study. Although
an American by birth, he spent thirteen years of his childhood in
a small town called Panchgani in western Maharashtra where his
father worked as the principal of an international residential
school. During this period he learnt the local language (Marathi)
and became familiar with the surrounding rural areas through
school activities. In 1995 he returned to the area as a McGill University doctoral student to undertake this study and he selected

two neighboring villages for this purpose. Thus he had the unique advantage of being an outsider (a foreigner) as well as an insider (like a native) with a knowledge of the local culture and society. This combination allows Johnson to observe and comment upon many nuances of people's attitudes and behavior. He is able to make note of many small details of behavior and mannerisms which a native often ignores due to familiarity; at the same time he is able to capture meanings of attitudes and behavior which are likely to be missed by a foreigner unfamiliar with the local language and culture.

Johnson chose to conduct an ethnographic study of two villages (one closer to the town and the other relatively remote) using the method of in-depth interviewing and participant observation appropriate to the field situation and the subject of study. This method enabled him to gain valuable insights into the villagers' lives. In the process, the people in his book come alive as individual human beings with distinct personalities rather than as mere numbers in tables. Moreover, Johnson has attempted a holistic study of village life while looking at the role of television in the ever-changing rural scenario affecting the aspirations, values, attitudes, relationships, and traditions of the villagers.

The study is based mainly on Danawli, a village in the Sahyadri hills once associated with the exploits of the 17th century Maratha hero, Shivaji. Johnson also introduces us briefly to Raj Puri, a village on the outskirts of Panchgani, to make some comparative observations. He describes the social structure of Danawli, including its caste system, landownership pattern, and the distribution of power. It is a small village of 104 households dominated by the regionally prominent caste, Maratha. The village is characterized by poor land, lack of irrigation facilities, and a relatively large population. Forty-seven per cent of the village men between 18 and 32 years of age migrate to work in Mumbai, nearly 300 km away.

After reviewing the literature on communication theory in general and television in particular, Johnson narrates the history of television in India since 1959 when it was first introduced. Color TV appeared in 1982, and the satellite explosion occurred in the early 1990s, offering viewers a choice of multiple channels and a variety of programs—a virtual revolution in the television field in India. The original objective of television programming was first to educate, then to inform, and last, to entertain the viewers. These priorities have been given up now in favor of entertainment, largely sustained by commercial sponsorship and advertising. The state-controlled Doordarshan is no exception to this. Its programs are by and large as entertainment-oriented as any other channel, although it does devote some time to programs useful to certain sections such as students and farmers.

Danawli was electrified in 1970, but the first television set appeared in the village only in 1985. By 1995, twenty-five of the 104 households had television sets. There is still no cable facility, so their viewing is confined to the national channel, Doordarshan. Only three landless households (out of twenty-three) possessed TV sets. All other television-owning households were of landowners. A television set has become an object of desire and status in the village, and several households were budgeting to buy one. A television set has also become an essential part of the dowry in village weddings.

While studying the role of television in the life of the villagers, Johnson proceeds systematically. He first describes the life of the villagers before the coming of television in the village. He gives a detailed account of the activities of members of a typical village household during the days prior to television. He then takes up five representative households which own televisions and spends one week with each of them for observation. He describes the day-long activities of a typical television-owning household. In addition, he selects a sample of fifty men, fifty women, and fifty children from households without televisions for in-depth interviews. Some of these people have access to TV programs in other people's houses in the village—their neighbors, friends or relatives, for instance. Much depends on the relationship between the households, because watching TV in another's house is like enjoying hospitality—people go only when they are sure that they are welcome. Such activities often lead to the creation of new relationships or the strengthening of existing ones.

Prior to the arrival of television in the village people followed what seemed like an age-old routine. They went to bed early, around 9.30 P.M., and woke early, around 5.00 A.M. On the whole they slept for longer hours. They also conversed more, talking among themselves in small groups according to age and gender.

Gossip was another means of passing time and of entertainment, and was also a source of information. Exposure to the external world was limited to radio programs (only a few households had radio sets) and to information conveyed by periodic visitors from Mumbai.

Information was also a source of power. It reinforced the economic and political power of the élite. The big landowners and village leaders enjoyed virtual monopoly over information due to their contacts with the outside world including the government bureaucracy and political leaders. They knew more about government rules and policies concerning land and agriculture, besides other matters. The poor and the landless learnt about these things only when the information percolated from the élite. The poorer sections on the whole suffered from a sense of dependence and deprivation.

The situation has changed with the arrival and spread of television in the village. Although less than 25 per cent of the households own television sets, in reality many others without them have access to TV programs. Thus, according to Johnson, only 11 per cent of the children, 32 per cent of the men, and 41 per cent of the women from non-owning households lack access to TV programs. Contrary to the belief in the literature, television in Danawli does not lead to social isolation or alienation of individuals. In fact, it cuts across age groups and gender, bringing people together. With television, there is now greater equality among villagers in acquiring useful information. However, a tiny information underclass has also emerged, a section lacking any access to television which suffers from a feeling of deprivation.

Life in the village is now not organized according to the sun's position, but according to the schedule of TV programs. People adjust their work and other activities so as not to miss their favorite programs. Men even share household chores to enable women to watch TV. The village is much quieter from the outside, but noisier within the homes, with the soundtrack of TV sets usually maintained at a high pitch.

Consumerism in general, and the desire for urban goods and an urban lifestyle in particular, have increased significantly. This is widely evident among the young whose aspirations are rising noticeably, so much so that the village elders are worried about the effects should these desires and aspirations fail to be met.

They also resent the increasing arrogance and lack of respect for elders among the village youth which they attribute to the evil effects of television. For these reasons some of them are not enthusiastic about the entry of television in the village. 'Television is ruining our culture,' they say.

Johnson makes another significant observation. There is now a palpable gap between verbal statements and actual behavior and action. Being exposed to enlightened views on various issues including caste, women, and marriage, the villagers have learnt to make politically correct statements, particularly in the presence of outsiders. But this does not mean that they follow or intend to follow these views in practice. They all express opposition to untouchability but practise it in subtle forms. Many of them, particularly the youth, favor what is called 'love marriage' or inter-caste marriage but no such marriage has been recorded in the village. Similarly, dowry is not openly defended, and sometimes it is even denigrated, but it is universally practised.

Johnson makes it clear that Danawli represents a transitional phase in the spread of television in rural India. Only twenty-five of the 104 households have TV sets at present, and that too with only one channel. But things are changing fast. Already TV has become an essential part of a girl's dowry. Very soon TV will become universal. Most households will have television sets in the near future, and that too with access to multiple channels. In Raj Puri, the village nearer Panchgani town, twenty-one of the forty-three Mahar (ex-untouchable) households have television sets, most of them with multiple channels. This is a sure indication of future developments in this area. The impact of such an expansion will be much more than what is currently happening in Danawli. It will have to be carefully observed and analyzed. Johnson's book will be a valuable and useful guide for future investigators.

The value of this book lies in the systematic and balanced analysis of television's impact on rural life. Johnson's preference for a qualitative approach yielded good results, including valuable insights into changes in village life. What helped him immensely was his familiarity with the local language and the fact that he had spent thirteen years in the area during childhood—a background that enabled him to approach the people under study with necessary empathy. As a result we have here a study which is

14 * *Television and Social Change in Rural India*

'educative, informative and entertaining,' to use the words which symbolized the original objectives of Indian television programming.

September 1999   B.S. Baviskar
                                                                 University of Delhi

Preface

India is a country marked by great contrasts. With the restructuring of the economy in recent years and a rapidly expanding middle class of close to a quarter of a billion people, India has emerged as an important and powerful player on the world scene. Today, millions of people living in India's cities are growing up in a culture familiar with cellular phones and pagers, luxurious cars, and lifestyles which mirror the values and goals of people living in places like London, Los Angeles, New York, Hong Kong, and Singapore. These Indian cities have elegant five-star hotels and restaurants, theaters, and museums. India boasts the largest cinema industry in the world, and major satellite companies are vying for control over the expanding television markets. Consumerism has reached unimaginable heights, and today Indians are growing up in an environment with goods, services, and economic mobility once only dreamed about.

What is happening in a village like Danawli or Raj Puri tucked away deep in the mountains of western India? Almost 75 per cent of India's one billion people live in villages such as these. How is this modernity that is now creeping into the daily lives of these villagers affecting them? What of the traditional and social institutions that date back centuries?

Television has, in recent years, changed India's villages forever. As India celebrated fifty years of Independence a variety of material improvements in village life could be cited. From electricity to water systems, health care to better roads, Indian villages are materially much improved from before. However, the one material commodity which has most dramatically influenced social change in rural India has been the television set.

This book is about the social environment of village life and the role of television in the ever-changing landscape of rural India. It delves into the lives of villagers and explores the impact of television on their aspirations, ideals, relationships, and traditions. It seeks to understand the role television plays in the social and economic development of these rural areas. With the focus on real people's lives and their voices, rather than a list of numbers and statistics, villages are described in the context of their evolving relationship with television and its role in the dynamics of social change. The student of development, its practitioners, and all those interested in topics such as media, social change, globalization, ethnographic methodologies, and rural India will find this book useful.

There are several processes at work in village India that relate to television's influence, and each has ramifications for development at the local level and beyond. These processes include consumerism, urban modeling, restructuring of human relationships, demographic change, linguistic hegemony, migration, and the emergence of an information underclass. Rural Maharashtrians are becoming active participants in the 'global village.'

This book presents data that illustrates change occurring on two levels, structural and psychological. The former centers on variables such as marriage, religion, and the relationships between people of different ages, castes, and genders, while the latter focuses on changes in attitudes, fears, values, images, opinions, and needs. To limit the analysis of the impact of television to psychological variables when trying to understand social change in general is to fall short of what is often its most significant aspect. An important element in any discussion of development communication is the social structure and the analysis of structural conflict. Too often discussions view villagers as a homogeneous group. These village studies make it evident that there is little to warrant such an assumption. Rural society is highly differentiated in terms of resource access, class, caste, and other divisions and is characterized by competition between various groups for scarce resources (Hartmann et al. 1989).

Most of the obstacles to change are structural rather than psychological or cultural; changing attitudes and ideas are important but insufficient on their own to make any real progress in altering the prevailing structures of inequality within village culture.

The arrival of television into the village has weakened many of these structural barriers.

Often researchers ask what the effects of television are on modernity, innovation, achievement motivation, and empathy. While these are important questions, they constitute a narrow approach which tells us little about village life and how television fits into that pattern. The focus is primarily on the individual without giving due consideration to structural forces. Such approaches are often criticized for their 'overriding emphasis on person-blame rather than system-blame' (Hartmann et al.,1989: 28). It is paramount for any research on processes of social change to analyze psychological variables along with the structural dynamics of community life. To more fully appreciate an individual's motivations and aspirations one must understand the structural context within which the individual lives. The problem of development is often in the system rather than in the psyche of the individual.

This is the framework in which the research was carried out. The research attempts to first understand the dynamics of village life and then explore the role of television in that context. An analysis of the political and economic aspects that determine television access, as well as the role of caste and gender in Indian rural life, it is hoped, will help contribute to a deeper understanding of the various processes at work in village India.

Acknowledgements

The years of research and writing that have culminated in this book have left me with many valuable friendships on two continents. Professor B.S. Baviskar, who is himself from rural Maharashtra, started me down this road with our initial meeting and discussions during a cold winter at McGill University in Montreal. He was gracious enough to visit me in Danawli during the research, and his advice and friendship were truly inspirational. I want to thank Professor Donald Von Eschen at McGill University for his keen insights, enthusiasm, and encouragement throughout the entire research process. He also provided valuable editorial and organizational assistance. I would like to recognize the department of sociology at McGill University for all its support through the years. In particular I would like to thank Luvana Di Francesco and Sharon Barqueiro for their enthusiastic assistance whenever I needed it. Professor Attwood's knowledge and experience of Indian culture, particularly in Maharashtra were invaluable, and his detailed editorial suggestions and other observations on village ethnographies are all much appreciated. I owe special thanks to Dr Eric Wager, a true mentor and friend from the earliest days of my graduate studies. His knowledge and guidance have been a source of constant encouragement and inspiration.

In India, there are more people than I can possibly acknowledge and thank in this short space. All those who were part of my life growing up in Panchgani have influenced me greatly. From my teachers and schoolmates, to my neighbors and friends, each played an important and unique role in shaping my life. After visiting the villages around Panchgani as a young boy and learning from the villagers about life, I can only say that if it were not for them I would not be the person I am today. I hesitate to name people individually for fear of overlooking some, but I must thank a few for their support and friendship in the early years of my life in India, and also those who acted as friends and family during the course of the research: the Whites, the Tafakiis, the Waites, the Millers, Viju Farahmand, the Javanmardis (particularly Shahram and Parvaneh), the Akhtarkavaris, the Mehrshais, the Karenchkas, the Afshins, and the Vasudevans. Finally, I would like to thank my childhood classmate, Mehraban Farahmand, who remains a cherished friend. His ability to find happiness and meaning in all aspects of daily life continues to inspire and amaze me.

This research would not have been possible if it were not for the people of Danawli and Raj Puri who welcomed me into their homes and lives and from whom I learned so much. I went to India to research the role of television in village life, but I gained much more. I developed an appreciation of the struggles and complexities of rural life. But more importantly I found the friendship of people who have forever made a lasting impression on me.

I am eternally grateful to Mary Wylie and John Ostlund for their continuous support, generosity, and encouragement over the years. I would also like to thank Alan and Connie Porth for sharing themselves and the farm with me. I am forever grateful to my parents, Ray and LaNelma Johnson, whose love and guidance have sustained me through the years. Their many sacrifices in India taught me to respect and learn from all people. Their firm beliefs, principles, and commitment to family remain an inspiration. To my sister LaRae, for her unconditional love and example of what it means to persevere. To my brother Craig, for his deep friendship, love, and his devotion to creativity, imagination, and adventure which taught me to live life to the fullest.

Finally, I would like to thank my wife Sarah because without her this book would never have been written. My numerous discussions with her helped bring much of the material into clearer focus, and her editorial advice helped me greatly. Her constant support throughout the years has allowed me to fulfill so many of my dreams. She gives my life meaning, is my spiritual companion, and she continues to be my best friend. I thank her with all my heart and soul.

Writing a book involves the minds and energies of a number of people besides the author. I would like to acknowledge my indebtedness to all my teachers, colleagues and friends who are scattered throughout the world from Asia to North America, and from the Middle East to the beautiful island nations of Micronesia. They have all been instrumental in my intellectual development and life's journey. I want to finally recognize the editorial team at Sage Publications in New Delhi—Rishi Iyengar, Abantika Chatterji, R.A.M. Brown and Santosh Rawat—for a job well done.

1

Introduction

The fresh air and morning dew cooled my face as I rode my motorcycle through the bazaar of Panchgani past the old temple and out over the mountainside. The mist and small clouds were beginning to rise far below in the surrounding valleys. This is the region in which the great Krishna River originates and where Shivaji, one of India's greatest warriors, fought and died. As I continued to ride along the narrow winding road I passed two old men herding water buffalo to the grassy hillsides for the day. Women made their way up the steep mountain slope balancing on their heads containers filled with milk to sell in town.

Upon entering Danawli, the village which soon became home, I noticed sights, smells, and sounds familiar to many small villages in this region. Smoke slowly seeped through the cracks in the walls of a few homes, a sign of breakfast on a wood stove. I could hear dogs barking in the distance, and the sound of clothes being beaten on rocks indicating that it was laundry day. And suddenly I wondered where the people were, and especially the children I was so used to seeing crowd the village streets at almost any time of the day. It was not uncommon for people to come up to me to begin a conversation as I entered a village. I stood out as a tall fair American. The children were usually most intrigued by me, sometimes even asking to touch my hair to see if it was real. But on this Sunday morning not a soul was to be found outside. The only time I remembered seeing a village this deserted was late at night, especially in these regions where leopards are known to roam at night catching the unsuspecting dog that wanders a little too far from home.

I had to investigate. I began walking through the village and heard some noise coming from inside one of the houses. I went up to the small doorway and bent over to look inside and what I saw fascinated me. It was a room full of people sitting on a cow dung floor with a thatch roof over their heads, all watching television. They did not acknowledge me until the commercial break, when their attention toward the small box in the corner decreased only slightly. They seemed to be enjoying the advertisements almost as much as the program itself. Suresh, whom I later discovered was the *Sarpanch* (headman) and who became a close friend, motioned for me to sit by him. When I did sit down I tried introducing myself with some small talk, but he simply gestured for me to be quiet and became engrossed in the television program that had begun.

I grew up not 20 miles from this village, at a time when television in the village was only a dream. It was an urban luxury. People in the small town where I grew up spent their leisure time with friends or family, enjoying the fresh mountain air while walking outside. When visiting villages we were welcomed into people's homes and would sit for hours drinking very hot, sweet milk tea, while talking about the weather, politics, or movies we had all seen when the *tamboo* (the traveling cinema) had last been in town.

Today television is not seen as an urban luxury but a necessity by many village families. It consumes people so much that farmers who used to go to bed shortly after sunset are now awake until 1:00 and 2:00 A.M. watching Hindi movies. Television has in the past decade become a very large part of most villagers' daily lives. Children run home from school during their lunch break to watch the latest developments in their favorite soap operas.

When I arrived in Mumbai from the United States in 1995, the first thing I noticed, after the heat, was a skyline not of rooftops but of television antennas. The drive from the Mumbai airport into Daadar runs through one of the most depressed slum and squatter areas I have ever seen. Yet, out of nearly every hut, shack, and cardboard box which lines the roadside emerges a television antenna climbing up like a blade of grass.

Of those villages I visited during my research in India, almost 25 per cent of homes owned television sets. Though primarily an urban phenomenon, the television set is rapidly becoming a common and mandatory fixture in many village homes across India.

As Indian villages continue to modernize and gain access to services once thought to be limited to an urban environment, basic human needs begin to change. What used to be an unattainable dream has become a luxury, and what was once a luxury is becoming a necessity. When I was growing up in Panchgani, a small town, the concept of television was not new. An occasional visit to Pune or Mumbai would be a time to watch TV with friends. Yet, the thought of having a TV set in our own homes in Panchgani was foolish, and not many considered it.

However, in December 1995 when I visited my old *mali's* (gardener's) house, which consisted of two small rooms no more than 7 by 8 feet each, no running water or gas stove, there sat in the corner a 21-inch color TV set made in India. He had spent an entire six month's salary to purchase the television. There I sat on a cow dung floor, eating dinner of caked rice with hot curry on a banana leaf, drinking water from the neighborhood well with things floating inside, which made me thankful it was a fairly dark room. I asked this man's 9-year-old son what his favorite television program was. His answer was not unique. He said he enjoyed three shows the most, *The Bold and the Beautiful, Beverly Hills 90210*, and *Bay Watch*, three shows which seemed to have no relevance in the life of a poor village boy. I strained to hear my host over the braying donkeys outside, and was told by his son dressed in rags, who had only a first grade education and had never ventured more than 10 miles from his town, that his favorite television shows were about rich American executives, teenagers with wealth and morals completely different from his own, and beach bums in string bikinis.

Research Question

Almost 75 per cent of India's one billion people live in villages, and agriculture is the primary occupation. India's rural society is marked by deeply held traditions in relation to caste, gender, and religion. Until recently, much of the rural population was isolated from external media influence. Over the past fifteen years, television has become widely accessible to most villagers.

The pertinent questions this book attempts to answer are: what role does television play in the process of social change in rural India? What influence has it had in relation to gender, caste, and family relationships? What are the aspirations, expectations, and concerns of villagers, and what influence has television had on these? What role (if any) do villagers see television playing in the social and economic development of the region?

The research focuses primarily on the advertising and entertainment aspects of television in the context of village life as a whole using qualitative in-depth interviews and participant observation.

Importance and Rationale

Unprecedented Access

Why is this study important? Today more than ever, rural Indians are increasingly coming into contact with the outside world through the mass media. Marshall McLuhan, referring to the communications revolution, wrote of the move toward a 'global village.' Radio, and to a lesser degree the print media, have contributed significantly to this shift. And with the coming of television the world seems to be a much smaller place. A farmer in India can sit down in his hut after a hard day of work in the rice paddies and watch the evening soap operas, the latest developments on local and national elections, and world headlines. At the same time he is bombarded by a variety of advertisements claiming to hold the key to a better way of life. Increasingly, Indian television is opting to buy foreign productions because of their low cost and popularity.

Television is by no means a new mass medium in India. Yet, only in the past ten to fifteen years has television become accessible to much of rural India. Only three decades ago, disseminating information throughout the country was an insurmount-able challenge. In 1962 a survey conducted by the National Insti-tute of Community Development three months after the war between India and China showed that only 22 per cent of Indi-ans had any knowledge of the war (Singhal and Rogers, 1989: 27). The government did not view the development of communi-cations systems as important as steel mills, power dams, and other conspicuous indicators of development (Pool, 1963).

This low priority was reflected in the budget allocations. Dur-ing India's First Five-Year Plan only 0.2 per cent of the national budget was allocated to radio broadcasting, and only half that was actually spent. Ten years later this minuscule broadcasting bud-get was cut in half (Rogers, 1969).

Television, introduced in 1959 as part of a UNESCO educa-tional project, has only recently become accessible to any sizable (in terms of percentage of population) number of Indians. In 1980 the rate of adoption of television by household was only 1 per cent, while five years later it was up to 5 per cent, and in 1990 it was at 15 per cent (Singhal and Rogers, 1989: 31). Today televi-sion transmission reaches as much as half of the total population (500 million people) (ibid.: 62). Vilanilam (1989: 487) argues that

Of the various media, it is the TV, which has registered the most sudden and spectacular growth in India. Up until 1982, TV was confined to four metropolitan cities and a few large towns. But today Doordarshan (India's TV network) has the technical capability of reaching 70 per cent of the population through 210 or more Low Power Transmitters (LPTs) and two dozen 10 kW production stations.

Entertainment Programming

A second rationale in support of the particular rural focus of this study centers on the lack of research in the area of entertainment programming and its influence on rural life. Mitra's (1993) study of television and popular culture in India is one of the few which addresses this lacuna. And though his study is important in many respects, it is narrowly focused and in no way serves as an eth-nography of television and village life. Television in most of rural

India is a relatively recent phenomenon. Research on this subject in urban settings is quite extensive including much interest in the Indian cinema industry. Dicky (1993) studied the role of cinema in the lives of the urban poor of Madurai in south India. I lived in Madurai for a month shortly after Dicky completed her research and observed how acutely people's lives were influenced by the cinema. As in most of India, the cinema is everywhere.

> Glittering billboards advertise the latest films, and smaller posters are slapped on to spare inches of wall space. Movie songs blare from horn speakers and cassette players at weddings, puberty rites, and temple and shrine festivals. Tapes of movie dialogue play at coffee stalls, while patrons join in reciting them. Rickshaws and shop boards are painted with movie stars' pictures. Young men and women follow dress and hairstyle fashions dictated by the latest films. Younger children trade movie star cards, learn to disco dance like the film actors, and recreate heroic battles in imitation of their favorite stars. Fan club members meet in the streets to boast about their star and make fun of his rivals (Dicky, 1993: 3).

Further, while several studies have been carried out in other countries on the impact of advertising, little has been published on the subject on rural India.[1]

Government television's purpose from its inception was first to educate, then to inform, and last, to entertain. Research has followed a similar order. While most programs on television today fall under the category of entertainment, the majority of research has focused on the educational and informational aspects of the medium. The first educational project using television (1959–60) was implemented in the villages around Delhi with agricultural programs to assist farmers in crop production. In 1975 the Satellite Instructional Television Experiment (SITE) project covering 2,400 villages in six states became a model for other Third World nations in implementing satellite-based television educational systems (Pokharapurkar, 1993). Television, at this initial stage, was 'not considered to be a medium of entertainment but primarily a pedagogic tool' (Mitra, 1993: 14). Entertainment programming, initially seen as a way to maintain viewers' attention and to satisfy urban populations has in recent years become the predominant force in Indian television. These programs produced primarily by and for urban viewers carry values and ideas which often run counter to the realities of rural life. As one critic perusing the literature on this subject points out:

> While the *effectiveness* of mainly informational material (usually emanating from government sources) has been studied, we still know comparatively little about the *effects* of mass communication more generally considered. In particular, there has been serious neglect of the role and importance of the entertainment material that tends to predominate in most media systems, even though popular entertainment quite obviously embodies values that may or may not be consistent with development goals (Hartmann et al.,1989: 27).

Hartmann and his research team (1989) conducted a comparatively large research project on the impact of the mass media on social change in rural India in the mid-1980s, focusing on the states of Kerala, Andhra Pradesh, and West Bengal. And though Hartmann acknowledges the important role entertainment media can play in the process of social change, his own team limited their focus to the educational and informational aspects of media, therefore leaving unanswered the questions about entertainment fare. Had their study followed a more holistic approach, more open to variables not considered at the outset, the role of entertainment media might have been more fully understood.[2]

It should be pointed out that Hartmann's (1989) as well as Rao's (1966) research both ask similar questions to the ones posed here. Both research projects attempted to understand the role of communication and media in the process of social change in rural India. Neither study included television in their equation, simply because it did not exist at the place and time that the research was carried out. In addition, both projects overlooked the role of entertainment and its impact on social change. The present research attempts to fill this void.

Television Advertising

In 1996, Unnikrishnan and Bajpai published their book titled *The Impact of Television Advertising on Children*. Their research consisted of a sample of 730 children in and around Delhi. They made sure to sample children from the lower socio-economic class as well as those from the middle and upper class. They concluded that 'consumerism is the new religion of the day and that its most devout followers are children' (Unnikrishnan and Bajpai, 1996: 19). Children's happiness is now defined by the products advertised by television and is intricately linked to them. These authors discovered that:

> Almost every child in Delhi is a regular television viewer; that children spend a good deal of their free time in front of the TV set; that most Indian children watch adult programming; that TV viewing is adversely affecting their reading, writing, and concentration skills; and that it is bringing about a major change in familial relationships by creating greater segregation between generations and individuals. Children are more aware today of products and brands in the marketplace and are re-orienting their priorities to keep abreast with the changing economic environment. They are looking to a well-equipped future home (they cannot envisage life without a TV set), clothes have become more important than ever before and levels of dissatisfaction with what they have are now noticeably high (Unnikrishnan and Bajpai, 1996: 20).

And though their study focused on an urban environment it is nonetheless important for understanding the role of television in modern India.

Advertising is the cornerstone and lifeblood of most entertainment mass media. 'The bulk of TV programs throughout the world are sponsored by big commercial establishments that are either multinational or closely linked to multinational corporations' (Vilanilam, 1989: 487). These corporations know that those who are going to spend the most on their products are the more affluent members of the society. Therefore, advertisements are geared toward that wealthy population. It has been argued that television has become an 'instrument of marketing goods, particularly consumer goods among the top 10 per cent of India's population' (ibid.: 488). The fact remains, however, that a large percentage of the viewers of these ads are rural villagers.

The question then arises: what influence have these advertisements, which are produced for and by the more affluent, had on village life? In what ways have television commercials influenced the desires and habits of villagers? A search of the literature on this subject found no in-depth studies of the influence of television advertising on village life in India. Several studies focus on the urban environment, with occasional reference to the rural farmer (Trivedi, 1991; Unnikrishnan and Bajpai, 1996,Vilanilam, 1989;). These studies agree that television 'advertisements created an adverse impact on the demands among children for new goods and items' (Trivedi, 1991: 54). In fact, Unnikrishnan and Bajpai (1996: 20) found that

> TV advertising is imposing an image of life that is completely alien to the vast majority of Indian children. Many children are beginning to believe that the India and the Indians they see in TV ads are the only ones worth emulating and learning from.... As a result, material aspirations are reaching unrealistic heights. Development has never appeared so disjointed. While consumerism is spreading like wildfire, access to the basics of life remains a serious problem for many.

Though there are great similarities among Indian children of both the upper and lower classes in urban environments, it is difficult to generalize this data to a rural setting. Therefore, the question asked in the present research is: what role is television advertising playing in the lives of *rural* children and adults?

Village Dynamics

Most research to date has focused on specific variables and how they are affected by the mass media. Researchers want to know the effects of television on variables such as modernity, innovation, achievement motivation, and empathy. Though important in many ways, this approach is extremely narrow. It tells us little about village life and how television fits into this pattern. It focuses primarily on the individual without giving due consideration to structural forces.

Furthermore, by focusing on such psychological variables as empathy and motivation, development communication studies are criticized for an 'overriding emphasis...on person-blame

rather than system-blame' (Hartmann et al.,1989: 28). By focusing only on psychological factors in attempting to understand the
processes of social change, many researchers often overlook
structural dynamics. Any social impact analysis must focus on
structural forces in order to appreciate more fully the individual's
motivations and aspirations, and the context within which the
individual lives. In many developing countries, 'existing patterns
of power and exploitation mean that poor people have little rea-
sonable prospect of self-betterment; and an attitude of fatalism
may be the only logical one' (ibid.: 28). Therefore, if a survey
finds a positive correlation between media exposure and motivation, one cannot be satisfied with this alone. One must look to the
structural factors of power and exploitation that might have
changed, influencing motivation among individual members of
the community. It would seem necessary then, to locate the problem of development in the system rather than in the psyche of
the individual.

In addition, many research projects have as their starting point
pre-conceived assumptions about the importance of media.
Hartmann et al. (1989) point out that the media acquire importance even prior to the onset of the research by placing them at
the center of the equation. The presumption is that media are
important, which produces findings supporting that statement.

Taking a step back in research, allowing the data to speak for
itself, allowing answers to create questions, allowing opinions and
assumptions to emerge from the field, and from the people we
are trying to understand, is a crucial starting point for any
research. Only after the research has begun do we know what the
important questions are and how many of our initial assumptions
were incorrect. One must attempt to understand the whole environment in order to grasp the dynamics of a certain variable.

Village life is not static or simple; it is complex and variable.
Relationships, whether inter-caste, gender, family, age, or between
landholder and tenant, are in constant flux. The romantic view of
traditional villages is one of harmony, solidarity, cooperation, and
simplicity. The more I learned about village society, the more I
realized its complexity. It is through this learning process that I
made sense of the role of television in rural life.[3]

In this research, an attempt is made to understand the dynamics of village life and then place television in that context. In

doing so, factors and processes not otherwise recognized are accounted for. An analysis of the political and economic aspects that determine television access, as well as the caste and gendered nature of Indian rural life, help contribute to a deeper under-standing of those processes.

Qualitative Interviews and Participant Observation

The final rationale for the methods and the particular design of this study originates from a review of the bulk of media audience studies. Research in this field has predominantly reflected the quantitative survey approach. Researchers attempt to isolate vari-ables that affect or are affected by media messages. And though such studies are acknowledged for their thoroughness and sophistication, one critic concludes that they have:

> produced a rather disembodied picture of patterns of relation-ships between variables with very few insights into why certain things go together. The variables are abstracted from the social processes that they are supposed to represent and, with only the sketchiest information about village life, the reader is left little the wiser about what it is that is facilitating modernization on the one hand or retarding it on the other. This is partly because of the over-reliance on the survey method (Hartmann et al., 1989: 34).

In recent years there has been a growing awareness of the need for a more holistic approach to understanding the role of televi-sion (Morley, 1990). As Hammersley and Atkinson point out, quantitative research, in so far as it is concerned centrally with the:

> mere establishment of a relationship among variables, [which providing a basis for prediction, does not constitute a theory]: A theory must include reference to mechanisms or processes by which the relationship among the variables identified is gener-ated (cited in Morley, 1990: 174).

Television in rural India is a recent phenomenon. There exist only a handful of studies on the impact of television on rural life and only one that focuses specifically on the entertainment aspects of the medium (Mitra, 1993). Therefore, at this exploratory stage, when hypotheses must still be developed and sharpened, a qualitative approach to the subject material is believed to be more appropriate.[4] Once a more detailed picture is developed and a deeper understanding of television in the context of village life emerges, then quantitative surveys covering larger populations may indeed become appropriate isolating specific variables.[5]

Overview

As I walked into a popular restaurant in downtown Chicago with my wife and parents, I smelt the delicious aroma of spice and herbs. This restaurant is located in an area of town called Little India. The restaurant was filled with a diversity of people, black and white, several Indians, and an African sitting behind me speaking French. I usually feel very much at home in Indian restaurants but not on this occasion. As the Indian waiter walked us to our table I noticed him giving me a strange look. I consider myself more Indian than American and usually take offense when people question my appropriateness in an Indian environment. And then it happened again. As I stood in line at the buffet table piling food onto my plate I noticed a young Indian lady staring at me. I was certain there was nothing wrong with my appearance and so I looked up at her in an almost confrontational way. She immediately asked: 'How do you know this song?' It suddenly all made sense. There I was as American looking as you can get, unknowingly singing along to the Hindi music coming through the speakers on the wall. The music was from the soundtrack to the movie titled *Dilwale Dulhania Le Jayenge*.[6] This was the most popular movie during the entire period of my research and was heard almost anywhere, any time of the day. Whether I was in the small barber shop or with old man Shinde on the mountainside herding his goats, or at Victoria train station in Mumbai, this particular soundtrack was often playing. Hearing this music transported me back to the beautiful mountainside in India and to the people who made such an impression on me.

The research was carried out in the Western *Ghats* (mountains) of Maharashtra between November 1995 and July 1996. Agriculture is the way of life for most people. Subsistence crops are grown to feed the family, and some farmers grow cash crops as well. In this hilly region, 4,000 feet above sea level, strawberries are the cash crop for five months of the year, mostly shipped to Mumbai for sale. Milk from cows and buffalo provides another means of livelihood. Farmers walk sometimes up to 20 miles to sell their liter or two of milk in town. Goats are occasionally raised and sold for a good profit. Most of the villages in this region are homogeneous in terms of caste composition with Maratha being the dominant caste.

The beauty of the mountains is breathtaking, but life is a constant struggle against the forces of nature and the countless structural forces which play such an important and critical role in an individual's and a families' well being. India has frequently been stereotyped as a timeless land with fatalistic people controlled by ancient traditions. But today the new position of this Indian subcontinent in world affairs is a mighty one.

With close to a billion people and a middle class rivaling that of the total population of the United States, this nation is steadily maneuvering into a powerful position on the world scene. India boasts the largest cinema industry in the world. And today major satellite companies are vying for control of the booming television markets. But what is happening in the Indian microcosm, in a village like Danawli? What about this modernity, primarily communicated through television, which is now more than ever creeping so rapidly into the daily lives of these villagers? What do they think about themselves and about their world? What is happening to the temporal and spatial boundaries of their universe? What of the traditional and social institutions that date back centuries? These are some of the questions I set out to explore.

Notes

1. There have been studies that focus on urban settings and articles that deal with the subject more generally. Refer to Lekshmi's (1987) unpublished Master's thesis and Vilanilam (1989).

2. Cynthia Miller, referring to this flaw in Hartmann's research, argues that, 'Had Hartmann's study been less focused on one particular use of media, and truly followed his own cautions, this dynamic would have emerged more clearly. This finding presents an important aspect of media in the lives of community members, and needs to be investigated more thoroughly' (1995: 57).

3. Miller, supporting this approach, writes: 'In order to obtain a fuller understanding of the interaction between mass media and society, one needs to look at not merely the individual and his or her usage and interpretation of mediated messages, but at the levels of family and community, as well, for media audiences are not simply aggregates of individuals—they are interpretive communities that collectively interact with the media in a variety of social settings. Through these interactions, audiences receive, accept, and resist mediated messages, and construct meanings based upon knowledge and experience' (1995: 2). Miller further argues that, 'the mass media's transformation of our social world requires a new approach to understanding communication and social power—an approach which fully utilizes ethnographic methodology—in order to better appreciate the nature of human interaction with mass media.... [This requires] an awareness of the range of practices and activities in which social subjects engage, and the role which the media play in the day-to-day experience' (ibid.).

4. The first four months of my research were spent in getting to know the people of the village and how everything worked. I soon realized that to understand certain aspects of village life and forces at play I would have to understand the regional political and economic structure as well. Therefore, an ethnographic approach to this subject at this time and in this environment was the most appropriate.

5. There are several approaches to media and audience research and Chapter 2 explores each one.

6. I saw this movie within days of arriving in India and found it very interesting that a movie with this particular plot received such popularity. *Dilwale Dulhania Le Jayenge* literally means 'the pure of heart wins the bride.' The entire plot centered on a girl who found herself in love with a man, but her father had already promised her hand to another. The tradition of arranged marriages is very strong in India, and the movie depicts the tragedy which comes along with that tradition. After much pain and struggle she gets the man she loves. And as I sat in the movie theater surrounded by couples who were probably in arranged marriages themselves, I was taken aback by the thousands in the audience cheering for the idea of true love. And after months of research this initial observation in a cinema was confirmed.

There is a gap between the changing ideas, beliefs, and values versus the reality and practices of people. People are more receptive to the idea of 'love marriage' but when asked if they themselves were in or knew of anyone not in an arranged marriage, the answer was invariably 'NO.'

2

Understanding Mass Media

The role of communication in development has become part of a much larger debate on the process of social change and the nature of development itself. There exist a wide variety of views about the role and relevance of mass communication to development. Theory and research suggest that mass communication can act as a positive agent of social change in some cases while impeding change in others. This chapter looks at some of these debates.

The central focus of this study will be the investigation of the experiences of villagers and of the process of social change in relation to television. Certain broad questions about communication and development must be discussed as a framework for this investigation. A brief overview of five related areas of inquiry is required to illustrate more fully the reasons for and methods of this study: (a) theoretical perspectives of mass media; (b) development and mass communication; (c) the methodological framework of television studies; (d) the cultural influence of television; and (e) television in India.

Theoretical Perspectives

An attempt to define or construct theories of mass communication must address questions of the relationship between mass communication and social change. Every theory offering insight into this relation shares a focus on three basic elements: an analysis of communication technology, the form and content of media messages, and social change in relation to media. Social change can occur at various levels including social structure, institutional arrangements, the distribution of public beliefs, values, and opinions. For the purposes of this discussion we limit the analysis to the third general set of theories (i.e.,theories about media and social change). Not all of these theories are 'mutually exclusive and no single theory can be expected to apply universally, given the variety of historical circumstances involved' (McQuail, 1983: 39).

According to McQuail (1994: 327), 'the entire study of mass communication is based on the premise that the media have significant effects, yet there is little agreement on the nature and extent of these assumed effects.' He argues that these effects take various forms. We choose what movie to go to based on what we see advertised in the newspaper, we dress in accordance to the weather broadcast, our buying habits are shaped by the advertisements we are exposed to, and opinions are formed by the news we watch on television every evening. Our minds are filled with media generated information. McQuail (1994) argues that in modern society media form a large part of people's lives, from billboards along highways, to radio programs, newspapers, magazines, films, and television.

Historical Evolution of Media Effects Research and Theories

The industrialized world depends on media for all kinds of entertainment and information. A major reason for this dependency is that we live in a society in which networks of interpersonal ties are not as deeply established as they once were (McQuail, 1994). In modern societies most of our information is not received through family ties and networks of friendships but rather through the mass media. Most people live in physical proximity to one another but with extensive differences based on ethnicity, race, education, income, religion, language, and other characteristics. Such social and cultural differences can impede interpersonal communication. This tends to inhibit the free flow of information between people and leads them to turn to other sources. As a result, the mass media, in satisfying this need for information, create a condition of dependency (DeFleur and Ball-Rokeach, 1982). People come to depend more and more on the media and less on each other.[1] The French sociologist Gustave Le Bon in 1895 saw an emergence of an age of crowds, without ties between people, as opposed to an age of community, in which people are linked by strong social bonds.

The development of thinking about media effects can be said to fall within four periods in history. This thinking was strongly shaped by the circumstances of time and place. Scholars in the first period (1900–1930) viewed media as all-powerful agents of change and developed the Magic Bullet Theory to explain media influence.[2] They predicted immediate, direct, and uniform effects on everyone who received a media message. The mass media was credited with considerable power to shape opinion and belief, and to mold behavior according to the will of those who controlled the media and their content (Bauer and Bauer, 1960). These conclusions were not based on any empirical research but on observations of the popularity and importance of media in people's lives.

Empirical research led to the second period of thinking about media effects. By 1929, feature-length films with soundtracks had become standard and were the primary media for family entertainment. The public had become concerned about the influence of movies on children. In the United States it was estimated that forty million minors, including more than seventeen million children under the age of fourteen, went to the movies weekly (Dale, 1970: 73). The Motion Picture Research Council called together a group of educators, psychologists, and sociologists to plan large-scale studies to probe the effects of motion pictures on youth. A private foundation called the Payne Fund was persuaded to supply the necessary money. The resulting Payne Fund Studies were the first large-scale, multi-disciplinary scientific efforts to assess the effects of a major mass medium. There was great criticism about the technical aspects of these research studies with claims that these were unsystematic and naïve. To the average person these technical criticisms about the research procedures were like debates about the finer points of navigation while the ship was already sinking. The conclusions confirmed the charges of the critics of movies and the worst fears of parents. One of the most interesting Payne Studies was done by sociologist Herbert Blumer (1933). According to Blumer, the movies had an especially powerful impact on children's play. Children impersonated cowboys and Indians, cops and robbers, pirates, soldiers, racecar drivers, and every conceivable hero and villain they had seen in films. More significantly, Blumer concluded that children and teenagers copied many mannerisms, speech patterns, dress, emotions, ambitions and temptations, career plans, ideas about romance, and other behavior portrayed on the screen.

Other Payne Fund Studies like Peterson and Thurstone's (1933) focused on how movies influenced children's attitudes toward social issues.[3] They concluded that attitudinal change due to exposure to movies was statistically significant.[4] The general research trend during this time focused on using media for planned persuasion as well as using information on political campaigns and assessing the possibility to control the effects of media on delinquency, aggression, and prejudice. But as McQuail (1994: 329) states:

Over the course of time the nature of research changed, as methods developed and evidence and theory suggested new kinds of variables, which should be taken into account. Initially, researchers began to differentiate possible effects according to social and psychological characteristics; subsequently they introduced variables relating to intervening effects from personal contacts and social environment, and latterly according to types of motive for attending to media.

Toward the end of the 1950s the notion of media as all-powerful was not a viable proposition. Joseph Klapper's (1960: 8) statement summarizes the final stages of this media research period: 'mass communication does not ordinarily serve as a necessary or sufficient cause of audience effects, but rather functions through a nexus of mediating factors.'

The third period of research on media effects was characterized by a rediscovery of the power of the media. According to McQuail (1994: 330) researchers were 'reluctant to dismiss the possibility that media might indeed have important social effects and be an instrument for exercising social and political power.' The leftist political philosophies of the 1960s made a significant contribution to the thinking about the powerful legitimating and controlling effects of the media in capitalist states. This was a time when television was gaining in popularity in the West. People were mesmerized by the box in the corner of their living rooms and were concerned about its effects on their children.

As fears of the consequences of television grew in the United States, public concern brought pressure on Congress to act. In March 1969, Senator John Pastore said he was 'exceedingly troubled by the lack of definitive information which would help resolve the question of whether there is a causal connection between televised...violence and antisocial behavior by individuals, especially children' (Surgeon General, 1971: 14). By 1971, the results of over sixty studies plus reviews of hundreds of prior investigations were published (ibid.). Many issues were addressed, including the impact of advertising, activities displaced by television, and the information learned from television. But the focus centered on the effects of television violence on the behavior of children. The Surgeon General concluded that televised violence might be dangerous to one's health. Media and particularly television were seen as powerful influences once again. Noelle-Neumann's (1973) article titled 'Return to the Concept of Powerful Mass Media' identifies this period of research.

The most notable aspect of this period was the clear contradiction between the findings of the studies by Schramm and his associates a decade earlier, and those of the report of the Surgeon General. Schramm, Lyle, and Parker (1960) published the first large-scale American investigation of children's uses of television. They concluded that television posed no danger to children, while the Surgeon General's report suggested that, for a few, the medium could be dangerous. Here was the classic situation that often confronts researchers: which is the correct interpretation?

Due to this dilemma the 1970s saw a sharp increase in research on the effects of television. In fact, 90 per cent of all research ever done on the effects of television viewing on behavior up to that time was carried out during the 1970s. So many research findings were available toward the end of the decade that Julius Richard, the new Surgeon General, requested a synthesis and evaluation of the mass of research evidence. Thus, in 1982, a decade after the first report, a second was published.

This initiated the fourth stage, which continues into the 1990s. This period is characterized by 'negotiated media influence.' Most research evidence reveals media have limited effects on behavior. This theoretical shift away from the notion of the 'all-powerful media' is coupled with a methodological shift, a move away from the more quantitative survey methods approach to more qualitatively based research models.

Dominant Paradigms

The direction of research and theories of audience studies then, varied from one period to another. The media have been seen as all-powerful agents of social change with their effects being not only direct and immediate but also uniform. Within this perspective audiences are seen as passive isolated individuals who are affected by messages sent by a source with a specific intention (*effects or stimulus response models*). On the other hand, audiences are seen as actively engaged in decoding and using media messages. This tradition falls within the *uses and gratifications perspective*. Between the 1970s and 1990s a third school of thought became increasingly popular. This new tradition attempted to 'synthesize insights from communication theory, sociology, semiology, and psychology to provide a more comprehensive understanding of the communicative circuits operating in social contexts' (Miller, 1995: 4).

This perspective, broadly labeled *cultural studies*, views the media–audience relationship in a much broader context. This involves two major propositions: that 'media "construct" social formations and history itself by framing images of reality (in fiction as well as news) in a predictable and patterned way; and second, that people in audiences construct for themselves their own view of social reality and their place in it, in interaction with the symbolic constructions offered by the media' (McQuail, 1994: 331). This perspective is not entirely inconsistent with earlier formulations of the 'effect' process. Yet, it does vary radically in terms of methods and research design calling for broader, more in-depth, and qualitative evidence in understanding the context within which media consumption occurs and the social environment which influences interpretations of media messages.

Effects Studies

The 'effects school' is concerned with the transmission of media messages, how senders and receivers encode and decode those messages, and what channels are used in this transmission. It views the process of transmission as linear. This stimulus-response model, also referred to as hypodermic needle model, can be illustrated as follows:

Who	Says What	In Which Channel	To Whom	With What Effect
Communicator	Message	Medium	Receiver	Effects

(McQuail and Windahl, 1981: 10)

It is because of this linear process that some have labeled this approach the 'process school' (Fiske, 1982). Let us take each stage and analyze it individually (Lasswell, 1948).

It is argued that mass communication begins with the senders, professional communicators who decide on the goals of the message to be produced in a form suitable to be transmitted via a particular medium. The intended meanings are then encoded by production specialists. This encoding process includes the selection of verbal and non-verbal symbols, and the special effects that are possible with a particular medium. The message is then transmitted through the use of specialized technologies characteristic of print, film, or broadcasting to disseminate it as widely as possible. The next stage centers on large and diverse audiences of individual receivers who attend to the medium and perceive the incoming message. Next, individual receivers construct interpretations of the message in such a way that they experience subjective meanings, which are to at least some degree parallel to those intended by the professional communicators. As a result of experiencing these meanings, receivers are influenced in their feelings, thoughts, or actions; that is, the communication has some *effect*.

This perspective has been heavily criticized, and modifications have been made in light of the growing research (DeFleur, 1970). It has been argued that individuals vary according to differences in their personality, background, attitude, intelligence, and interests. According to DeFleur (1970: 122), 'media messages contain particular stimulus attributes that have differential interaction with personality characteristics of audience members.' Second, it became accepted knowledge that response was linked directly to social category. Thus a response to the same media message varies according to age, class, sex, occupation, educational status, and religion. DeFleur (ibid.: 123) notes that 'members of a particular category will select more or less the same communication content and will respond to it in roughly equal ways.'

This model of 'communication effects' privileges the text over the audience. The message is viewed as a fixed entity that is received by an audience incapable of deciding for itself what meaning to give to the message. The intended meaning results in an intended response, and the audience members are seen as passive non-negotiators. Within this model there is no room for feedback by the audience, an element deemed critical to understanding media effects (Fowles, 1992). Issues like motivations for watching, the role of the social environment, or the potential needs that are being satisfied by media consumption are not addressed. Questions such as these form the basis of a theoretical perspective developed in response to the effects model of communication.

Uses and Gratifications

Attempts to understand the uses audiences made of the available media and the gratifications they derived from exposure to their selections resulted in the uses and gratifications theory. This begins with the audience making a conscious and motivated choice as to the content of the media. Another key assumption is that 'the meaning of media experience can be learned only from people themselves. [Within this approach] media use is most suitably characterized as an interactive process, relating media content, individual needs, perceptions, roles and values, and the social context in which a person is situated' (McQuail, 1994: 318).

The earliest and most dominant form of this theory has tended to be functionalist in formulation. Katz et al. (1974: 20) describe the theory as being concerned with

(a) the social psychological origins of (b) needs, which generate (c) expectations of (d) the mass media or other sources which lead to (e) differential patterns of media exposure (or engagement in other activities), resulting in (f) need gratifications and (g) other consequences, perhaps mostly unintended ones.

Therefore, media use is seen as a problem-solving, functional, activity to solve social and psychological circumstances.

Since Katz et al. published their work in 1974, certain modifications have been made (Rosengren et al., 1985). First, the emphasis on needs has been reduced, since this proved more often than not to be theoretically and methodologically problematic. Second, 'there is a much lower expectation that differentiation of the audience according to their perceived use and gratification would help in explaining differences in degree or kind of effects' (McQuail, 1994: 319). A reformulated, less mechanistic or functionalist version of the statement of Katz et al. would now look something like this:

(a) Personal social circumstances and psychological dispositions together influence both (b) general habits of media use and also (c) beliefs and expectations about the benefits offered by media, which shape (d) specific acts of media choice and consumption, followed by (e) assessments of the value of the experience (with consequences for further media use) and, possibly, (f) applications of benefits acquired in other areas of experience and social activity.

As compared to the effects theories already discussed, the new approach, instead of privileging the text, strives to assess media consumption from the audience's point of view. Some theorists assess audience needs and attempt to determine the extent to which those needs are being met by media. Others begin their analysis by focusing on the social context within which audience needs and expectations originate, while others attempt to understand how audiences use media to satisfy their needs.

Whatever the starting point for research within this perspective, there is a common set of assumptions about the audience that combine to form the model called uses and gratifications (Carey and Kreiling 1974; Liebes and Katz, 1989; McQuail 1972, 1984):

1. The audience is conceived of as active, that is, an important part of mass media use is assumed to be goal directed (McQuail, Blumler, and Brown, 1972). The question here is whether patterns of media use are shaped by more or less definite expectations of what certain kinds of content have to offer the audience member.

2. In the mass communication process, initiative in linking need gratification and media choice lies with the audience member. This places a strong limitation on earlier theories which saw a linear effect of media content on attitudes and behavior. According to Schramm, Lyle, and Parker (1961: 68): 'In a sense the term "effect" is misleading because it suggests that television "does something" to children.... Nothing can be further from the fact. It is the children who are most active in this relationship. It is they who use television rather than television using them.'

3. The media compete with other sources of need satisfaction. The needs served by mass media constitute only one segment of the wider range of human needs, and the degree to which they can be adequately met through mass media consumption varies.

4. In terms of methodology, information about the goals of mass media use can be derived from data supplied by the audience members themselves—that is, people are sufficiently self-aware to be able to report their interests and motives.

5. Value judgments about the cultural significance of mass media should be suspended while audience orientations are explored on their own terms (Miller, 1995: 9–10).

This new approach took into account the fact that different people selected different content from the media and interpreted it in different ways. Thus, the media had both selected and limited influences (as opposed to the previous Magic Bullet perspective which saw the media as powerful, uniform, and having immediate effects) on people who are exposed to a particular message.

However, the central question underlying this perspective is: 'Why do people use media?' Why do audiences deliberately seek out certain types of media and ignore others? Why do people buy a particular book? Why do people first turn to a particular section in the newspaper? Why do people select one television program over another? This is goal-oriented behavior, which indicates that audiences are not passive but active in their interaction with media. They are in fact *using* the media for some purpose and not vice versa.

The uses and gratifications theory was developed to try to explain why audiences do not passively wait for media messages to arrive. It seeks to understand why audiences are active, deliberately seeking out forms of content that provide them with information that they need, like, and use (DeFleur, 1970). This psychological theory focuses on the audience's interests, needs, attitudes, and values that influence media selection.

To explain the reasons why people select certain media, McQuail, Blumler, and Brown (1972) developed a typology consisting of four categories: diversion (including escape from routine and the burden of daily life); personal relationships (including substitute companionships); personal identity (including reality exploration and value reinforcement); and surveillance (informing ourselves about the world around us). The authors argue that people use media and consciously select media content to *gratify* one of these four needs.

Katz, Gurevitch, and Haas (1973: 122), take this argument a step further and state that besides these reasons for media use, individuals engage in media consumption in order to connect (or sometimes disconnect) themselves 'via instrumental, affective, or integrative relations' with different kinds of others (self, family, friends, nation, etc.). My own research in part supports this argument. While talking with villagers about their uses of television, I asked: 'What are some of the reasons you watch television?' Some responses were:

- *Television is fun to watch, but sometimes I am bored with it, but I still watch it because my friends watch it, and I might get lost and not know what happened to Nisha and her baby (reference to a story line in a soap opera).*
- *Before television came to the village, my husband would leave the house every night after dinner to go talk to his friends or drink. But now that there is television he stays here and watches with me, and that is good. He spends more time here now. He even spent money on a good antenna, so we get a clearer picture.*
- *Sometimes the programs go very late, but I watch it with my husband, and we spend time together.*

This theory is not without its criticisms, however. For example, it is too simplistic to believe that if a behavior exists, it must be gratifying a pre-existing need. Is it not possible that media consumption occurs by individuals for no particular reason? As one young villager confided:

- *The only reason I sometimes watch the afternoon show (soap opera) during lunch is because my mother and sister are watching it. I hate that show, I think its for girls, but there is nothing else to do… so I watch it and eat my lunch.*

The theorists within this perspective have done a good job in bringing the focus back from the text to the audience, but they limit their analysis by viewing audience interaction with media in isolation from other social forces. In addition, they fail to consider one's position within the social order and possible external social forces which may influence the level of consumption, the type and the motivation for interaction with media.

Cultural Studies

The origins of cultural studies date back to the founding of the post-graduate research center at the University of Birmingham by Richard Hoggart in 1964. Stuart Hall was the director of the center from 1968 to 1981. Hall's work greatly influenced the theoretical perspectives of much of the research that was done through the center. And though Hall claims that there was no political or theoretical orthodoxy at the center, and that the research undertaken there was conducted in a democratic, non-dogmatic atmosphere, it is clear that Marxism was the reference point with which work produced at the center was considered and compared (Lull, 1990: 6).

Dennis McQuail (1994: 297–298) has outlined the salient features of the culturalist tradition of audience research:

1. The media has to be 'read' through the perceptions of its audience, which constructs meanings and pleasures from the media texts offered (and these are never fixed or predictable).
2. The very process of media use as a set of practices and the way in which it unfolds are the central objects of interest.
3. Audiences for particular genres often comprise 'interpretative communities' which share much the same experience, forms of discourse, and frameworks for making sense of media.
4. Audiences are never passive, nor are their members all equal, since some will be more experienced or more active fans than others.
5. Methods have to be 'qualitative' and deep, often ethnographic, taking account of content, act of reception, and context together.

Though many of these features have been borrowed from other perspectives, this approach to media research is most distinctive in its emphasis on hegemony. As Lull (1990: 7) argues, the 'pre-eminent theoretical contribution to cultural studies came from elaborations of Antonio Gramsci's theory of ideological hegemony.' It is advocated that focus be given to media experience and how the audience relates to it. This allows the 'reader' more interpretative power while 'consuming,' 'decoding,' and 'reading' the media texts. Cultural studies 'attempt to understand these texts' role in society and culture, especially among oppositional or marginalized groups' (Miller, 1995: 22). For Fiske (1988: 272) the methodological strategies of the culturalist school have their origin in semiotics and structuralist traditions, and are also derived from 'ethnography and requires us to study the meanings [that audiences make of certain texts]. This involves listening to them, reading the letters they write to fan magazines, or observing their behavior at home or in public.'

However, cultural studies research is interdisciplinary and its key concepts are based on critical approaches to mass media. Gramsci's concepts of hegemony, ideology, and consensus are important in understanding the process of the ruling class establishing and maintaining dominance not just by force, but by encouraging consensus among diverse social groups.

Hegemony is attained through the myriad ways in which the institutions of civil society operate to shape, directly or indirectly, the cognitive and affective structures whereby men perceive and evaluate problematic social reality (Femia, 1981: 24).

Gramsci believed that the production of meanings is closely connected to the social structure and hence, to understand those meanings one must understand the structure and history which have produced them. On the other hand the social structure is maintained by the meanings which culture produces.

Another underlying theme of this perspective is that:

properly fitted within the basic terms of materialist theory hegemony is a construct encompassing factors central to cultural studies' theorizing: culture and ideology placed in relation to economic and social class, a focus on processes of ideological influence, historical specificity, a concept of social power that is dynamic and open-ended, and a social theory that is appropriate for study of advanced industrial societies (Lull,1990: 7).

Society and its various divisions are not seen as an organic whole but as a series of interconnected parts. Social relations are analyzed in terms of power, 'in terms of a structure of domination and subordination that is never static, but is always the site of contestation and struggle' (Miller, 1995: 23).

In the domain of culture, this contestation takes the form of the struggle for meaning, in which the dominant classes attempt to 'naturalize' the meanings that serve their interests into the 'common sense' of the society as a whole. Subordinate classes, for their part, resist this process in various ways, and try to make meanings that serve their own interests. Cultural studies acknowledges the relative independence of ideology (from the economic base) and emphasize ideology's mechanisms of signification, expression, and consent creation (Miller, 1995: 23–24).

It follows then, that the mass media and its output are areas of ideological struggle.

David Morley (1980a, 1980b, and 1986) was one of the first whose research tested this theoretical perspective. Others like Angela McRobbie (1984), Dorothy Hobson (1981), and John Fiske (1987), point to the influence of social and cultural factors, with special attention given to gender and domestic relations, on media consumption. Morley (1980a) argues that texts are polysemic and messages are essentially open to several possible interpretations, but concludes that media texts contain preferred readings consistent with dominant ideologies. Morley's *Family Television* (1986) and Lull's *Inside Family Viewing* (1990) both observe that television viewing and its cultural influence can be understood only by analyzing the overall context of family structure and leisure activity.

Though cultural studies originated in Britain and was influenced to a great extent by the people associated with the University of Birmingham, adaptations have been made from North American (Lull, 1988, 1990; Radway, 1984, 1987, 1988) and Latin American (Barrios, 1988; Canclini, 1993) scholars. Feminist criticisms have also made great contributions to the study of communications (Kaplan 1987; Ang, 1983, 1985, and 1990). Even so, this particular perspective remains limited both theoretically and practically. This is because cultural studies research is based in Marxist ideology with specific reference to class, power, and hegemony. This is no doubt useful especially in the Indian context. Issues of marginalization and disempowerment are important concerns and valid agendas for research. Yet, if research begins with a class-ideological focus it is possible that other key variables may be overlooked. The researcher runs the risk of producing agenda-laden ethnography, which may lead to distorted conclusions (Miller, 1995).

Cultural studies remains to a great extent a perspective favoring theory over practice (Collins, 1986; Allen 1987). There have, however, been worthy attempts to rectify this in the recent past. Moores and Lull are two scholars grounded in this theoretical perspective and carrying out ethnographic fieldwork. They both argue for the ethnographic approach as researchers in cultural studies pursue questions of meaning and social context in relation to media.

Communication and Development

At a time when communication technologies are spreading to the most isolated regions of the world, and the development of the poorest of the poor is a dominant political issue, many Third World nations see development communication as a viable strategy for modernization.

This link between communication and modernization dates back to the 1950s and 1960s. Many countries in the Third World during that time had recently gained or were gaining their independence, and were considering various development options. Development was seen as a process of change 'to be set in motion and guided towards the objective of eradicating the hunger, disease, injustice, exploitation, and related ills' that afflict the majority of the planet's population (Hartmann et al., 1989: 17). Illiteracy rates, the number of malnourished children, and deaths by curable disease were high, in spite of the great advances in nutrition, health care, and educational programs. Attempts to understand the dynamics of these problems resulted in considerable debate. Numerous solutions and methodologies were proposed, and one in particular centered on the role of the mass media.

Daniel Lerner, Wilbur Schramm, and Everett Rogers are considered among the most influential early writers in the field of development communications. Lerner (1958), a sociologist at MIT, argued in *The Passing of Traditional Society* that urbanization leads to an increase in the literacy rate of a country which in turn leads to an increase in mass media exposure, which results in wider economic and political participation. As the title of his book indicates, he saw the problem as one of 'modernizing' traditional societies. Central to Lerner's argument was the idea that development failed to occur because peasants did not easily identify with new roles and a better way of life. This lack of 'empathy', he argued, could be righted through the use of the mass media. 'Empathy endows a person with capacity to imagine himself as proprietor of a bigger grocery store in a city, to wear nice clothes, and live in a nice house, to be interested in "what is going on in the world" and to "get out of his hole"' (Lerner, 1958: 342).

Rogers (1962, 1969) developed the 'diffusion model' to understand communication processes. His conclusion, based on his research among farmers in the United States, was that people did not interpret and respond to messages in the same way. He also found that not all people were equally exposed to media messages. He argued that mass media influence occurred in a two-step flow process. Higher status members of a group, who were more exposed to media messages, spread those messages to others. Statistically measuring antecedent and consequent variables, he argued the existence of a positive correlation between media exposure and various social psychological variables. His paradigm of the role of mass media exposure in modernization is as follows:

Antecedents	>>>> Process >>>>	Consequence
Literacy		Empathy
Education	Mass	Agricultural and home innovations
Social status	Media	Political knowledge
Age	Exposure	Achievement motivation
Cosmopoliteness		Educational and occupational aspirations

(Rogers, 1969: 102)

Rogers believed that 'communication processes are integral, vital elements of modernization and development.' In fact, he argued that 'all analysis of social change must ultimately focus upon communication processes' (Rogers, 1969: 8).

Both Lerner and Rogers are criticized for failing to consider the structural dynamics in their psychological characterization of the problem of stimulating development (Grunig, 1971). Hartmann argues that psychological states exist due to structural variables. Much of the research in development communication, though, tends to focus on 'person-blame' rather than 'system-blame.' Psychological variables are important to an understanding of the dynamics of change, but can in no way be singled out and analyzed in a vacuum. A tendency to focus on the individual without considering the processes and mechanisms behind certain behavioral or psychological variables is a major shortcoming in the early research. In referring to the relative 'neglect of social structure and structural conflict in discussion of development', Hartmann et al. (1989: 256), state:

> Too often discussions treat the people as an amorphous mass; where distinction is made between social strata, it is usually between the city-based elite and the rural masses. This leads easily to the assumption of a harmony of interests among the rural population.... Village society is highly differentiated in terms of access to resources and by caste and other divisions.... The unequal distribution of wealth, power, and esteem in the community leads to a state of incipient conflict between different sections where the relative advantage of some is maintained through the disadvantage of others. The problem of landlessness, for instance, cannot be alleviated without harming the interests of the landed.... The key point is that there are structural conflicts of interest even at village level that no [research] can ignore.

Another important criticism points to the elite bias of the two-step flow process of communication. This often results in what has been termed the 'communication effects gap' (Shingi and Mody, 1976). In recent years it has become known that development campaigns most often result in advantages for the 'haves' of a society and disadvantages for the 'have nots.' Research supports the idea that village elites are often able to monopolize information for their own advantage (Rao, 1966). For example, village elite often keep the 'community radio' or television in their own homes and limit others' access to it. However, the bulk of the research fails to address this complexity in the communication process and instead relies on a simplistic analysis of social and political structures.

This research was designed with these criticisms in mind. The 'overriding emphasis... of person-blame' is corrected by first understanding the dynamics of village life, the social structures, institutions, and power relationships. This will allow for a more meaningful appreciation of the individual's place in the community and the role of television in that pattern. Second, replacing the 'over-reliance of the survey method' with a qualitative approach will remedy the 'disembodied picture' produced by many survey researches.

Wilbur Schramm (1964), the final early theorist to be analyzed in this section, became one of the leading intellectuals in this field with the publication of *The Mass Media and National Development*. The book became the accepted blueprint for development planners interested in tapping into communication resources. His basic thesis was that, 'We must share information, we must share it widely... for development to occur.' Schramm saw the mass media as 'magic multipliers' of information. And while Lerner saw all media messages as having modernizing effects, Schramm was more interested in their 'informational' content, which he saw as the key to national development. According to Schramm (1964: 231):

> It is hard to argue that these [entertainment programs] have much to do with economic development. On the other hand, in a given country it may be highly desirable, at a given point in development, to offer some of this relaxing program fare, and it may be that the bonus of news, public affairs, and instruction mixed with the entertainment programs might be enough to justify the expenditure for television in development terms as well as entertainment terms.

In fact, much of the early research had taken for granted that 'mass media in less developed countries... carry mainly pro-development messages' (Rogers, 1969: 52). It was a given and not considered something to be examined. But in recent years this assumption has been widely challenged. How far, many ask, does 'communication serve mainly to manipulate the masses into compliance with the wishes of the powerful' (Hartmann et al., 1989: 28)?

One challenge to the 'top-down' model and its assumptions has been what Bordenave (1976) has called the 'Freire revolution.' Freire has argued that education (and communication) is usually conceived and practiced as a form of 'banking' in which the teacher (or communicator) 'make[s] deposits, which the students patiently receive, memorize, and repeat' (cited in Bordenave, 1976: 22). This process merely transfers 'content from a knowledgeable and authoritative source to a passive receiver... which does nothing to promote the receiver's growth as a person with an autonomous and critical conscience capable of contributing to and influencing his society' (ibid.: 21). Therefore the process of communication and the content of the messages being communicated become central to any discussion on the role of the media (as conveyors of information) and social change.

In addition, social change may be of various kinds, and not all change, even though it might represent 'development,' is necessarily beneficial to everyone.

> Changes that benefit one section of the community may leave others untouched or even damage their interests. Improved agricultural technology, for instance, may benefit landholders but weaken the position of landless laborers. So we should beware of regarding all progressive change as unproblematic (Hartmann et al., 1989: 255).

The data presented in later chapters supports this argument by illustrating that change which benefits one section of the village can also harm others.

Many studies on the developmental impact of mass communication have been satisfied with limiting their analysis to the informational, educational, and developmental aspects of the messages, which is understandable since many villagers speak of these aspects of television. As one villager stated on one of my initial visits to the village:

> • *I like television very much.... I watch it for the weather to help me know how to plan my day and my week. When the rain comes, when*

it will be sunny, and dry. I also have learned a lot about Jersey cows and why they get sick all time (Water Buffalo are the indigenous cattle of this region and Jersey cows from New Zealand were introduced approximately fifteen years ago due to their high milk yield). *They teach us how to take care of our cows, what vaccines to give them. I have learned about new fertilizers.*

'Yet,' 'there has been serious neglect of the role and importance of the entertainment material that tends to predominate in most media systems...' (Hartmann et al., 1989: 27) And though Hartmann et al., acknowledge that their own research focused solely on the informational aspects of media, in their conclusion they briefly allude to the power of entertainment media in fostering social change in terms of clothing and certain behavior. It would be logical to concentrate more of our energies on this aspect of the media. Though Hartmann et al. (1989) are avid critics of many studies on the impact of mass media on rural life, and while they point out that little work has been done on the entertainment aspects of the media, their own study on rural India was conducted apparently during a time and place in which television was not present. Their 'mass media' included radio, newspapers, magazines, films, and folk media. Their study, though published in 1989, was carried out in 1982, while television access has only recently become widespread.

Hartmann et al. (1989), following the lead of Rao (1966), conducted a large study in rural India on the impact of mass media. Many of the findings of Hartmann et al. (1989: 263), do not differ greatly from those described by Rao more than twenty years earlier.

Radio and film may have come into greater prominence and the effects of government initiatives (in agriculture and elected Panchayats, for instance) become more noticeable, but the impact of the media as forces of change does not appear dramatically greater and social patterns in villages remain similar to those reported by Rao.

Hartmann et al. (1989: 260) found that 'interpersonal communication' was a much greater source of information than mass media, yet the latter did prove to have certain developmental consequences.

Media exposure emerged as a significant factor influencing the adoption of better agricultural and health practices and in promoting more positive attitudes towards women and greater awareness of social problems affecting respondents. The media proved a particularly important source of political and other news from the outside world (Hartmann et al., 1989: 260).

However, it is important to reiterate that their findings, like Rao's (1966), do not support the idea of media as an all-powerful change agent. At most, they argue that media messages have a 'comparatively marginal' impact (ibid.: 35). It must also be borne in mind that both of these studies did not include television into their analyses, simply because it did not exist in the villages at the time of the research.

Now that a brief history of the field of development communications and its relates to this proposed research is complete, a discussion of the methodological frameworks within the field of television studies is necessary.

Some Methodological Considerations

The tradition of audience studies has predominantly been one of quantitative empirical investigation. Researchers attempt to isolate variables that affect or are affected by television messages. Many of these studies have contributed significantly to our understanding of the dynamics of television and culture. In recent years, however, there has been a growing awareness of the need for a more qualitative and holistic approach to understanding the role of television (Lull, 1988; Morley, 1990). Following the argument of Glaser and Strauss (1967), Lull (1988: 16) states:

> what I have learned through my own experience collecting and analyzing naturalistic data, I believe strongly that the theoretical essence of our work emerges quite spontaneously within each research project. I believe that we should not simply conduct research that is programmatically influenced by any fixed theoretical perspective if we are to really 'let the data speak to us.' .... Social research that focuses on communication is especially well suited to this theoretical and methodological stance.

It is this growing awareness that has produced a body of literature that seeks to understand television viewing as a family activity. Supporting this type of approach Reddi (1989: 395) points
out that:

> the relationship between media and culture is both all-pervasive
> and symbiotic; it is impossible to analyze one in isolation from
> the other. The boundary between the two is difficult to de-
> marcate and if the two areas of contemporary life are divided
> arbitrarily, it must be done with a full recognition of their inter-
> dependence.

Thus it is clear that television needs to be understood within the
'structure and dynamics of the... process of consumption of
which it is but a part' (Morley, 1990: 173).

It is for this reason that I have chosen a research design that
best fits this model. By first understanding the dynamics of village life and then placing television into that pattern I hope to
account for factors and processes not otherwise recognized.
These include an analysis of the political and economic aspects
that determine television access as well as the gendered nature of
Indian family life.

Agrawal (1981) has made a further argument for the qualitative design for research on this subject. In referring to the decision to supplement survey methods with qualitative field studies,
Agrawal (ibid.: 54) argues:

> I firmly believe that most of the research tools available to
> 'measure impact' or to investigate problem-oriented areas of a
> society are 'culture specific.' These are designed keeping in
> view a particular culture milieu and in other cultural contexts,
> they fail to yield true results.... Earlier surveys conducted in
> rural India had serious problems in eliciting correct responses
> from respondents. During SITE, in spite of the fact that the
> schedules were prepared in the local languages, investigators
> with rural backgrounds and good command of local language
> found it at times very difficult to elicit information from struc-
> tured questions in a formal interview situation. Therefore it
> was felt that the anthropological method that allows for deep
> probing and understanding of communication process *in situ*

should be followed as an alternative approach for social evaluation of SITE.

Furthermore, Hartmann et al. (1989: 35), in referring to research methodologies on communications and development, argue that:

> In-depth village studies with comparatively 'open' methodology have probably more to offer media research than the more orthodox survey approach on its own, in spite of the seeming scientific rigor and analytical elegance of the latter. Yet, in spite of Rao's pioneering work now over two decades old, hardly any research in India or elsewhere on the effects of mass communication has followed this lead. The sample survey reigned supreme as the main method of investigation, and the rich tradition of Indian anthropology has seldom been brought to bear upon the role of mass communication in Indian society.... There has been a distinct preference for data that can be collected by hiring interviewers, and processed in a comfortable office. A further reason is the attraction of the neat relationships that survey research tends to reveal, both for the bureaucrats who may commission the research and use its findings, and for the social scientists unconcerned that they may be offering a picture of reality that is over-neat and therefore misleading.

However, the more important rationale in choosing the qualitative approach is the lack of research. Television is a relatively recent phenomenon in rural India, and there exists only one study that focuses on the entertainment aspect (Mitra, 1993). Therefore, at this early exploratory stage when hypotheses are still being developed, an appropriate design for this study must have a qualitative orientation. The findings of this research will contribute to the development of our understanding of the role of entertainment television in rural life, which will enable hypotheses to be developed and tested on a larger scale.

The Cultural Influences of Television

Earlier research has concluded that media have little impact on social change. Rao's (1966) research in two villages in rural India found that patterns of interaction and conflict and the role of elites were central determinants of change, and that the media had a comparatively marginal role in effecting change. Hartmann et al. (1989) have similarly concluded that interpersonal communication played a much greater role in effecting social change than the mass media. However, it is crucial to highlight the fact that both studies were carried out in villages without television. The question that emerges is this: 'Since its arrival in villages, what has been the role of television in the process of social change?'

Is television a more powerful agent of change than other media? According to one researcher it is. Salzman (1993) argues that because of the particular form of the medium, television is in fact a much more powerful cultural influence than any previous mass medium. He points to three 'unprecedented' characteristics of television that 'make it a particularly effective medium of cultural influence' (ibid.: 3). The *easy availability* of television programs is due in part to the relatively low purchase and maintenance cost of television receivers. In addition, there is no 'financial constraint on how much one watches, for watching more costs nothing more; rather the more one watches the more 'value' one gains from one's investment [and], the low economic cost of watching TV is matched by the low personal energy costs and the general convenience' (Salzman, 1993: 2). Watching television requires no work, and, unlike a movie theater, TV is often located in people's homes or the homes of friends or relatives. In addition, Hollywood television programs that might cost $One million to produce, cost many Third World countries only $300 or $400 to buy (Hedebro, 1982: 41). These programs are not only popular but cost almost nothing. Therefore, more and more Western productions are being aired on Indian television.

Second, Salzman points to the *broad scope* of television as another characteristic in explaining its unprecedented cultural influence. The increased number of hours of programming, the diversity of programs, and the advances in satellite technologies have all contributed to the expanding scope of television. Indian television, which has traditionally been limited to one channel and criticized for its 'boring, stodgy, government controlled fare,' is opening five 'new channels to private producers [which is hoped] will result in flashier sports, entertainment and news programs' (*Montreal Gazette*, 21 July 1993: A4). Indians are now quite familiar with 'such international fare as MTV, British comedies, American soap operas and Japanese entertainment shows' (ibid.).

Finally, television is marked by its *benign presence*. Salzman (1993: 3) argues that television viewing is apparently 'a pleasant, gratifying, and unthreatening activity.' The viewer appears to choose when and what to watch, how long to watch, and when to turn off the television. Therefore, the television 'is, or appears to be, "under the control" of the viewer' (Salzman, 1993: 3). It is these three characteristics that Salzman argues account for television's cultural influence.

A general survey of the existing literature on the subject of television and its cultural influence is now necessary. Singhal and Rogers (1989: 76–77) point to the adoption of Maggi 2–minute Noodles in diets as a consequence of television advertising.

> The success story of Maggi 2–Minute Noodles in India demonstrates how rapid diffusion of television, the great popularity of an indigenous soap opera, and organizational innovations in marketing and advertising can launch an alien product in a Third World country.... In fact the Maggi noodles story is considered to be the most successful use of advertising in India during the 1980s.

I was living in India during this time and observed the rapid acceptance of this new product. Villagers were eating noodles for the first time and enjoying them. On one weekend trip to a village, I looked in the local store and next to the soap powder, oil, *gur*, flour, rice, and salt were packets of Maggi Noodles. Within a period of less than five years these noodles had become part of the daily local diet.

Another research study referring to the effects of television advertising states that, 'Doctors who work in villages of Mexico report that it is not uncommon ... for a family to sell the few eggs and chickens it raises to buy a Coke for the father while the children waste away for lack of protein' (cited in Vilanilam, 1989: 490). Candy and soft drinks are the most regularly advertised products on Indian television. A soft drink in India costs what the average worker makes in two hours of work. According to Vilanilam (1989: 493),

Someone can easily say that those who cannot afford them
need not buy soft drinks. But advertising persuasion is not
class specific. The passport to the new life style offered by the
soft drink and candy advertisements appeals to all classes, and
a villager who believes in the goodness of the cola for his
'healthy and modern life style' is not aware of the big economic
gap between him and his counterpart in countries which promote these kinds of products.

Kent (1985), studying the cross-cultural influence of television on
rural Navajo families, found that television viewing reduced the
diversity of activities. Families *without* television engaged in a
much greater variety of activities such as family discussions,
butchering, weaving baskets and blankets, making quilts and
inexpensive necklaces, playing with young children, talking, and
grooming horses. Television viewing also 'reduced the number of
loci at which activities occurred, since the set was usually located
in the living room and most activities revolved around it' (Kent,
1985: 124). As Comstock et al. (1978: 154), argue, 'television
reduces involvement in other activities when it is a novelty, and
there is a possibility of a lasting decrease in involvement in more
frequently engaged-in activities. Television is not without its price.'
    Kottak (1990: 70), studying the impact of television in rural
Brazil, concludes that, 'the length of time residents had had
access to television, rather than their current levels of viewing,
provides the best measure of television's cumulative effects.'
Among the variables analyzed were trust, fear, and sex–gender
attitudes. Kottak found that the more people had been exposed
to television the less they trusted the government, and the more
they feared the world around them. A finding, which especially
relates to the present research, concerns the sex–gender views.
This particular finding was 'one of the strongest statistical indicators of television's impact on attitudes...Television made a strong
contribution to [liberal/modern] sex–gender views, independent
of other inter-correlated predictor variables, such as respondents'
sex, education, and income' (ibid.: 81). A very important question
that Kottak poses is whether these findings are really 'effects' or
just 'correlations.' Does 'Brazilian TV make people more liberal,
or do already liberal people, seeking reinforcement for their

views, simply watch more television' (Kottak, 1990: 82)? Kottak concluded that:

> Liberalization is both a correlation and an effect. There is a strong correlation between liberal social views and current viewing hours. Liberal small-town Brazilians may well watch more TV to validate non-traditional personal views that the local setting suppresses. However, there is an even stronger correlation between liberal social views and years of home viewing. Just as the cumulative effects of formal education are assumed to increase with years of schooling, it seems reasonable that the cumulative effects of television increase with years of home exposure.
>
> Thus, heavy viewers are probably predisposed to liberal views; however, over time, their viewing reinforces those views. TV-biased and TV-reinforced opinions and attitudes spread in the community as viewers take courage from the daily validation of their unorthodox (local) views in (national) programming. More and more townsfolk encounter nontraditional views and come to accept them (Kottak, 1990).

Kottak also found that television possession increases social status in the community and that it acts as a source of privileged information. The research concluded that people with high socioeconomic status watch TV 'attentively and frequently because it brings them special information, which they gain prestige and authority by disseminating' (ibid.: 83).

Rao (1966), on the other hand, found that village elites in India with privileged access to media information used that information to manipulate and maintain that position in the community. The community radio in one village was housed in the *Sarpanch's* home resulting only in a handful of people knowing about its existence.

Other research cited by Salzman (1993), supports the thesis of television's strong cultural impact. A study conducted in rural Italy (Silverman, 1975) found that television had a greater influence than newspapers, magazines, or radio. Silverman (1975: 146) found that upon the arrival of television, media messages are no longer filtered through the elite, and that these messages are 'directly accessible to all classes.'

This broadened participation is changing the definition of civilta [i.e. civic culture]. Increasingly, to be 'civile' is coming to mean the ability to take one's place as a citizen in national life and to subscribe to acceptable standards of behavior. Increasingly, those standards are external ones, the national models projected via television and magazines (Silverman, 1975: 147).

Salzman (1993) points to several other studies in support of his argument that television strongly influences cultural change. In surveying this literature, he highlights certain processes that relate to television's influence. According to Salzman (1993: 7), these include:

> The bypassing of elites in the flow of information; the cathecting of consumption as an appropriate orientation; the legitimization of urban, metropolitan, and cosmopolitan models of living and working; the authoritative advocacy of established scientific and state ideologies; and the privileging of certain languages, dialects, concepts, and terms.

These processes — democratization, consumerism, urban modeling, and linguistic hegemony — are a few of the foci of this research and are discussed at greater length in Chapters Seven and Eight.

Television in India

This section analyzes the historical development of television in India. Indian television is now approximately forty years old and has experienced considerable changes in that short time. Shortly after independence, Prime Minister Jawaharlal Nehru urged for the development of television and placed it on the national agenda (Mitra, 1993). Doordarshan, which literally translates as 'distant vision,' was the name given to the television network in India owned and controlled by the government. Until recently there existed only one network, but now cable operators have introduced other channels which are still mostly restricted to the urban environments. The initial objectives visualized by the government for television were:

1. to act as a catalyst for social change,
2. to promote national integration,
3. to stimulate scientific temper among the people,
4. to disseminate the message of family planning as a means of population control and family welfare,
5. to stimulate greater agricultural production by providing essential information and knowledge,
6. to promote and help preservation of environmental ecological balance,
7. to highlight the need for social welfare measures including welfare of women, children, and the less privileged,
8. to promote interest in games and sports,
9. to stimulate appreciation of our artistic and cultural heritage, and,
10. to educate the masses (cited in Pokharapurka, 1993: 16–17).

Entertainment was a very low priority for the government. It can be argued that the medium has grown along two paths. First, advances in technology, mostly over the last fifteen years, have resulted in Doordarshan's reception range covering 85 per cent of the total urban population and 56 per cent of the rural population (Pokharapurka, 1993: 57). Second, programs became more refined as television moved from a merely educational medium to one of entertainment paid for by advertising revenues. There continues to be debate as to the ownership and control of television. Each government party has promised to deregulate but upon coming into power realizes the advantages to their continued control over the medium.

This debate over ownership and control is complicated and will be dealt with at greater length in subsequent discussion. Here the discussion is limited to an examination of the evolution of television in relation to urban versus rural audiences. As Mitra (1993: 25), referring to this evolution points out, 'The connection between "education" and "rural" indicated that the benefits of didactic television were predominantly for the rural population, as opposed to entertainment television which was assumed to cater primarily to urban culture.'

Initially, television was a medium developed to benefit the rural population. Television was perceived only in terms of its educational potentialities (Rao, 1992). The Chanda Commission made it clear that 'television was to be a medium of education and any other programs were relatively unimportant within the future plans of television' (Mitra, 1993: 14). Community viewing (i.e. one television set per village) was the method by which villagers watched television. Sets were usually placed in the headman's house or in the village school. There was one half-hour program nightly, which soon developed into a full hour.

By the early 1970s, however, programs were being telecast daily between 6:30 and 10:30 P.M. At the same time, 'television receiver technology was being indigenously developed and an increasing number of domestically built black-and-white sets were available in the market' (Mitra, 1993: 15). Middle- to upper-class urban families began to acquire these sets and lobby for more entertainment programming. The importance in the shift in viewer demographics became evident as programs began to appeal to both the villager as well as the urban household. Mitra (1993) makes it clear that satisfying these two polarities was no easy task. And it is these changes in television audiences which led to a number of changes in the nature of television programming over the next decade. However, no discussion of television in India would be complete without reference to SITE.

The inauguration of the Satellite Instructional Television Experiment (SITE) on August 1, 1975, is considered the most significant landmark in the history of TV, not only in India but all over the world (Rao, 1992). The experiment was set up in conjunction with the US National Aeronautical and Space Administration (NASA) for reaching the rural audience with developmental messages. The primary purpose of the project was:

> to gain experience in development, testing, and management of satellite-based instructional television systems, particularly in rural areas, to demonstrate the potential of satellites in developing countries, and to stimulate national development in India... to contribute to health, hygiene, and family planning, national integration, to improve agricultural practices, to contribute to general school and adult education, and improve occupational skills (Mirchandani, 1976: 74).

The experiment involved 2,400 villages in six states. Numerous research studies documented its effects. Agrawal (1978, 1980) illustrated the role of SITE in bringing about changes in rural audiences. Shukla (1979) researched the learning levels of children exposed to SITE and compared them to those not exposed. Most of the research involved educational evaluations (Chaudhuri, 1986; Coldevin and Amundsen, 1985) and did not consider the impact of television in reshaping rural culture.

The research considered 'television purely as a channel of communication... [without] much concern for the nature in which [the medium] could impinge upon social and cultural formations' within the rural audience (Mitra, 1993: 34). At most, Eppan (1979) considered the seating patterns for TV viewing at community centers, with the higher status members of the community seated in front while the less fortunate ones (mostly women, poorer men, and children) sat in the back or on the sides of the room. Seating arrangements reflect the village hierarchical structure. The most prominent persons like the village headman or priest are usually placed in front and even sometimes on chairs while others gather around them. Women are segregated from men and are usually found peering through windows and doorways.

The early 1980s witnessed an increase in transmission capabilities as well as the development of a variety of genres of programs on television. Educational programs evolved from 'head-and-shoulder lectures on family planning... to talk shows where a set of guests and a host would discuss various aspects of birth control. In a similar spirit, quiz programs began to present educational information in the form of competitive quizzes which not only entertained but also educated' (Mitra, 1993: 16). Television sets were soon becoming a common addition to the living room furniture of middle- and upper-class urban families. And by the mid-1980s urban television was no more an elite phenomenon.

Today, Doordarshan broadcasts are available throughout the country. In analyzing the medium's current place in Indian society, Mitra (1993: 38) states:

The original priority of education has been supplemented by an entertainment orientation, particularly aided by the commercial sponsors. Consequently, television is now established as primarily an urban phenomenon.... Television is accepted as a quasi-commercial medium, as the advertisers recognize television's potential of reaching the affluent urban [viewer]. Television is more widespread, with a large number of people having access to television receivers. [And] finally, television has emerged as a popular cultural form... and a large number of people across the country now consider watching television a part of their everyday material practices and activities.

Since Mitra's research, television has permeated the Indian countryside even further. Some of the most remote areas of the country now have access to entertainment, news, and information that is watched by people all over the world. In the late 1990s, villagers are rapidly becoming full participants in the television age, and this is dramatically reshaping village life.

Notes

1. This explanation of the relationship between the content of the mass media, the nature of society, and the communications behavior of audiences is called media dependency theory, and its major propositions can be summed up in the following terms: (a) people in all societies need information in order to make decisions about such matters as food, shelter, employment, and other aspects of family life; (b) in traditional societies, people tend to pursue similar ways of life and are linked by word-of-mouth networks of extended families, deeply established friendships, long-term neighbors, and other social ties from which they obtain the information that they need; (c) in urban-industrial societies, populations are composed of unlike people brought together through internal migrations and immigrations from outside; they are greatly differentiated by such factors as race, ethnicity, occupational specialization, and economic class; (d) because of their far greater social differentiation, people in urban-industrial societies have fewer effective word-of-mouth channels; (e) thus, people in urban-industrial societies are dependent on mass communication for information needed to make many kinds of decisions. From the media, they obtain a flow of information advice, and role models in the news, entertainment, and advertising that they use as a basis for those decisions (DeFleur and Ball-Rokeach, 1982: 240–50).

2. This simple belief in the direct effects of media (the hypodermic needle model) has its roots in psychology and behaviorism.
3. This study resembles today's research procedures using a field experiment design but failing to use a control group in any of the experiments.
4. Showing a film to children about a fine young Chinese-American who was not accepted by his non-Chinese neighbors resulted in more positive attitudes toward Chinese. Other youngsters watched a clearly anti-black film which was sympathetic toward the Ku Klux Klan that resulted in the subject's attitudes toward African-Americans becoming more negative.

3

Research on the Frontiers

The research problem and question dictate the research methods. What does a mango taste like? You can break it down chemically and analyze its various components, but if you don't put it in your mouth you will never know how it really tastes. My goal is to understand the role of television within the context of village life from the villager's perspective. An ethnographic approach is best suited for this endeavor. Ethnography 'is the work of describing a culture' (Spradley, 1979: 3). The aim of any ethnography is to see and understand through the eyes and minds of the people from whom we are trying to learn. As Malinowski put it, the goal of ethnography is 'to grasp the native's point of view, his relation to life, to realize *his* vision of *his* world' (1922: 25). According to Spradley (1979: 3), 'Field work, then, involves the disciplined study of what the world is like to people who have learned to see, hear, speak, think, and act in ways that are different.' The emphasis is on the native point of view, because culture is not an autonomous or generalized force that determines behavior. Rather culture emerges from the myriad of decisions made by intelligent individuals within the constraints of their social context.

Spradley (1979: 3,5) argues that:

Rather than studying people, ethnography means learning from people.... The essential core of ethnography is the concern with the meaning of actions and events to the people we seek to understand.

This fact became clear upon entering the field and remained so throughout the duration of the research. I became the student and the Indian villagers the teachers. I was there to learn and grasp meanings from their point of view, from their perspective. Ethnography encompasses a wide range of techniques and methods. How data is gathered affects what data is gathered.

This chapter will detail the methods initially proposed to explore the research questions. The rationale behind the selection of these methods is discussed along with certain modifications which had to be made after entering the field. The procedures for village selection, the unforeseen problems faced during that process, and the rationale for choosing participant observation and in-depth interviewing as the instruments for investigation are described. In addition, an outline of the procedures for the selection of informants to be interviewed, the interview process, and procedures for interpretation and analysis of the data are delineated.

Point of View

Ethnographic fieldwork is subjective for two reasons. First, the ethnographer selectively reports what he is exposed to from the flood of information he hears, sees, and records every day. And second, the information and understanding gained depend largely on the kind and quality of relationships between the researcher and his informants. Each field experience is different not only because the 'cultural environment or the nature of the research problem may differ, but because each depends upon an interaction between the personality of a particular [researcher] and those of his or her hosts' (Ellen, 1984: 100).

My interests, values, and close acquaintance with the research problem are the sources of motivation for this study. I grew up in rural India, in a small town called Panchgani not far from the research villages. The particular culture of rural Maharashtra that most Westerners would consider extremely foreign, I consider home.

I attended an International Baha'i school that had as an integral part of its curriculum the idea of 'service to the community.' This involved various development projects in the surrounding villages (assisting in building a road, literacy classes, etc.), as well as sporting events like soccer, cricket, and *kabaddi*, a local game. The village gained by having additional manpower to do the projects, and the students gained an appreciation of the life of villagers and the knowledge they imparted. I visited these villages on a weekly basis for thirteen years.

In the 1970s and early 1980s Panchgani was a town of approximately 30,000 people. For most of the year it was a quiet town, but during the summer months when the heat was unbearable in Mumbai and Pune, the city folk would flock to this 'hill station.' I moved to Panchgani at the age of three when my parents began working at the New Era School. I completed all my schooling there and returned to the United States for university in 1985.

Most of my friends, playmates, and neighbors came from nearby villages for school or work. Most of my time out of school was spent playing with village kids. And though I often felt like one of them and was often treated as such, I would never argue that I am an Indian. Being white and in comparison more wealthy, I could never completely know what it was like to be a villager. But in many ways my personality reflects the culture in which I was raised.

I returned for a visit in 1988–89, by which time television had finally arrived in the area. And it was this trip which spurred my interest in the research topic. On a visit to a nearby village, I noticed that instead of people sitting outside their huts talking and sharing their experiences of the day, almost everyone had gathered in and around the headman's home to watch television. Daily conversation included discussions of the TV shows of the previous evening and anticipation of the next shows. There also seemed to be more political discussion going on due to news and information gleaned from television.

Ethnographic Methodology

For investigation of the research problem, a quantitative experimental design could not illustrate adequately what village society is like, what role television plays in that context, what the experiences of villagers are in relation to television, and how people think and feel about that experience. A qualitative approach aids in accessing the more subjective aspects of research.

Though both quantitative and qualitative approaches to research should go hand in hand, at this early stage of the arrival of television in villages, qualitative studies are needed to identify questions, formulate preliminary hypotheses, and provide essential context before adequate quantitative studies can be designed, which will be necessary to confirm the judgments of qualitative researchers. For this reason an ethnographic methodological approach to explore the research questions seemed most appropriate. The methods for data gathering were in-depth interviewing and participant observation. The research paradigm chosen is influenced by a variety of perspectives.

This paradigm is naturalistic in that it 'proposes that the indigenous behaviors and meanings of a people can be understood only through a close analysis of natural settings' (Lindlof, 1995: 19). It also takes 'full advantage of the not inconsiderable power of the human-as-instrument, providing a more than adequate trade-off for the presumably more objective approach that characterizes rationalistic inquiry' (Guba and Lincoln, 1982: 235). It is ethnographic in the sense that it seeks the 'thick description' (Geertz, 1973, 1983) of village life and the role of television in that context. The more 'detail that goes into the description, the more multidimensional our understanding, and the more meaning each element of the culture holds for the reader' (Lindlof, 1995: 20). And finally, it is qualitative in that it seeks to answer:

> What kinds of things are going on here? What are the forms of this phenomenon? What variations do we find in this phenomenon? That is, qualitative analysis is addressed to the task of delineating forms, kinds and types of social phenomenon; of documenting the things that exist (Lofland, 1971: 13).

It is this paradigm that directs the focus and delineates the structure and scope of this research project. It is important to enter an area as it exists to obtain data without any deliberate intervention to alter the setting. The focus of attention is on the perceptions, behavior, and experiences of the informants. Their beliefs, feelings, and explanations of those feelings are treated as significant realities.

An ethnographic approach can be seen as interpretive social science. This is due to the fact that the ethnographer does not simply observe but interprets meaning. As Ellen (1984: 28) points out, this

> notion stems directly from the idea that the social world is not a real objective world external to man in the same sense as any other objectively existing reality (natural world) but is a world constituted by meaning. It does not exist independently of the social meanings that its members use to account for it and, hence to constitute it. Social facts are thus not things, which can be simply observed.

Therefore, it is not only behavior, customs, objects, and emotions that are important but their meaning. The ethnographer:

> observes behavior, but goes beyond it to inquire about the meaning of that behavior. The ethnographer sees artifacts and natural objects but goes beyond them to discover what meanings people assign to these objects. The ethnographer observes and records emotional states, but goes beyond them to discover the meaning of fear, anxiety, anger, and other feelings (Spradley, 1979: 6).

Behavior, customs, and people's general way of living can be interpreted and described from more than one perspective. That is why the definition of culture is so important.

For example, at a certain level, 'the culture concept comes down to behavior patterns associated with particular groups of people that is to "customs," or to a people's way of life' (Harris, 1968: 16). However, this definition 'obscures the crucial distinction between the outsider's and insider's points of view' (Spradley, 1979: 5). Members of two different groups might observe the same event or behavior with completely different interpretations.

This can be seen in a simple example from a childhood experience during a visit to the United States when I was ten or eleven years old. I was walking down the street with my grandfather in Oklahoma, and a jogger passed us at a fast pace. This simple behavior was interpreted by my grandfather as normal and produced no reaction from him. I, on the other hand, interpreted it very differently based on the knowledge from growing up in India. Seeing someone in Panchgani, India running down the road meant one thing: the individual was running from something, usually a wild dog. So, based on my knowledge of what running meant, I took off running as well to try and get away from the 'wild dog' which I thought was chasing this jogger. This demonstrates how we use our culture to interpret what we hear, see, and feel.

It is the ethnographer's task to understand and report meanings of behavior, customs, events, and emotions not from his own experience and cultural background but from the perspective and point of view of the people from which he is trying to learn. It is for this reason that Spradley's definition of culture is more appropriate for the purposes of ethnography. 'Culture.... refers to the acquired knowledge that people use to interpret experience and generate social behavior' (Spradley, 1979: 5).

Selection of Villages

It made sense to carry out the research close to Panchgani, India where I spent thirteen years of my childhood. Growing up in this mountain region made me very familiar with the local customs, language, beliefs, and values. I therefore felt that as an ethnographer my research findings would be more accurate and offer greater insights from this environment more than any other.

During a four-week selection period I visited eighteen villages. Through readings of ethnographic materials and consultations with my colleagues in Montreal, Delhi, and Pune it was clear that the villages under study would have to meet certain criteria. The villages would have to be small enough to carry out ethnographic research. They would also have to be large enough to be fairly representative of other villages in the region. Therefore, a village of only a few families, of which there were many, is not representative of most of the villages in the Satara district of Maharashtra. *The Statistical Handbook of Maharashtra* (1994) estimated that the average size of a village in Satara district consisted of approx- imately 950 people. The selected village would have to be hetero- geneous in terms of caste, class, and religion in order to explore power relations within the village. It was also important to find a village with the least urban influence so as to isolate as much as possible the influence of television.

The following list includes the selection criteria developed prior to the initial visits:

1. Size (approximately 100 households).
2. Heterogeneous in terms of caste, class, and religion.
3. Most villagers live and work in the village.
4. Location of village at least 3 miles from the main highway.

After the first week of visiting villages, true to the warnings of my mentor back in Montreal, I soon had to re-evaluate some of the criteria originally set. I had thought that television would be pres- ent in all the villages, but this was not the case. Location had a lot to do with whether or not television was found in a village. In this mountainous region of Maharashtra, reception is limited to those villages at higher elevations or those not surrounded by moun- tains. Some valleys are very narrow and deep which severely lim- its television reception.

On my third day out in the field I visited a very remote village. There was no road to the village, just a small dirt path that bicy- cles could traverse. It was so remote that on the way there I was sure that this would be a great place to carry out the research due to the limiting influences of other external forces. After about three hours in the village and several cups of *chai* (sweet milk tea), it became clear that this village was rather well off. Every house had a gobar gas[1] tank by which they cooked their meals and heated their water on a gas stove. The village also had four latrines, which is rare in this part of the country. Every house I entered had a television set, yet there was an absence of TV antennas. This village did not receive television reception but had instead purchased televisions and VCRs to watch movies every evening. So even in places where television reception was non- existent, the modern medium of the VCR served as a substitute.

In addition, after the first several visits it became clear that most of the villages in this region were not multi-caste but made up mostly of the dominant caste of Maharashtra, the Maratha caste. All small to medium villages in this region comprised only Hindus. This realization created a great deal of anxiety, since my original plan was to focus on caste relations. The more villages visited the more it became obvious that only larger villages and towns contained different castes. One possibility was to travel much farther away from Panchgani to locate small multi-caste villages. This posed several problems among which were language barriers, customs, and accessibility. To have the greatest depth of understanding of village life I had to restrict myself to this mountain region where I grew up.

And finally, I observed what Dandekar (1986) had discovered fifteen years earlier in a village not too far from the area I was visiting. Approximately 40–80 per cent of the males between the ages of 18–35 had migrated to Pune and Mumbai for work. Many of these men would be gone up to five or six months at a time. They mainly worked in construction, transportation, or the textile industries. In attempting to limit other modernizing forces on village life in the hope to isolate to a greater degree the influences of television, I set out to find a village with little or no migration to the cities, but of the eighteen villages I visited in this entire process, not one was immune from this trend.

This discovery again resulted in high levels of anxiety. How was I supposed to know the degree to which television is influencing these people's lives if there are other very strong modernizing forces at play? I came to the conclusion that to explore 'rural life' in India, I would have to accept that urban influences are part of that life, and it would be foolish, almost impossible, and not representative if I were to find a village with no modernizing forces except for television. I decided to find a village with moderate levels of urban migration.

Therefore, after visiting several villages the selection criteria were changed to the following:

1. Presence of television for at least five years, preferably more (electricity is assumed).
2. Size (approximately 100 households, small enough to handle yet large enough to make the task of generalizing more accurate)
3. Economically stratified.

4. Moderate to low political intervention.
5. At least 3 to 7 miles off a main highway or bus route.

The research was confined to the highlands of the Wai and Maha-baleshwar *talukas* of the Satara district in the state of Maharashtra. Panchgani acted as my base of operation, and I selected the village of Danawli to begin the research.

Participant Observation

The principal method of data collection was in-depth interview-ing. However, interviewing ought not to be used exclusively but in combination with 'participant observation.' The latter refers to living in the presence of others over a period of time and having some nominal status among them as one who is part of their daily lives. When used in combination with interviewing it offered a powerful way to call into question the relationship between words and deeds. By becoming a participant observer, I was in a posi-tion to see if people 'say what they mean and mean what they say' (Schwartz and Jacobs, 1979: 46).

Upon entering the field it became clear how intimately these two processes (observation and interview) are interconnected. It is impossible for an interview to exist in a vacuum. Observations are continually influencing not only who should be interviewed but also the questions that need to be asked. The moment I entered the field my observations began. For the first month and a half I did not attempt any deliberate or in-depth interviews. I began by making broad descriptive observations, trying to come to some understanding about the social forces that were most dominant. I got to know people on a personal level, and they slowly became comfortable with my daily presence. After a while I no longer was a novelty to them. Whenever they saw me they greeted me and went on with their daily activities. It is crucial for the ethnographer prior to venturing into in-depth interviews to settle in, become accepted, and be viewed as non-threatening. It is this initial period which allows the ethnographer to get an overview of the social situation. Once he is accepted, at least partly, into the group then he can begin asking questions based on the early observations.

This, of course, does not happen overnight. It took several weeks for children to stop being amused by my blonde hair or my fair skin. During this period I was the talk of the village. Young and old were curious about me both physically and personally. I expected this initial reaction, but during my third week something happened that really worried me.

A boy from Danawli, my research village, was getting married to a girl from a village in the valley about 20 miles away. It is the custom for the girl's family to prepare and organize the wedding. It is always held in the bride's village. On the day of the marriage I was very excited because this was the first big event I would have the opportunity to observe. At about noon, all of Danawli made its way down the mountain slope toward this neighboring village to attend the wedding. By this time, the people of Danawli were comfortable with my presence, and I was beginning to feel part of the group, though being a tall Caucasian I never completely felt unnoticed.

As the wedding ceremony began, Shahir[2] began to welcome everyone over the loudspeakers. There were approximately 4,000 people in attendance. I situated myself deep in the crowd trying very hard not to attract attention. Shahir then began introducing the important personages in attendance including important people visiting from Mumbai, the priest, and some others. People around me were not noticing me and were watching the stage. All of a sudden, I heard my name over the loud speaker. I felt myself go whiter than I normally appear. Shahir, pointing in my direction with an enormous smile on his face, was telling the crowd that I had come all the way from America to learn how Indian villagers live. And that I had chosen Danawli out of all the villages as the place to focus on and I would make Danawli famous.

I was, sitting with everyone else on the ground and felt myself sink deep below. My knees locked and then I turned bright red. I managed to make my way through the thousands of villagers all cheering me on up to the stage and, as quietly as I could, accepted the coconut and garland. What kept me secure was the thought of returning into the crowd and becoming invisible again, but then Shahir ordered a chair to be brought on stage for me to sit on throughout the entire two-hour ceremony. I was the only one on stage sitting in a chair. This is a sign of utmost respect and a practice I never became comfortable with. Shahir continued to brag over the loudspeakers how I was part of the Danawli people and how proud they all were of that fact.

I was of course flattered that the people of Danawli accepted me to the point that they would boast about it to others, but I also felt as if this might be the end of me as an ethnographer. I soon realized that this behavior occurred only outside Danawli. When there were no other outsiders around I felt very much part of the group and was never singled out for special treatment.[3] I did learn to use this special treatment I received at times to my advantage. I would occasionally be exposed to certain individuals of regional importance whom I normally would not have met and I also got the opportunity to interview an important politician.

However, the most significant reason to use participant observation is that only through observations can the ethnographer know what questions to ask and what the responses really mean. According to Black and Metzger:

It is basic to communication theory that you don't start getting any information from an utterance or event until you know what it is in response to—you must know what question is being answered. It could be said of ethnography that until you know the question that someone in the culture is responding to you can't know many things about the responses. Yet the ethnographer is greeted, in the field, with an array of responses. He needs to know what question people are answering in their every act. He needs to know which questions are being taken for granted because they are what 'everybody knows' without thinking.... Thus the task of the ethnographer is to discover questions that seek the relationships among entities that are conceptually meaningful to the people under investigation (quoted in Spradley, 1980: 32).

Therefore in using participant observation for ethnographic purposes, Spradley (1980: 32) argues that, as far as possible, 'both questions and answers must be discovered in the social situation being studied.'

I documented observations and casual conversations as often as possible and made notes about impressions, feelings, and reactions to certain events or situations. After lunch the villagers often relaxed for an hour or two before going back to work, which I used to catch up on my notes. I also set aside a few hours every evening and morning for writing. This was a time for analyzing, organizing, and cataloging the notes. The morning was the busiest time of the day for the villagers, with children going to school, women preparing the food for the day and cleaning the house, and men milking the cows and taking the milk to market. It was during this busy period that I did most of the observing. People did not have time and were not in the mood to talk. I observed the morning bustling activities of the villagers' lives with as little interference as possible. Late morning was a very productive time of the day; I reviewed the notes from the day before and reflected on the increasingly complex data. This was also when I discussed material with my assistant, who proved to be a great resource and friend.[4] It was usually during these mornings that I had the opportunity to visit with the few elders of the village.[5]

My notes also consisted of a detailed description in chronological terms of the events and sites of the day: who was interviewed, where it occurred, what was observed, what was heard within the interview as well as outside the interview, and my own impressions and feelings. These notes also included references to past observations. These field notes, along with the interview notes, become the data for analysis and interpretation, which was an ongoing and continual process of re-coding, refining, and reformulating.

In-depth Interviewing

In-depth interviewing was the other primary method of data collection. I began interviewing after almost six weeks of participant observation. By this time the villagers were comfortable with my presence and did not see me as a threat. All interviews were carried out according to a three-phase method. The first interview was used to establish rapport and to begin understanding the more general questions of the research. The second interview was a time in which more in-depth questions were discussed. The last interview was used to reflect on what had already been learned and any other subjects that had arisen since the last interview. The third interview was also a time to relate back to the informant any conclusions and hypotheses I had developed. I would state what had been my understanding based on the interview and my observations and allow the informant to respond.

The reason for this three-phase approach is to ensure that areas are fully explored. As Whyte (1984: 104) points out:

> The researcher should not hope to cover all relevant areas in the first interview. Often we are greeted with suspicion... if we venture into the touchiest emotional areas at the outset, we find people responding in a guarded and superficial manner and observe unmistakable signs that they would be happier if we left them alone.

The initial interview often yielded, at most, a normative picture. It was only through additional interviews, once rapport had been established, that materials become more descriptive, more confidential, and more reflective of 'what things were really like.' I quickly realized that the first interview must remain as light as possible. Before the informant trusted me, any excessive curiosity about particular individuals, about conflict situations, money, or taxes could have proved dangerous. As Ellen (1984: 195) cautions, the ethnographer:

> needs to continually be reminded that he or she is an uninvited stranger. Therefore, the gamut of questions put to informants must be severely limited. Issues which are likely to offend, embarrass, or arouse suspicions, or which may result in the early termination of fieldwork, are obviously unwise.

Notes were analyzed after every interview to prepare for the next. Questions were open-ended, allowing the informant to cover areas and issues which I did not directly elicit. The length of each interview varied, but the average interview extended between ninety minutes to two and a half hours. I had originally proposed to tape-record all my interviews. This decision was made prior to entering the field. I soon realized that not only did my presence have an impact upon what people said and how they behaved, but the moment the tape-recorder was brought out things changed even more dramatically. Therefore only certain informants and discussions were taped. For example, most of my conversations and all the interviews with Shahir were taped since it was not a novelty to him, and since he had no fear that his recording would come back later to haunt him. At the same time, I chose not to record the Panchayat meetings because to do so would be very intrusive. None of the women I interviewed wanted to be tape-recorded. I took notes of interviews which were not taped. Every night and morning I set aside a few hours to rewrite my notes and observations. I was fortunate to have an assistant to recheck interview materials for accuracy. He acted as a constant support for the first couple of months when I was still reacquainting myself with Marathi and the various terms and phrases that are only used in this mountain region.

A 'good research interview is structured in terms of the research problem. The interview structure is not fixed by predetermined questions, as in a questionnaire, but is designed to provide the informant with freedom to introduce materials that were not anticipated by the interviewer' (Whyte, 1985: 97). Whyte points out that a 'genuinely non-directive interviewing approach simply is not appropriate for research [as it may be for therapists]. Far from putting the informants at their ease, it actually produces anxieties' (ibid.). My interviews followed Whyte's scheme on the flow and direction of each interview. His scale goes from low to high directiveness and is reproduced in edited form below (Whyte, 1985: 99–100):

1. 'Uh-huh,' a nod of the head, or 'That's interesting.' Such responses simply encourage informants to continue and do not exert any overt influence on the direction of their conversation.

2. Reflection. Let us say the informant concludes his or her statement with these words: 'So I didn't feel too good about the job.' The interviewer then says: 'You didn't feel too good about the job?' This adds a bit more direction than response 1, since it implies that the informant should continue discussing the thought which has just been reflected.

3. Probe the informant's last remark. Here, as in response 2, attention is directed to the last idea expressed... the interviewer raises some question about this last remark or makes a statement about it.

4. Probe an idea preceding the last remark by the informant, but still within the scope of a single informant statement. The interviewer probes on an idea expressed earlier in the informant's last statement.

5. Probe an idea expressed by informant or interviewer in an earlier part of the interview.

6. Introduction of a new topic. Here the interviewer raises a question on a topic which has not been referred to before.

The parameters of each interview were demarcated by a set of broad questions. However, it must be borne in mind that due to the ethnographic nature of this research the interview strategy often emerged out of the data itself. Thus the parameters were flexible and were being readjusted constantly as more data were gathered and analyzed.

After a month-and-a-half of participant observation within the village community the initial interview parameters were based on the following five broad questions:

1. Could you tell me about your life in this village before television arrived?
2. What is life like now since television has been introduced?
3. What does this experience mean to you in your life?
4. What do you think of the programs you see on television?
5. What aspects of your life have been influenced by television, and which have not?

These questions were flexible as to wording and were rephrased when the meaning of the question seemed unclear. It is important to reiterate that

Far from being a robot-like data collector, the interviewer, not an interview schedule or protocol, is the research tool. The role entails not merely obtaining answers, but learning what questions to ask and how to ask them (Bogdan and Taylor, 1975: 77).

This learning process spanned the entire period of my stay in India. I was constantly learning what to ask, how to ask it, and when and whom to ask.

At the completion of each interview, I either transcribed the tape or rewrote my notes and highlighted the recurring themes I found. Data was categorized according to these themes and sub-themes. Since the analysis in a qualitative study is ongoing and simultaneous with data gathering, themes were constantly re-evaluated and re-ordered. Each piece of data was coded as to the village, informant, and theme.

In addition, the development of 'theoretical memos' (Glaser, 1978) accompanied every aspect of the analysis. The memos were continually reread for further theoretical ideas. Each memo was categorized according to subject and coded as such along with the code of the data it originated from. No material was discarded in case it was needed for future reference.

Selection of Informants

Qualitative research employing both participant observation and in-depth interviewing techniques calls for a flexible design. 'Neither the number nor type of informants is specified beforehand' (Bogdan and Taylor, 1975: 83). Glaser and Strauss' (1967) strategy of 'theoretical sampling' was used as a guide in the selection of people to interview. What is important is not the number of interviews but the potential of each interview to aid in developing theoretical insights into village life and the role of television.

Informants were limited to those who were permanent residents of the village, and an effort was made to limit the selection to those who seldom visit the towns or cities. The easiest way to 'build a pool of informants is 'snowballing': getting to know some informants and having them introduce [me] to others' (Bogdan and Taylor, 1975). A total of thirty informants were interviewed in Danawli, taking special care that the pool of informants was representative of the village in relation to gender, age, caste, and economic and educational status.

Comparative Data

My initial plan was to spend a few months in one village and then decide on the criteria for the selection of the second village. One possible option was to use the second village as a comparison of the first, holding as many variables constant except television exposure. Another plan was to locate a multi-caste village to compare it to Danawli to see if caste relations were changing due to television.

After entering the field it became clear that most of the smaller villages in this region were homogeneous in relation to caste. Maratha is the dominant caste of Maharashtra, and most of the smaller to medium size villages were populated only by the Maratha caste. This caste is the traditional landholding elite who, though ranking lower than Brahmins, are community leaders and historically the warrior caste. It was observed that almost every villager was exposed to television at some level. I had originally thought that I might find one village with television and one without and make a simple comparison. But even if a village was situated deep in a valley and was unable to receive television broadcasts, the villagers would visit neighboring villages with reception or buy VCRs to watch movies every night of the week.

After several months of research I made a decision based on the knowledge I had gained. Most people had weekly access to television. However, there were two types of television. A TV antenna limited the first type of television reception. With only an antenna a villager could watch the national and regional stations: DD1 and DD2. These are government owned and operated channels, and the TV fare on these channels varies from that of the second type of television reception: Cable television, beamed in from Hong Kong and accessed through a satellite dish or connection.

The majority of the villagers can afford only a TV antenna, and this was the case in Danawli. However, most people in Panchgani and in the nearby villages can afford monthly cable fees, and some can afford to buy a satellite dish themselves. I found a village on the outskirts of Panchgani which had access to satellite television. This village also had a large population that belonged to the Mahar or untouchable caste. This caste converted to Buddhism *en masse* several years ago in an effort to break out of the rigid caste structure. Dhangars are another prominent caste in this region but are much closer to Marathas in the hierarchical structure. The village, Raj Puri, was too large to attempt an ethnographic study.[6] But I decided to conduct numerous indepth interviews in this village with both Marathas and Mahars to understand the caste dynamics. Raj Puri was also not a typical farming village. It was so close to Panchgani that a large percentage of villagers held full time jobs in town and commuted on the bus daily. I chose to interview Mahars and Marathas since the former were traditionally the untouchables and the latter were the landholding elite. I was interested to see if television was influencing the relations between these very distant castes and to discover the role of television on the Mahar caste identity and consciousness.

Notes

1. 'Gobar Gas' is a term used to describe the technology by which cow manure is transformed to methane gas, which is used for cooking.
2. 'Shahir' is a title given to someone who is a folk singer or poet. This was not only his title but a name by which everyone referred to him. He was also the police patil of Danawli.
3. When I say I did not receive special treatment I mean not any more than a person with relatively high status in the village. The mere fact that I was male gave me special privileges which will be discussed later.
4. Prakash, my assistant, was 35 years old. He belonged to the Mahar caste. He had a tenth grade education and was from Panchgani. He was quite familiar with village life since he visited his brother regularly in a nearby village. He was conversant in English as well as Hindi and Marathi. I decided to hire an assistant to help me with several things. I had been away from India for seven years and needed help brushing up on my Marathi. I also felt I needed a friend to initiate contacts within the villages. Though I grew up in the region I was still considered a foreigner, and any help I could get was essential. His companionship and help proved to be so essential that I kept him on for the duration of the research.

5. The few old men and women who did not economically contribute anymore to the family used to sit outside alone after breakfast. The reason the morning was the best time to visit with these elders was because later in the day other villagers would gather around making the elders less comfortable. Though older people are respected to a certain degree they are increasingly thought of by the younger generations as uninformed, conservative, and non-productive members of the village. Younger people sometimes taunted them and created confrontational situations, which I usually tried to avoid as much as possible.

6. There were approximately 300 people who belonged to the Mahar caste and about 2,400 Marathas. There were a few other castes represented in smaller numbers as well.

4

Village Danawli

This chapter attempts to paint a general picture of Danawli, which will set the stage for a more in-depth analysis in Chapter 5 of the social dynamics of the village and its structure.

The Setting

Danawli village is located in the Deccan region of the state of Maharashtra. Under British rule, the inland plateau region of western Maharashtra where Danawli is located was designated the administrative territory of the Bombay Deccan (Attwood, 1992: 23). In 1960, the independent state of Maharashtra was formed when it split from Gujarat. Maharashtra sits on the western coast of India and is flanked by the Arabian Sea to the west, Goa to the southwest, Karnataka to the south, the Eastern Ghats, Andhra Pradesh to the southeast, Madhya Pradesh to the north, and Gujarat to the northwest (Appendix A).

Historically, this region looked westward beyond the Arabian Sea for commercial contacts with Egypt, Arabia, Greece, and Rome. During the fifteenth and sixteenth centuries this region was politically divided under the control of several kings. In the seventeenth century the Maratha Empire reigned sovereign with Shivaji as its first and most memorable leader. With the formation of the state of Maharashtra the region has for the first time emerged as a cohesive political and administrative unit (Dandekar, 1986).

During the British period, rail and road networks elevated the city of Bombay (now Mumbai) to a major center of commerce and industry. In particular the textile mills with their link to London brought Mumbai onto the international scene. Today the city acts as the nerve center of not only the state but the entire region and has had a tremendous impact on the microcosms of village life and its economy. This impact will be shown with reference to Danawli.

Physical Characteristics of Maharashtra

Maharashtra belongs to the basaltic formation called the Deccan lavas which formed about seventy million years ago. A plateau covers almost nine-tenths of the state, with a rim to the west slowly decreasing in elevation east and southeastward. The Western Ghats, also called the Sahyadris, are a mountain range, which form the western rim of the plateau. This mountain range, running through the entire state from north to south, peaks at almost 4,500 feet in Mahabaleshwar 15 miles from Danawli.

These mountains rise quickly in elevation from the coast and have a few passes, which have historically served as main routes from the interior to the coastline. Swift flowing rivers cut deep ravines into the steep west facing mountainsides. The slower eastern flowing rivers have cut wide river valleys throughout the expanse of the Deccan plateau. Huge, almost perfectly flat plateaus of which the Mahabaleshwar plateau is the most significant, mark the tops of the Ghats. The eastern slope of this plateau sits in stark contrast to the steep almost impassable western side.

Rainfall

Maharashtra is generally divided into two broad regions, the Konkan coastal belt and the eastern interior. The climate of both regions is directly linked to the monsoons. Over 80 per cent of the annual precipitation occurs during the monsoons (June to September). The Konkan belt receives the highest precipitation, which decreases east of the Ghats. Mahabaleshwar, the highest peak of the belt, receives an average rainfall of 243 inches (6,182 mm.) annually. This sharply decreases just 15 miles away in Panchgani to 73 inches (1,865 mm.), and Wai, which is at the foot of the Ghat just east of Panchgani, receives only 28 inches (710 mm.) of rain per year. Wai sits in the shadow of the Sahyadri crest and is therefore relatively dry.

Maharashtra: Basic Facts

Maharashtra, at 187,387 square miles, is the third largest state in India (Government of India, 1992). The total population of the state is close to sixty-five million with 48 per cent being female. There has been an almost 25 per cent increase in population since 1971. Maharashtra primarily consists of a rural population (65 per cent of the total) most of whom are engaged in agriculture. However, less than 15 per cent of cultivated land in the state is irrigated. The main food crops are wheat, rice, jowar, maize, bajra, and pulses. The main cash crops are sugarcane, tobacco, cotton and groundnut. The main industries of the state are sugar and textiles (the latter of which is almost exclusively located in Mumbai).

Maharashtra is divided into four administrative units: Mumbai, Pune, Aurangabad, and Nagpur. The state is further divided into thirty districts. Each district has its headquarters in the main town or city of that district. Each district is further divided into smaller divisions called *talukas*. There are eleven *talukas* in Satara district. Danawli is located in the Mahabaleshwar taluka in Satara district, in the administrative unit of Pune.

Satara District

The Satara kingdom predated the British and was seized by them in 1848. The present day district of Satara dates back to 1960; today the district is approximately 90 miles east–west and 75 miles north–south with a total land area of 6,384 square miles (Appendix B). The Satara district is primarily rural with 87 per cent of its population in villages. The Pune district borders to the north, Sholapur to the east, Sangli to the south, and Ratnagiri to the west. Natural features help demarcate the borders of the district. The Nira River runs over almost the entire northern border, the Sahyadri range lies on the west and southwest borders, and the Mahadeo hills border the east. The low lands of the district are part of the larger drainage system of the Krishna River, which originates from the mouth of a cow statue in an ancient temple in old Mahabaleshwar. The Krishna River is one of the main rivers that runs east through the Deccan region.

The physical features of this region remind one of a huge medeival fort surrounded by battlefields. The Sahyadris and the Mahadeo form the hill complex of Satara district with its table-like plateaus set on the peaks throughout the mountains. Sixty miles of the Sahyadris are within Satara district with several fort-like peaks; two of these were major Maratha forts under Shivaji (Pratapgad and Makrandgad). The western face of the Sahyadri range falls steeply into the coastal region of the Konkan. The eastern face falls much more gently into the Krishna valley. Danawli is nestled on the east face deep within the Sahyadris mountain range.

Satara District Economy

About 77 per cent of the total land area in the district is cultivated, and another 11 per cent is covered by forests. Agriculture depends heavily on rainfall, since only about 15–18 per cent of the cultivated land is irrigated. In the past two decades there have been major canal development projects to increase irrigated land. The Neera and Krishna rivers supply these canal projects. However, almost all mountain village lands are not within reach of canal irrigation and have to resort to wells and rain for water.

There are varying soil types within the district with medium black to deep black soils generally found close to riverbanks, which are rich and suitable for garden crops. In the mountains there is generally one type of soil, which is a bright red suitable for rice and fruits. The major crops grown in the district are sugarcane, jowar, rice, wheat, pulses, fruits, vegetables, groundnuts, chilies, and cotton. *Gur* (unrefined brown sugar called jaggery) is a major article of export to the bigger cities. Also exported out of the district are coriander, groundnuts, turmeric, chilies, onions, and garlic. The major trading centers are concentrated in a few towns such as Satara, Lonand, Phaltan, and Wai.

Location of the Village

Off the Pune–Bangalore national highway runs a smaller highway to the east that joins Wai, an important regional town with economic ties to most of the villages in a 12 mile radius. A narrow two-lane road from Wai winds its way back and forth up the steep mountain slope toward Panchgani 9 miles away. Panchgani was a hill station where the British from Bombay and the wealthy Indians would flock during the sweltering summer months. In fact, for several months Mahatma Gandhi rented a villa there. The town sits approximately 4,000 feet above sea level and other than three months of heavy monsoon has a mild climate throughout the year. It was once a refuge for the ailing and sick. Today Panchgani together with Mahabaleshwar, a neighboring town 15 miles to the west, is one of the most popular vacation spots in central India.

On 17 December, 1995 I began my day like any other. I awoke in my small room in Panchgani to spend another day in search of a village which would become my life for several months. I had arrived in India in late November and had spent the last few weeks visiting numerous villages striving to determine which would satisfy the objectives of my research project. The search was beginning to frustrate me. The villages were either too big or too small, lacked television or had obtained access very recently. In two villages I was not at all welcome especially when one Sarpanch recognized me as being the boy responsible for sinking his fishing boat almost sixteen years ago, which was an accident in my view but a careless prank in his. So on this particular crisp morning in December I set out as I had for several weeks in search of the perfect village.

I had ascertained the location of Danawli, 8 miles outside Panchgani, but did not yet know of its beauty. It is located not more than 2 miles from Bhilar, a larger village which acts as the transportation link to the other commercial centers like Panchgani, Wai, Mahabaleshwar, and Satara. Bhilar is only 2 miles from the Panchgani-Mahabaleshwar road. The farmland adjacent to Bhilar has become some of the most sought after real estate for many *Mumbaikars'* summer homes. A tar road installed in 1992 makes its way south from Bhilar through the strawberry fields and wraps itself around the mountainside over the huge cliffs to the village Danawli tucked below them. This is the only road in and out of the village. Danawli is located in Mahabaleshwar taluka in Satara district in the state of Maharashtra. Mahabaleshwar and Panchgani are the closest social and commercial centers to Danawli.

Village Settlement

The villagers of Danawli are mostly farmers of the Maratha caste. There are two main patrilineal groups which make up the majority of the village population. The Yadav and Jadhav clans trace their lineage back to the Yadav Dynasty, which fell in the fourteenth century. There is a third smaller group which migrated to Danawli in 1974 when the government relocated them from the Kikli valley due to the construction of the Dhom Dam. Thousands of villagers were displaced because of this dam project and the Kasurdes were each given a couple of acres of land and a small displacement fee to settle on the outskirts of Danawli in what was then uncultivated land. The main road of the village that runs north–south separates the Yadav and Jadhav houses.[1] The village is divided into three separate wadis. Table 4.1 gives a break down of the population and number of households per wadi.

Table 4.1: Danawli Village Settlement (1996)

Wadi	Households	Population
West	22	194
Central	74	604
East	8	65
Total	104	863

The western wadi is approximately 300 meters from the village center with twenty-two households (194 people) from the Yadav clan. The village proper surrounds the school (KG to fifth grade) and is populated by 604 people (seventy-four households). All of the Jadhav clan live in this village center as well as some of the Yadav and five Dhangar families. The eastern Wadi with eight households is where the Kasurdes (sixty-five people) were relocated to and is situated 500 meters from the village center (Appendix D).

Only the five Dhangar families do not belong to the Maratha caste. The lower caste Mahars left the village about twenty-five years ago. This small group of approximately forty individuals were landless laborers who managed to make a living by working in other's fields in exchange for rice or wheat. They were responsible for most of the clean up of the village in exchange for tax exempt housing. Suresh, one of the elders of Danawli, explained that they ate any livestock that died due to illness or disease. When asked where they used to live, he said, *on the other side of the wadi past the area where we defecate*.

The village temple, which houses the mother god *Jani Mata Kambarji*, is located several hundred yards down the mountainside. The village used to surround the temple but over the years people moved their houses up the hillside to flatter land and closer to the cliffs for protection during the heavy monsoons.

For the first two months of my research I thought that all the villagers belonged to the Maratha caste. This is what they told me when I asked them several times to be certain. But one day when I was talking to an old woman outside her house in the Jadhav area of the village, my assistant asked her if she was from the Dhangar caste. She immediately put her finger over her mouth as a sign to hush up and very angrily went into the house and closed the door. Was she a Dhangar or wasn't she? And if she was indeed a Dhangar why had the villagers said there were none?

After consulting with my assistant and a few Maratha elders in Panchgani, I asked Shahir about what had happened. He acknowledged that indeed she was a Dhangar and that there were four other families that were also Dhangar living next to her (a total of twenty-nine people). This is the conversation that followed:

I was under the impression that the village was fully Maratha.

Shahir: Well, yes it is.

But what about these four Dhangar families?

Shahir: Kirk Baba, it is difficult for you to understand how we live.

I am trying to. Please help me understand.

Shahir: A long time ago there used to be many Dhangars living in Danawli. Actually, they lived all over this region. They are goat herders and that is how they live. But over the years most of the land in this region has been occupied by Marathas or the Mumbaiwalas. These rich people from the city come here and buy up the land because of the nice climate. During the hot season they all come up here from Mumbai and Pune and other places. They are all smugglers. They are rich people. They buy the land and build houses and fence their property. The Dhangars do not have many places anymore for their goats to graze. They do not own much land, we own all the land here and so they have moved to the towns and cities to try and make a living. See, I own 15 acres. Five of those acres I lease to one of the Dhangar families. I could not cultivate all 15 acres by myself even if I wanted to. I only have my son and wife to help me. My daughter is lazy. So I lease it to them. That is the only reason they have stayed in Danawli.

But why did everyone tell me that only Marathas live in Danawli?

Shahir: Marathas are the ones who own the land. They are the rightful inhabitants of Danawli. The Dhangars, poor things, are poor people. But they are like us. They work hard, and even though they don't own any land they are part of our village. They are treated like everyone else. Most people probably don't even know they are Dhangar. It's not like it used to be. In the old days people used to do everything according to caste. Things have changed. The Dhangars are like us now.

What about other caste like Mahars?

Shahir: The Dhangars are not untouchables like the Mahars. They are dirty (Clearing his throat he quickly added). No, no they are OK. But there are no Mahars here in Danawli. There used to be when I was a small boy. But they left many years ago. There are many Mahars in Panchgani.

Are there any other castes in Danawli besides Dhangars and Marathas?

Shahir: No.[2]

Regional Connections

The highways in India are generally poorly tarred two-lane roads which crisscross the country and connect all sizes of cities and towns. They cut through the slow and routine life of the village with the farmer plowing his fields using bullocks and a wooden plow, or harvesting his crop with his family using only a sickle and their hands. Blaring horns from trucks, buses, cars, and motorcycles continually remind the villagers that they are not alone. Along with the noise and pollution, India's highways bring with them everything that is urban. From magazines to films, from tourists to politicians, India's roads and highways are continually exposing rural India to urban life.

Of all the villages I visited during my research, without fail, a road was the deciding factor of the level of development of a village. With access to a road villagers can get their produce to market and students can get to schools. The road joining Danawli to Bhilar was constructed during the 1972 drought. Due to the desperate shortage of food supplies the government employed the villagers to construct the road and paid them 2 kg of wheat per day and 1 liter of cooking oil per week. They managed to survive the drought because of this. In 1992 the road was paved. Before this, the rocky road and landslides from the monsoons made it very difficult for the villagers to use the road. They had to negotiate the extremely steep rough road with their bullock carts and bicycles. If someone fell sick they had to carry him or her on a bamboo stretcher to Bhilar.

Since the paving of the road the village has acquired fifteen motorcycles and one jeep. Access to the outside is becoming easier every day and occurs more often. Shahir used to carry 15 liters of milk to Panchgani every morning on his bicycle, which took most of the morning. Now his son uses a moped to finish the job in a couple of hours. Shahir himself takes another trip into town for police or other business. For any real shopping or business villagers go to Panchgani. Dillip, his wife, and child, go in to town at least twice a week on their moped.

Mumbai seems a million miles away while standing in Danawli's strawberry fields, listening to the birds sing in the serene atmosphere that is characteristic of this region. Yet, Danawli is intimately linked with the big city. Not only do 47 per cent of the males between the ages of 18–32 live and work in Mumbai and return home to Danawli during the harvest season and special festive occasions, most farmers in this village grow cash crops for sale in Mumbai. Strawberries are the number one grossing cash crop. Due to the high elevation and cool temperature, this hilly region of Maharashtra is the sole producer of strawberries in the state, and the famous Malas Jam Company relies heavily on the strawberries from villages like Danawli.

Twice a week during strawberry season a truck is loaded with strawberries from Danawli and driven to Mumbai. Some farmers wanting to make a larger profit on their crop cut out the middleman and sell it themselves in Panchgani, Mahabaleshwar, or Wai. They fill their baskets and make their way to town first thing in the morning, sitting on the side of the main road in town and selling small bunches of strawberries to locals and tourists, with the tourists paying three to four times as much as the locals.

Even though Danawli is located within Mahabaleshwar *taluka* it is much closer to Panchgani and therefore the villages carry out most of their business here. On days that I was not in Danawli but in Panchgani I would continually see people from the village. Wednesday is market day in Panchgani, which is a time when farmers from surrounding villages bring their produce and other items to sell in town. Panchgani doubles in size and traffic on market day. Villagers from Danawli sell anything from tomatoes to strawberries to green beans depending on the season. Some villagers journey down to Wai on Monday for its market day. Wai is a bigger town than Panchgani and is therefore even more attractive. Villages in the valley around Wai do not grow strawberries, so the mountain villagers enjoy the lack of competition in Wai.

Market days are a time to sell one's produce and to gather socially. Villagers get dressed up to see their friends and to be seen. They eat food they do not get every day, visit the tailor in preparation for an upcoming special event, network with potential business associates, or even take in a movie. This is also the time where information and gossip about weddings, politicians, and festivals are exchanged and spread. Prospective marriage partners and dowry are sometimes negotiated.

Public Amenities

The drinking water for the entire village comes from six hand-operated water pumps that were installed throughout the village in 1983. Prior to 1983 the villagers' only source of drinking water were open wells which were a cause of several parasitic maladies. Illnesses caused by unclean water are very common in India, which led my mother to boil and filter our home drinking water the entire thirteen years that my family lived in India. A common parasitic malady caused by unclean water is a terrible infection as a result of long tapeworm called *naroo*. One often sees this tapeworm in the human excrement that lines some of the roads in Panchgani.[3] Water pumps are a major reason for the decreased incidence of water-borne diseases such as cholera, and various intestinal parasites like roundworm and hookworm.[4]

A common sight every morning in Danawli and other villages is the large group of women and children around the water pumps filling their pots for the day. A pecking order existed among the women as to who should get water and when. On one occasion I witnessed a heated argument between a group of young girls and an older woman about whose turn it was to get water. I spoke to the older woman later, and she complained about the lack of respect and deference shown to adults and the elderly by the younger generations. She said:

- *When I was their age I would have never spoken to an older person like those girls speak to me. They even talk back to their parents. They have all become junglies (hooligans). No one can control them anymore. Times are changing and soon there will be no order.*

During the summer drinking water is usually kept in clay pots to keep the water cool and in copper pots the rest of the year. The villagers believe that copper carries certain medicinal properties and therefore the water stored in these pots also carries those same properties.

In September of 1994 the village managed to get the regional development office to grant them Rs. 20,000 to construct two water tanks to hold drinking water. The water was to be pumped from underground and held in these two tanks. The tanks and the pipes were delivered and the people delivering the material were supposed to install it as well. They talked the Sarpanch into accepting five extra pipes instead. A year later the pipes still lay in the middle of the village and continued to be a source of great disagreement among the village leaders.

The village has one communal well which is located by the village temple. The water from this well is used for washing clothes and dishes, bathing, and watering animals but is not for drinking. The water is pumped to sixteen taps throughout the village for three hours every morning. One or several individuals privately or communally own the other wells in the village. A total of fifteen wells surround the village in nearby fields, and sixteen wells are located above the cliffs where many villagers own land. Many of these wells sit dry most of the year and fill up only during the monsoon. Water was by far the most discussed topic among villagers throughout my research, and it became very obvious how life sustaining and important it was. Most Gram Panchayat meetings dealt at length with water issues, and often the discussions were extremely heated.

There is no real sewage system in Danawli today, and the level of sanitation is low. The well water that is piped throughout the village runs into the streets after it is used. There were only two taps with gutters that allowed this run-off to make its way to the fields. A few homes have attempted to manage their used water, but the vast majority wash their dishes outside their homes and let the dishwater and bath water run into the streets. Villagers keep their livestock in the front room of their homes. The excretions from the animals are often moved to the outside of the house, but homes with gobar gas tanks direct this waste into the tanks.

Medical facilities in Danawli are almost non-existent. Tukaram, an elder of the village, acts as the village 'doctor' who treats most small injuries and illnesses. For anything as serious as childbirth or chronic illness villagers go to the several local clinics or the government hospital in Panchgani. In addition, the government provides annual mobile vaccination clinics free of charge. During my stay in Danawli one mobile clinic came into the village for two days and vaccinated all children for polio. Prior to their arrival of the mobile clinic, advertising, which consisted of posters and writing on walls, informed and reminded the villagers of this program in their village. Most people in the village go to Panchgani for medical treatment because it is easily accessible now. However, this is not always the case. One day, Deepak, the Sarpanch's 7-year-old son broke his arm and was treated by the village doctor. Instead of having a cast on his arm he had a few bamboo splints wrapped around it with a sling holding his arm up to his chest. I asked Deepak's father Suresh why he had not taken his son to the hospital in town. He replied that the village doctor did not think it was that serious, so he treated it by applying a turmeric paste to the arm and wrapping it.

The village school is located at the village center. The school was first started in 1957 and provides education from kindergarten (KG) through grade five. There are a total of forty-eight boys and thirty-nine girls.

Table 4.2: School Age Children

Total number of children	Number attending school			Number not attending
	Danawli	Bhilar	Panchgani	
258	87	36	9	126

The school principal and one of the teachers are from Bhilar, and the second teacher is from Panchgani. Thirty-six children from Danawli go to Bhilar every day for school up to eighth grade. Nine children go to Panchgani every morning for ninth to tenth grades. Therefore, out of a total of 258 school-aged children, 126 do not attend school. The principal of the school in Danawli said that very few students attend class regularly. Children are kept at home for a variety of reasons throughout the year. According to the principal:

- *Sometimes the class is full, and sometimes its like this. Now is the harvest season so many children are staying at home to help their parents with the farm work.*

Technological Advances

Danawli, like most other villages scattered throughout the Western Ghats of Maharashtra, is fairly small and in recent years has made significant advances in technological improvements. Today when one enters Danawli, one observes developments which were non-existent twenty years ago.

Whether it is piped water supply to various corners of the village, a paved road, electricity to every house, street lights, tiled floors in several homes, electrical fans for the hot summers, television antennas climbing out of homes owned by rich landowners and landless laborers, or elaborate stereo systems playing popular film songs throughout the day, these mountainous villages are demanding a standard of living commensurate with that in the cities.

Village electrification in Maharashtra has been extensive; in the late 1950s only a fraction of the villages received electricity; by the early 1980s almost 72 per cent of the villages had electricity, and by 1992, 87 per cent of the villages in the state had electricity (Bureau of Economics and Statistics, 1994). Maharashtra has done well in comparison to the rest of the country. In 1980 only 48 per cent of villages throughout India were electrified (Dandekar, 1986: 85). Danawli received electricity in 1970. At first only a few homes in Danawli could afford this new luxury. But only a decade later half of all homes had electricity and today all of Danawli's homes are electrified; it is now seen as a necessity rather than a luxury. Initially electricity was mainly used for lighting, but today it is used for everything from irrigation to television.

One of the first uses of electricity in Danawli was street lighting, installed in 1969, which extends to all three wadis. Leopards roam the mountainsides in this region, which was one of the main reasons given for the installation of the lights. Most house doors are closed and bolted tightly soon after dark because of the waags. A month after I began my research a father and son were attacked by a leopard. They both survived, because they managed to shoot the leopard before any serious injury. I saw the dead animal the next morning. The father said that they were walking to the village when the leopard pounced on the father. He managed to get free, but it caught the boy. The father ran to the village, got his gun, came back to the site and shot the leopard before it could do any real damage to the boy. There are, however, two sides to this story. It is illegal to harm a leopard because they are endangered. Those who harm or kill a leopard can be fined several hundred thousand rupees and sentenced to life in prison. I heard the other side of the story in a café in Panchgani: The father and son were sitting in the dark night waiting for a wild boar, which are quite numerous in these mountains and make very good meat. They saw something move in the tall grass and assumed it was a boar, so they shot it. When they approached the animal which was lying on the ground it grabbed the boy, giving him deep gashes in his back and arms, and the father shot it again, this time killing it. From that day on it was very difficult to convince my assistant, Prakash, to ride back home on my motorcycle in the countryside after dark.

A tax is levied on all homes to pay for these street lights (Rs. 40 annually). Most villagers do not dispute this tax, but some argue that they never use the lights and therefore should not have to pay. They claim that they are indoors before sunset and do not require the use of streetlights. Several times, an older widow argued with the Sarpanch about the tax because the light was so far from her house and she could barely see the light. She argued that only those houses which are near the lights should pay the tax.

When I was growing up in Panchgani in the 1970s and 1980s, gobar gas technology was just being introduced. My school installed one behind the dining hall and used it for several years. This technology uses cow dung and other wastes, include human excreta, to create methane gas for fuel purposes. The fuel is mainly used for cooking, lighting, and heating water for bathing. It was argued that this new technology would lead to healthier living conditions because more sanitary disposal of human and animal wastes would reduce insects and parasites. It would also create cleaner cooking fuel.[5]

In an article titled 'Gobar-gas Plants: How Appropriate Are They?' Hemalata Dandekar (1980) argues that this technology is more suited for some villages than others. Her own research (ibid., 1980: 83) in Sugao, a village in the neighboring Wai *Taluka*, showed that 'scarcity of cattle, the shortage of water, and a lack of land on which to build plants, as well as the dubious gains from an individual farmer's perspective, made the plants unattractive.' In Danawli, Shahir and his family bought the first facility in 1985.

Today, the village has seventeen gobar gas tanks, with a few homes sharing tanks. In two cases, one family had the capital and space but no cattle for cow dung. They approached their neighbor who owned cattle to negotiate a deal. The former proposed that he would put up the capital and space if the latter agreed to maintain the tank by supplying cow dung on a regular basis. They both agreed to use the tank and share the used manure for fertilizer. Another family had an agreement with two other families to deliver the cow dung from their own cows every morning in exchange for a bag of rice every three months.

In all my years visiting villages in this region I never once observed the presence of a latrine. So, one day when I was visiting the eastern wadi in Danawli and saw a little square structure made of cement I commented to my assistant, Prakash, 'how poor this person must be living in such a small house.' To our amazement, it was an outdoor latrine. It was this more than any other thing, whether it was television, stereos, motorcycles or *Time* magazine, which symbolized to me the course and rapidity of rural development in India. I began to understand that the rural people were beginning to see themselves in a different light and to believe that they were equally worthy of the luxuries of urban life. Television is an important contributor toward this rationalization because it shows what urban people consider necessities and makes village people wonder why they do not have the same lifestyle.

Mass Communications

At first Danawli appears to be a fairly isolated village tucked away deep in the Western Ghats of Maharashtra. It sits at the end of a very narrow road which wraps itself around the mountainside and over cliffs, and the village cannot be seen until you are upon it. Yet, Danawli, like so many other small villages scattered throughout this region, is seen as an important part of a larger system.

Villagers do not know only about their village and the regional towns but are becoming more aware of the outside world. An example of this growing awareness occurred one morning when I was sitting with a group of young men sorting potatoes. We were talking about the snake that Rajesh had killed the night before when one of them suddenly asked me: *Who is O.J. Simpson?* Sitting in a potato field on the side of a mountain in western India, I was surprised to hear a young farmer ask about an American football star on trial for murder in Los Angeles.

Television, radio, newspapers, and magazines are common sights in Danawli homes. These media bring information about local, national, and international politics, economics, and weather forecasts. But the primary use of these forms of media is entertainment. From soap operas to sporting events, Hindi movies to stories about their favorite stars, villagers spend as much as five or six hours every day enjoying these media.

Five homes receive the daily Marathi newspaper. These papers are read out loud by a literate member of the family, usually the father or the eldest son, during the morning household activities. The family members go about their business but pay attention to items in the paper that most interest them. Biramneh, the vice-Sarpanch, receives the national Hindi newspaper. Most people can understand a fair amount of Hindi, but only those who have studied it can read. Biramneh has a tenth standard degree from Wai College and is fluent in Hindi. For those who do not have access to the newspaper in Danawli, the teashop in Bhilar is the closest alternative.

Most people, however, rely on the morning and evening television newscasts for their information. The newspaper is seen as a status symbol reserved for those with a greater education; people who receive the newspaper are thought of as intelligent and are sought for advice in important matters. Magazines are a common sight in villages as well. They are usually very old and have been read by many people. Most of the magazines I observed fell into the entertainment category, focusing on film stars and popular musicians. .

Hartmann's (1989: 195) study of villages in Andhra Pradesh, West Bengal, and Kerala found that radios were owned only by those villagers of higher economic, caste, and educational status.[6]

Table 4.3: Ownership of Media

Media	Number of households
Marathi newspaper	5
Hindi newspaper	1
Radio	86
Television	25

In Danawli television had replaced radio as a status symbol. Only the more influential members of the village, who also happened to be the wealthier and better educated owned television sets. Eighty three per cent of homes (out of 104 households) boasted a radio. Since the arrival of television, however, people listen to their radios less and less. As one villager told me:

- *The radio used to be on all the time. We would listen to songs, the news and even to the cricket matches on the radio. But now that we can watch it on television why listen to radio. Television is much better.... And I have seen the color TV set in Panchgani and will get one like that soon.*

The people who do not have much access to television tend to listen to the radio much more often. When I arrived in Danawli twenty-three homes owned television sets, and during my stay two more homes acquired sets. TV sets are becoming cheaper and more affordable to many, so it would not be surprising if by the end of the century 60 per cent of homes in Danawli own television sets.

There are two kinds of television reception in India. Doordarshan, the government-owned station, can be seen using only an antenna, but there is a growing cable market as well. The way the cable industry works is very simple at the local level. A wealthier member of the community can buy a satellite dish, which receives Star TV (a number of channels beamed in from Hong Kong) and Doordarshan. He can charge a monthly fee to anyone who would like access to this cable, and a wire is then run from his dish into their homes. This was common in the various neighborhoods in Panchgani and the wealthier villages connected to the town.

At this point in time Danawli has access only to Doordarshan, because no one has bought a satellite dish yet. Bhilar has had satellite dishes for three years now. In 1996 one could purchase a dish for approximately Rs. 5,000 which equals about $150.[7] A few villagers from Danawli were considering their options. Within three years Danawli, and many villages like it, will own satellite dishes, and people will be watching even more television. All the television sets in the village are still black and white, but color sets, especially those made in India, are becoming much more affordable. There is not a single phone in Danawli; the closest one is in Bhilar.

Institutions and Offices

After Independence the Indian government, in an effort to effectively decentralize, formed an institution called the Panchayat. This new formation of an old concept was an attempt to democratize the village community. Whereas the old Panchayat membership was limited to dominant caste males, the representation in this newly-formed institution was supposed to be more egalitarian. The old Panchayat's decisions were based on maintaining the status quo. In their eyes the village was a social unit based on a social hierarchy, and their decisions supported that existing hierarchy. As Dandekar (1986: 66) notes in her ethnography of a village in Satara district only 30 miles from Danawli:

> The Panchayat heard of a dispute about cultivation rights to a particular piece of village land dedicated to the temple. The protagonist, who clearly had no substantial claim to the land, clinched his argument by asking, 'Are you going to believe me, Ganpat Tukaram Yadav, your kinsman, or this low-caste, no account *teli*?' (*Telies* are oil pressers by occupation and much lower in caste hierarchy than the Yadavs.) The case was decided in his favor.

This new government institution with two reserved seats, one for a woman and the other for a representative of the lower castes, was an effort to empower people at the grassroots to make development initiatives on their own. The Panchayats have the responsibility of carrying out economic development programs envisaged under the national Five-Year Plans. The original village Panchayat was developed to carry out the following responsibilities:

1. Develop farm production programs for the village.
2. Secure funding needed in order to carry out these programs.
3. Act as the channel through which the governments' assistance, given through agencies like co-operatives, reaches the village.
4. Set a minimum standard of cultivation to be observed in the village with a view to increase production.
5. Bring wasteland under cultivation.
6. Arrange for the cultivation of land not cultivated or managed by owners.
7. Organize voluntary labor for community works.
8. Make arrangements for co-operative management of land and other resources in the village according to the terms of the prevailing land management legislation.
9. Assist in the implementation of land reform measures in the village.

(First Five-Year Plan, 1954: 133).

The main sources of income of the Panchayat are taxes levied on property, houses, fairs, festivals, and an octroi tax which is a tax on goods entering the village (Madan, 1990: 344). In addition, the Panchayat is entitled to receive grants from the government for development purposes.

Though there are two seats reserved on the Panchayat, one for a woman and the other for a representative of a lower caste, in Danawli the only active members are from the Yadav and Jadhav clans. Tarabai, the only woman member, is a member only by name. She did not attend any of the Panchayat meetings during the course of my research.

The first Gram Panchayat of Danawli was established on 2 November, 1958.[8] The present Gram Panchayat was elected on 14 November, 1994. There are a total of eight members. There are three members from the Yadav group, three from the Jadhav group, and one from the newly-arrived Kasurde group. The only woman member, Tarabai, belongs to the Yadav group. And though it is required by law to have representation of a lower caste group, the Dhangar are not represented. During the course of my research I attended three meetings of this institution. It does not have its own building, so it uses the schoolhouse as its meeting place.

The formal political structure of the village comprises a variety of offices. The brother of the Sarpanch currently holds the office of Patil, the sole representative of the legal system at the village level. The Sarpanch is the chairman of the village Panchayat and is responsible for ensuring the implementation of the development initiatives of the Panchayat. The up-Sarpanch or vice-chairman is another important officer in the Panchayat. The block development officer (BDO) is a major figure in this region. He is generally based in the taluka headquarters. The BDO for Danawli was stationed in Mahabaleshwar. For the entire period of my research in Danawli he never once visited the village. There are two representatives of the government at the village level. The village level worker (VLW) represents the development component of the government and is usually informed about technology and programs which are beneficial to farmers. The VLW was an older man who lived in Danawli who did a commendable job informing farmers about various agricultural supplements and government programs to aid farming. And though he made efforts to meet with those disadvantaged members of the village, I observed him more with the higher status members. The village *talathi* is the revenue collector. The talathi for Danawli lives in Bhilar. He visited Danawli regularly and met with the Panchayat twice during my stay. This position is often held by Brahmins who have 'traditionally monopolized revenue positions to exploit the poor and ill-informed' (Dandekar, 1986: 70). However, this talathi belonged to the Maratha caste and seemed to be welcome and at ease in the village.

Now that I have laid out some of the more tangible aspects of the village, I will attempt to give the reader a sense of the social fabric of Danawli. I will describe the social structure and power relations in terms of caste, class, and family life.

Notes

1. This type of village arrangement is common in this part of Maharashtra. (see Dandekar, 1986; Kamble, 1979; Valunjkar, 1966).
2. In later chapters I will refer to this conversation again. We discussed caste relations at great length. One thing I learned over the months of research is that when it came to the topic of caste few were completely honest because people knew the politically correct thing to say. But their beliefs and actions often contradicted what they professed. This is why participant observation was so critical to this type of research.
3. During my time in Danawli one child died of dysentery related to unclean water.
4. The original communal well that Danawli villagers used to drink from was an open water well, approximately 15 meters in diameter. The water level would vary from 8 feet below ground level to 40 feet. The well walls are lined with steps leading down into it. Instead of drawing the water out with rope, women and children would walk down into the well. The water became infected in this way by feces and other organic matter carried on the soles of their feet. Today this well is used to pump water throughout the village for washing and other various needs but not for drinking.
5. There is a high rate of lung cancer and various respiratory illnesses due to the heavy smoke from wood stoves.
6. It is important to note here that Hartmann's villages did not have television and radios were the most advanced technological equipment they owned. Dandekar's (1986) research in Sugao was also carried out prior to the introduction of television.
7. The value of the rupee is in constant flux. When I arrived in India the value of the rupee fluctuated between 33 and 38 rupees per U.S. dollar. The average family income in Danawli was between 1,000 and 1,300 rupees per month, although some made as little as 600 rupees per month.
8. The concept of the Panchayat is not new. It is a very old institution which predates the British. The present form of the Panchayat dates back to a few years after India's Independence when the state of Maharashtra was formed (see Madan, 1990).

5

Social Change and Village Society

Introduction

This chapter takes a close look at the social dynamics of village life in this region of Maharashtra. I analyze rural social institutions and deal with the stratification systems of caste, class, and power. The village is placed in the context of the larger socio economic system to better understand the changing forces at the local level. At the outset I would like to discuss two myths about village life which have been dispelled by others. Certain writers have made great strides in disproving the idea that rural society is self-sufficient and haromonious. Therefore my effort here is to lend support to these scholars. Over the duration of my research a picture of village society emerged as a community that is inter-connected with the outside world and marked by great divisions and hierarchies.

Myth No. 1: Self-sufficiency

According to Dumont (1966: 158–59), the early accounts of the 'village community' by the English administrators in the first few decades of the nineteenth century describe the 'village as a little republic, self-sufficient, having its own functionaries, and surviving the ruin of empires.' This romantic view of village life persisted due to the idealized notion espoused by those writing the history books. The popular belief centered on village life as having existed without much change or adaptation from time immemorial. Whether it was village boundaries or names, interests, families, or economies, the romanticized idea of a 'village community' being self-sufficient and autonomous was very real. Dumont further argues that this 'can be seen even more clearly from the fact that the inegalitarian aspect[s]' of village life go unmentioned and unrecorded (Dumont, 1966: 158–59).

This represents both an oversimplified and idealized picture of village life and this notion continued, with few alterations, for the next 150 years (Srinivas, 1994: 21). As recently as 1968, Kumar argued that the village was a 'miniature world, self-sufficient in itself... and that the absence of sharp differences in incomes in the villages of Maharashtra created a climate devoid of conflict and strife. [Even the untouchable Mahars] possessed an important voice in the community despite their low social ranking' (quoted in Attwood, 1992: 31).

Villages were thought to be self-sufficient economic units. Crops provided food and seeds for the next season, taxes to the State, and the means to pay essential artisan and servicing castes such as the carpenter, blacksmith, potter, barber, washerman, and priest. And the appearance of self-sufficiency was enhanced by caste-wise division of labor. Yet, as Srinivas (1994: 55) points out the traditional village community was far from being economically self-sufficient. A closer look reveals several gaps. Salt, for instance, was not produced in most villages, and most spices had to be imported into the village. Gadgil (1948) recognized that sugar-cane farming was limited to certain regions with favorable irrigation, soil, and climatic conditions. Both oil and gur, the raw product of sugar cane known as jaggery, widely used by villagers, had to be purchased in towns and weekly markets.

The romantic view that village life is harmonious, in equilibrium, self-sufficient, and politically autonomous is one which has been disputed by many scholars (Attwood, 1992; Bandyopadhyay and Von Eschen, 1988; Baviskar, 1980; Sháh, 1974; Srinivas and Sháh, 1960; Srinivas, 1994; Wade, 1988). Through my own research I came to understand village society as part of a larger system, economically, politically, and socially interconnected and interdependent with other villages, towns, and cities of the region.

In reiterating these connections, one can not overlook the vital role which the city of Mumbai plays in the lives of villagers in western Maharashtra. Mumbai has always been an important city in the region and has its own distinct character. The largest city in the state, it is dominated by Gujaratis, Parsis, Marwaris, and others from outside Maharashtra (Attwood, 1992: 293). Mumbai is 'not really a Maharashtrian city in terms of language and culture of its elites. This can be explained, in part, by the steep mountains which separate the inland plateau from the coast' (ibid.: 294). The pre-colonial élite of the region were the Marathas and the Brahmins, and in recent years the Marathas have dominated state politics.[1] In referring to the process of political activism over the past several decades, Attwood (1992: 295) argues that the 'progression of movements, trends, and events served to create a strong sense of political identity and potency in the countryside, in opposition to urban interests. By the same token, it muted consciousness of conflicting interests within rural society.'

Though it is an entire day's journey away and what seems like a entirely different planet in terms of lifestyle, work, technology, and language, one cannot escape the dominating impact Mumbai has had on the lives of most of the villagers in the ghat villages of this region. Not only are cash crops exported to the city but labor is as well.[2] Dandekar's data from Sugao, a low-lying village only 50 miles away, shows the trend in migration. 'In 1942, 17 per cent of the resident population had migrated; by 1958 this was up to 24 per cent, and by 1977, 29 per cent of Sugao people lived outside the village. The primary movement of Sugao men continues to be to Bombay' (Dandekar, 1986: 221). Sugao is a village located not far from the main highway leading to Pune and Mumbai, and this trend in migration dates back several decades. The mountain villages of Danawli and Raj Puri are more isolated, and hence the impact of migration began only some twenty years ago. Today, 47 per cent of the male population in Danawli ages 18–32 live and work in Mumbai and return home occasionally for harvest or special religious and family functions. In sum, village society is by no means self-sufficient. It is very much interconnected and interdependent with the outside world.

Myth No. 2:
Harmony and Cooperation

The second myth which has been dispelled is the idea that harmony and cooperation characterize village society. In reality the opposite is true. The study villages resembled any other larger society, with all the complexities of power struggles, factionalism, politics, and crime. In the village I found a society that was striving for change and doing everything in its power to achieve it. Instead of harmony and an idealized communal living arrangement, I found a culture replete with conflict. Each farmer was interested in his own success and considered a gain by a neighbor to be a loss for himself.

I do, however, understand how an uninformed visitor could form a romantic view of village society. Initially, there seems to be a natural equilibrium within village life. Women and men have certain responsibilities, as do the young and the old. Landlords hire the landless and poorer laborers to work their land. By law the Panchayat membership should represent all segments of the village. Both boys and girls sit together in school and learn the same material, and there is a great deal of cooperation which takes place between villagers.

As the months of research rolled by, I came to understand that cooperation among villagers is highly selective and occurs mostly out of necessity. Farmers with adjoining plots consult and negotiate with each other during sowing season in order to plant complementary crops. During the harvest villagers pool their resources and hire trucks to transport their crops to local towns and to Pune and Mumbai. Farmers share the water and energy costs from common wells. These common wells which were once owned by single families are now shared due to partible inheritance. For instance, two brothers who now live and farm separately share the same family well for irrigation. Examples like these demonstrate that some cooperation does occur in the village but mainly out of necessity. According to Attwood, this type of selective and limited cooperation has characterized western Maharashtra for centuries (1988: 187).

When one analyzes the micro relationships within the system itself one finds a myriad of relations characterized by competition and conflict. Villagers are constantly striving against each other for patronage by higher status members of the community. Others see the establishment of a patron–client relationship as a loss for themselves. This is referred to as a 'zero-sum game.' The idea or theory of 'limited good' characterizes village society. Any gain by one member of the community is seen as a loss for others. Therefore, conflict is a daily occurrence within the village. The form and magnitude of the conflict varies and is usually insignificant. But occasionally it can spiral upward to involve the entire village. I observed numerous instances of conflict among villagers during my research. One in particular illustrates how a misunderstanding or miscommunication can escalate.

As we sat in the dimly lit, smoke-filled room no bigger than 6 by 6 feet, my host, Narayan (a Maratha), began to speak about the injustices of village life. He spoke in great depth of inequalities of power, that a few men of the village controlled almost everything in the community. His anger was apparent not only in his words, his tone, and his eyes but also by his actions during the previous day. Narayan owned only a half an acre of land. In addition to growing what crops he could on the small plot, he raised chickens and goats to support his family.

His anger was spurred by the injustice he had experienced which resulted in his actions the day before. A few weeks prior some of his *kombdi* (chickens) had ventured into one of Shahir's fields and had died from pesticide poisoning. Narayan had approached Shahir, who was the village Patil, with this problem and asked for compensation. Shahir told him that he had announced to his neighbors that he was putting pesticides on his fields and to keep their livestock out. Narayan was unaware of this and had therefore sought compensation to no avail. Narayan took this matter to the Panchayat. They listened to his complaint but told him there was nothing they could do. With great time and expense he went to the police in both Mahabaleshwar and Panchgani and had received no help. Narayan decided to take the law into his own hands. He was determined that if he could not get compensation for his loss, Shahir would not benefit either. The evening of the previous day, Narayan allegedly set a number of Shahir's bushels of wheat on fire.

I was visiting with Biramneh in his house when we heard the shouting and commotion outside. As I emerged from the hut a flood of villagers rushed to the burning field. Though Narayan never admitted it, and no one witnessed the crime, Shahir and the entire village suspected him. He claimed he would never do such a thing, but the villagers had already decided. During the rest of my time in Danawli, Narayan was viewed as an outcast. He was ridiculed and ostracized and was never seen associating with other villagers. He spoke of selling his land and leaving the village with all its injustices and moving to the city.

These and other events confirmed the complexity of village life and that its power relations are marked by conflict and suspicion. Far from being simple, static, and harmonious, village society is a 'fiercely competitive environment, one of confrontation and suspicion, each farmer assumes a defensive stance vis-à-vis the rest of the village, spending his energy defending his land and optimizing his return from it' (Dandekar, 1986: 264).

The Social Institutions of Marriage and Family

Traditionally the family is the most important social institution within the village. If there must be a choice made by any member of the family, between family duties and outside obligations, family duties come first (Wiser, 1971: 152). Research has demonstrated the importance and documented the influence the family has on the individual. According to Mandelbaum (1970: 41):

Each person learns the fundamentals of his culture and society from his family; he experiences his main satisfactions and shares his personal achievements with other family members. In his jati-group he is primarily identified as a member of his family, and he assumes the reputation of his family in the village. His whole life experience is embedded in his family relations. The main transitions of the life cycle are family celebrations, and the grand occasions of a person's life are mainly those that occur in the context of the family.

In this mountain region of western Maharashtra the family remains a very important social institution. It remains the primary unit of production and consumption. Land is worked by the family, and the exchange of services is largely carried out between families. Although the family remains a vital institution and an important influence in an individual's life, in recent years there has been a shift in its role. Today, individual achievement is highly respected. One does not automatically 'assume the reputation of one's family' anymore (Mandelbaum, 1970: 41). What one achieves based on one's own initiative is an important and valued aspect of life. Mahendra was born into a very poor family, and his father cleaned the public toilets and sewage in a nearby town. He belonged to the lowest untouchable caste (Mahar). He is now an educated man working as a clerk in the town's post office. He is highly respected within his caste and among the Marathas of the village. People from all strata of the village come to him for advice and assistance.

Another change in recent years is reflected in the source of knowledge and learning. Traditionally 'each person learned the fundamentals of his culture and society from his family' (Mandelbaum, 1970: 41). Today, television is an important conveyor of culture, and children learn many of their values by watching hours of television every week. Their aspirations, goals, and ideals often reflect more of what they see on television than what they learn from their parents and grandparents.

Family Type

In India the structure of the family unit varies considerably and is determined by numerous variables. Caldwell et al., (1988) identify four major family types which include (1) *a nuclear family* which is a conjugal couple with their unmarried children; (2) *a stem family* includes two married couples in different generations; (3) *a joint family* includes married siblings living together; and finally (4) *a joint-stem* family is the classical full pyramid where the older couple have with them more than one of their married children and usually grandchildren. Any of these can be *extended* if other persons, usually relatives live with them. There is also the possibility of *eroded families*. For instance, 'if a widowed mother lives with a younger couple because both couples shared residence before the death of the widow's husband, this is an eroded stem family; but if the widow joined the younger couple for support only after the death of her husband, this could be regarded as an extended nuclear family... Any family structure more complex than a nuclear family [is] called a large family, irrespective of relative numbers of members' (Caldwell et al., 1988: 111). Each of these family types are represented in Danawli.

As Table 5.1 illustrates, the majority of the families in Danawli are nuclear. Sixty-two families (59.6 per cent) were intact nuclear types, five of which had relatives living with them. Twenty-two families were characterized as stem families with several housing relatives. A stem family with at least one broken couple signified migration or death.[3] There were three joint families and five joint-stem families. The latter representing the full pyramid often spanned three generations living in one household.

Table 5.1: Household Structure of Danawli

Type of household	Distribution of households (actual number)		
	Not extended	Extended	
		Agnatic	Non-agnatic
Full Classification:			
Nuclear			
• Both parents living with unmarried children.	57	3	2
• One parent living with unmarried children.	7	1	1
• Married couple without children.	1	1	
• Single adult living alone.	1		

Table 5.1 continued

Table 5.1 continued

Stem			
• Two or more married couples of different generations.	7	1	2
• At least one couple broken.	8	1	3
Joint			
• Two or more married siblings.	1		1
• At least one couple broken.	1		
Joint-stem			
• Parent/s with two or more married siblings with or without children.	2	1	2
Summary:			
Nuclear	66	5	3
Stem	15	2	5
Joint	2	–	1
Joint-stem	2	1	2
Totals	85	8	11

In all but four of the cases where non-agnatic relatives were living in the household, when asked why they were living there the response always involved financial reasons. All said this was a very temporary situation that would last only a few months. In the other four cases the non-agnatic members had moved into the household permanently and were contributing financially to the maintenance of the family through outside employment.

According to many elders of the village, this classification of family types has not changed much over the years. Nuclear families have always been in the majority with few joint-stem families. As one man in his late seventies explained:

- *Families have always been small. There are only three or four families in Danawli which are big. Those are the powerful ones with many acres of land. Most of the families here own just a few acres of land and have always been small. Some have no land at all. At times they get big, when their son gets married and has children or an uncle comes to live with them.*

Caldwell et al. (1988: 129) illustrates the relationship between family type and landholdings:

Among those with no land at all, 71 per cent are found in nuclear families; with land up to 1 acre, 65 per cent; with land from 1 to 4 acres, 58 per cent; and with over 4 acres, 46 per cent. With more resources and a need for more labor, there is more point in keeping a larger family together.

Mandelbaum (1970: 54) argues along these same lines, 'people tend to remain in joint families longer when economic factors favor such families. The poorest and lowest groups tend to have fewest joint families, but even at these social levels, most families become joint for at least a time after a son marries.'

Table 5.2: Land Distribution by Family Type

Acres	Nuclear (%)	Nuclear	Stem	Joint	Joint-stem	Total
0	91	21	2			23
1–2	81	18	4			22
3–4	75	15	5			20
5–10	57	11	5	2	1	19
11–15	46	7	6	1	1	15
> 15	40	2			3	5
Totals		74	22	3	5	104

My own data show a similar trend, but in Danawli there seems to be a higher percentage of landless nuclear families. As illustrated in Table 5.2, 62 per cent of the families in Danawli each own less than 5 acres of land. Of those, 83 per cent live in nuclear families. Following Caldwell's line of analysis, 91 per cent of landless families, 81 per cent owning land up to 2 acres, 75 per cent owning three to 4 acres, 57 per cent owning 5 to 10 acres, and 45 per cent owning 11 acres of land belong to nuclear families. The figures from Danawli are higher than Caldwell's, but the trend remains the same. The more land a family owns the less likely it is to be found among the nuclear families.

Attwood (1992: 17) referring specifically to rural families in Maharashtra states that:

> The *ideal* family is the patrilineal, patrilocal joint family, consisting of a senior married couple, their sons, and their sons' wives and children. Owing to various contingencies of fertility and mortality (and economic opportunity), this ideal is often not attained in practice; and when it is, it appears only as a phase in a long cycle of family growth and dissolution. Nevertheless, there are good economic reasons why this family type serves as a conscious goal for many villagers. In brief, the family can be more productive and more secure if it combines the skills and experience of a senior couple with the vigorous toil of one or more junior couples. It is vital to combine the specialized efforts of men and women, and equally vital to combine those of the senior and junior generation of adults.

Several of the nuclear families that I interviewed stated that at one time they were a joint or joint-stem family. Family types are constantly changing, but most strive to attain the ideal joint-stem family type. My data, similar to Attwood's (1992) arguments, suggest that the ideal that most villagers strive for is a joint family type, which they believe to be more productive and secure. But in reality few families remain joint for very long due to the developmental cycle or process of growth and dissolution. A joint family requires a substantial amount of land not only for sustainable agriculture but to grow cash crops as well.

I now present an example which illustrates how a family type can change under varying circumstances. Sunjeet and his wife Sunita married in 1963. They lived with his parents who both died within five years. Sunjeet was the only son, and his one sister had married before him outside the village. Sunjeet inherited 16 acres of land from his father. They were relatively wealthy compared to most other villagers and had brought Sunita's parents and brother to live with them. They farmed 12 acres and leased out the rest. Within ten years of marriage they had three daughters. And with the marriage of each daughter they lost 5 acres of land due to the dowry system. When I met them Sunjeet was working in a pharmacy in Panchgani and the half-acre of land they still had possession of in Danawli was up for sale. They owed the bank Rs. 60,000 and had no way to pay it off. The only people living in Sunjeet's ancestral home were he and his wife.

Family Size

The families in Danawli were grouped into four classes: (*a*) small, consisting of one to four persons, (*b*) medium, consisting of five to six persons, (*c*) large, consisting of seven to eight persons, and (*d*) very large, consisting of eleven to fourteen persons, with fourteen members forming the largest family in Danawli.

As shown in Table 5.3, only 4.9 per cent of the households in Danawli were classified as large (having seven or more members), while 50.9 per cent had between one to four members. According to one woman:

- *I would love to have my husband's brother come live with us, he is a good man and is good to my children. But we only have enough land to grow rice for five people and not any more. Before he left we were really suffering. We tried to find outside work to make more money. But since he left two years ago we are doing much better. Smaller families are more economical. This is also why you won't find people anymore having five or eight children. I only have three and I sometimes wish I had only had two.*

The data does not always support the idea that large families are less cost effective than smaller ones. Some villagers argue that large families are more cost effective because they provide more free labor. Smaller families are upset about having to hire labor to help with the farm work. According to one villager:

- *I can never get good help. I hired a certain woman from Bhilar yesterday, and she did not do any work. At the end of the day I had to give her seven rupees.*

Table 5.3: Family Size in Danawli

Family size	Number of families
1–4 persons	53 (50.9%)
5–6 persons	30 (28.8%)
7–10 persons	16 (15.4%)
11–14 persons	5 (4.9%)
Total	104 (100%)

Some families stay together not out of necessity but out of fear of losing their share of the inheritance of the family land if they leave too early. Others break up the family for personal reasons. Rajesh moved out of the village in 1992 with his wife, found a job in Panchgani, and bought a small piece of land on which to build his house. He explained:

- *I moved out of my house in Danawli because I had no privacy with my wife. I was also treated badly by my father because I was the youngest of four children. I was always having to do the worst jobs, so I finally said 'no' one day and moved into my friend's house in Panchgani.... I never had my own money, but now I do and I can do anything with it that I want.*

According to Rajesh, he could not have improved his life in the original situation. His only option was to get out and start on his own. He maintains good relations with his family in Danawli but has no economic ties to them.

Family Relations

Traditionally, brothers remained together within the parental home after they married, equally sharing the economic responsibility of the household and helping each other to the best of their abilities. Traditionally age and sex were:

the main ordering principles in family hierarchy. The men have the more decisive authority in the traditional Indian family as compared with women, and elders have greater authority as compared with younger persons. Difference of a year or two in age is sufficient to establish firmly who is the formal superior. As between the authority of an elder woman and a younger man, sex is the more important determinant. Men have the formal property rights, and so the formal authority of a younger man—not necessarily his actual influence—is higher than that of his older sister, though he is expected to respect and cherish her (Mandelbaum, 1970: 38).

The importance of age and sex has been changing over time. Young people are more informed and are more defiant toward their elders than before. Teenagers are often as knowledgeable as their elders about various regional, state, and national affairs. Young adults are often more aware of new business opportunities and investment possibilities. Young men frequently talk about ways of making money off the farm. The older generations are more tied to agricultural labor and are beginning to respect the younger generations more. But there are some that are not happy with the changing attitudes of the young as the following comments illustrate:

- *These young people today have no shame. They do not respect anyone. They think they know everything.*
- *I would have never talked like that to my father when I was his age. Times are changing. See how young Suresh is and he was elected Sarpanch.*

In addition, gender relations have been changing in recent years. According to one young woman who was soon to be married:

- *I have more opportunities than my mother and grandmother had. My parents listened to me when they were going to pick a man for me to marry. I did not want just any man. I wanted a man who would treat me well, and my parents listened to me. And even though my brother is older than me he also has to do work in the house and not sit like an old buffalo. My father makes him work just as hard as me.... You know, the man I am going to marry is not very rich and so my father has said that he would give me one acre of land when he dies and so it will not all go to my brother.*

According to Mayer (1960), 'the dominant note in the formal pattern of relations in the household is that of restraint. There is restraint between people of different ages and restraint between those of opposite sex' (quoted in Mandelbaum, 1970: 40–41). And though this restraint and hierarchy that has traditionally characterized relations within the family unit is still evident today, it is becoming less obvious. I saw fathers and their sons playing and being affectionate toward one another. Unrelated men and women were seen joking and laughing while watching television. And teenage boys sneak out of their homes after dinner *to watch television with the girls.*

The husband wife relationship is another area of discussion. As Wiser and Wiser (1971: 79) has stated,

No matter how humble a man's position may be in village society, he becomes a personage when he enters his own courtyard. His wife, and any other women who are junior to him, are ready to do his bidding with head bowed and voices subdued. To the young husband, this authority is most pleasing. He who has always been dependent upon others, suddenly finds a human being under his control.

To demonstrate this point I have recreated a scene from my field notes. These notes were taken 20 March 1996 on *Gudhi Paadva*, the Hindu New Year:

After the meeting at the Temple, Shahir and I went back to his house for some lunch, and we walked in to find his wife sleeping. He acknowledged that she had been very sick the night before. Obviously in a lot of pain, she began preparing food for us as we sat there and watched. I felt terrible as I watched this woman who was badly ill cook us lunch as we just sat there. To make things worse she sat there while we ate (a custom that I never became comfortable with) and continued to serve us. She even fetched water for us. She returned to the bedroom only after we had finished everything. The entire time Shahir did not raise a hand to help her. His 17-year-old son just sat there.

While there are certain visible changes within family relation-ships, the family remains an extremely important institution within the village and within an individual's life. Although the individual spends most of his time interacting with members of his family, and these relationships are very important to him, other types of relationships based on class and caste also greatly influence a person.

Caste

The caste system of India has been defined as a system of 'endur-ing groups whose mutual relations are governed by certain broad principles. Castes as enduring groups can be located with relative ease, since they are named and have fairly well defined bound-aries. The principles which govern these mutual relations, how-ever, are complex in nature' (Beteille, 1996: 3–4). It is first and foremost a system of stratification in which the status of the indi-vidual is determined by his birth and ritual purity. Caste has been defined as a 'small and named group of persons characterized by endogamy, hereditary membership, and a specific style of life which sometimes includes the pursuit by tradition of a particular occupation and is usually associated with more or less distinct rit-ual status in a hierarchical system' (Beteille, 1996: 46).

The majority of smaller villages scattered throughout the Ghats of western Maharashtra mainly comprise Marathas, so I selected a much larger village, Raj Puri, on the outskirts of Pan-chgani where a variety of castes were represented. Interviews and observations with these people helped me understand caste dynamics in more depth and gave me insight into the history of caste relations and changes that have occurred over time.

While Raj Puri, a village with a population close to 4,300, is cat-egorized as a farming village, the majority of its working adults hold full-time or part-time jobs in Panchgani. A bus leaves the vil-lage four times a day for the short trip into Panchgani. Many vil-lagers own mopeds, bicycles, and a few own and operate taxis. Raj Puri has a variety of castes represented besides the Marathas the largest of which are the Mahars or 'Buddhists.'

Both dependence and interdependence characterize caste relations. In referring to this two-sided system, Sharma (1978: 62) states:

> The formal political relations among castes involve a differential access to power and are governed by the idea of dominance, which is ritualized economic interaction...mutually binds individual members of one caste to individuals of another in exchange of goods and services.

Historically village society in Deccan Maharashtra was hierarchical. It consisted of three major groupings: (*a*) a dominant class of cultivating landowners who usually belonged to upper castes such as Brahmins and Marathas; (*b*) a subordinate class of individuals belonging to the lowest castes (considered untouchable) who acted as village servants, performing the menial and ritually polluting tasks essential to the community, and were paid by revenue-exempt tenure on village lands; and (*c*) a group of artisans who provided services to the village as a whole for which they were paid by revenue-exempt tenancy on village lands (Attwood, 1992; Dandekar, 1986).

Today villages in this region consist mostly of farmers of the Maratha caste. The Marathas are traditionally the land-holding élite, and though ranking lower than Brahmins, they are the community leaders. The Marathas are:

> known for their cooperatives and politics, that is, in enterprises which depend on organizing public support. Unlike their counterparts in Gujurat, they are not known for their business skills, nor for migrating to other regions in pursuit of commercial profit (Attwood, 1992: 294).

Marathas are strongly represented in Satara district, which is the heartland of the Maratha peasantry (Sirsikar, 1970: 40). According to Gadgil (1955), this region of western Maharashtra has for centuries been the stronghold of the Maratha caste, and it is the peasantry who are responsible for the power wielded by the Marathas at the state level.

In the early stages of the freedom struggle the political leadership was in the hands of the Brahmins. However, for almost half a century the Marathas, who constitute approximately 40 per cent of the total population, have led state politics. According to Karve and Damle (1963: 156), who has written extensively on rural Maharashtra, the Marathas, 'though neither educationally advanced nor wealthy, have always been conscious of themselves as a fighting and a ruling class.' In addition to their power at the state level, the Marathas dominate the leadership positions through the Panchayati Raj institutions because of their numerical strength, and make up the bulk of the peasantry, as well. To quote Sirsikar (1970: 24), 'the Marathas have numerical strength, economic and political power, and ritual status on their side.' All this in addition to the historical positions of power occupied by the Marathas 'combine to give to this caste group a very dominating position in the political and social life of Maharashtra, specially in the rural areas' (ibid.: 25). This triple Maratha monopoly (caste, class, and political party) distinguishes Maharashtra as unique within the Indian Union.

A lower caste also residing in the area is the Dhangar. Five Dhangar families lived in Danawli and were the only other caste there beside the dominant Marathas. The Dhangars are traditionally a caste of sheep and goat herders. The Mahar caste, now often known as the Buddhists, is the largest untouchable caste in the state (Attwood, 1992). The Mahars' traditional occupation was village servant. In order to break free from the rigid caste hierarchy, Mahars collectively converted to Buddhism several decades ago. Attwood (1992: 99) describes the Mahars' early political struggle led by one of their own:

B.R. Ambedkar (1891–1956), with doctorates from Columbia and London University, was the most remarkable leader from an untouchable caste. Born a Mahar, Ambedkar received support for his education from Sayajirao Gaikwad. Ambedkar organized conferences and demonstrations for the 'Depressed Classes,' demanding the right to enter temples and take water from tanks used by higher castes. As a gesture of defiance, he once burned a copy of the Manusmriti, the ancient Hindu code of laws. He was supported at this time by Jedhe and Jawalkar, the militant non-Brahmin leaders. Ambedkar fought bitterly with Gandhi and the Congress leaders because they treated issues of social justice as secondary to political freedom.

However, he joined Nehru's first cabinet after drafting India's Constitution. He resigned from the cabinet in 1951 and led the Republican Party in opposition to the Congress. As his final gesture of defiance against Hindu society, he led his own caste to convert to Buddhism in 1956.

Under Ambedkar's leadership, Mahars embraced the path of education as a route toward individual and social emancipation. However, their status as a small minority with little land prevented them from gaining political or economic power in the countryside. Individual Mahars found better opportunities through education and urban employment, and some went on to express their frustration with the caste system by founding the Dalit Panther movement.

Today, having little or no land to make a living in the villages and few opportunities with any political influence, many Mahars have migrated *en masse* to the urban centers.

Panchgani has substantial Mahar populations who are employed throughout the town in varying capacities. Sharad, a Mahar whose family migrated to Panchgani from a nearby village when he was only 8 years old, is now a powerful political figure in the town. In fact, like many politicians, he has managed to earn a substantial income (official or not). During my stay he held a big celebration for his new house which attracted many powerful townsfolk to the heart of the Mahar residential area. He is so influential today that he helped me on several occasions with government papers and visa.

The Mahars of Raj Puri on the other hand, are still struggling with little power or political influence. Most of them work what little land they have and hold jobs in Panchgani. Shankar, a man I became very close to and who was instrumental in helping me gain access to the village, works in a general store in town as an assistant. He has had this job for over thirteen years, and though he still owns only two acres of land in Raj Puri, he is financially stable.

Like the Mahars, Brahmins are numerically insignificant in most villages of this region. They are located mainly in urban centers like Pune. Today Brahmins number about 3 per cent of the total population of the state. Historically Brahmins have, due to their 'dominant position during the Peshwa Rule, and the greater part of British period, been able to maintain their hold on professions, civil services, and in recent times the industrial and commercial bureaucracies' (Sirsikar, 1970: 25). This is less true today. Mahars have made great inroads into the professions and commercial bureaucracies because of their strong emphasis on education. Federal and state legislation has also created opportunities for lower castes to enter the civil service. The Brahmins, of whom six families live in Raj Puri, who do reside in villages are often the most literate, carry out administrative functions, and are generally quite powerful. Brahmins in the countryside are also known for large land holdings (Attwood, 1992).

From historical accounts of some of the older villagers of Danawli it became clear that at one time there might have been a sizable population of Mahars living in the village. According to an 83-year-old ex-Sarpanch of the village, many years ago the Mahars once numbered close to 200 or 300 people. The last few Mahar families left the village some thirty years ago. Since the Mahar caste is so wide spread in Maharashtra some scholars have speculated that its members are the original inhabitants of the area (Zelliot, 1970). In fact, some evidence suggests that they may have been the original land owning class in the villages (ibid.).

There were six untouchable or scheduled castes in Raj Puri. They were the Mahar (village servant), the Mang (rope makers and musicians), the Ramoshi (village watchman), the Holar or Chambhar (cobbler), the Dhor (leather tanning), and the Wadar (supplier of stones and earth). Few of these people retained their traditional caste occupations and instead opted for jobs in Panchgani or farmed their family's or other's land in the village. Mina, a daughter of a widowed Mahar, was educated up to tenth grade in Panchgani and then went to Wai for college. She now works as a school teacher in one of the boarding schools in Panchgani and lives with her mother and brother in their home in Raj Puri.

Another very good example demonstrating the fact that traditional caste occupations are not set in stone and that there is always room for upward mobility concerns a friend of mine. Prakash (not to be confused with my assistant), a classmate of mine, was the son of a Dhobi (washerman) in Panchgani. His family was very poor and could not afford some of the luxuries of other Dhobis. Every morning as a child he, along with his father and mother, would carry heavy loads of dirty laundry 2 miles out of Panchgani to wash. Every morning on my way to school I would see Prakash running home to get ready for school. By the time I had woken up he had already put in a good three hours of work washing clothes. He graduated at the top of our class and completed his teaching degree in Wai. As I sat drinking tea one evening in Panchgani I heard my name called and turned to find Prakash, a handsome, well dressed young man sporting a necktie and expensive looking eye glasses. He is a teacher at one of the local schools and is married with two children. His father continues today to wash clothes for a living.

My discussions with villagers about caste and caste relations proved to be intriguing and puzzling. I interviewed several individuals and groups in Raj Puri. This village has a fairly large Mahar population which lives on its outskirts, and it was on this group that I focused. On my first visit to this section of the village I noticed that the road we used to get there was the defecating area of the villagers. It had such a repulsive odor that I had to cover my face until we had passed. One particular afternoon as I sat with three Mahar men and one Mahar woman under the shade of a mango tree, I asked them about caste relations in the village. Malan bai, the woman in the group, was very outspoken. She assured me that caste relations were very good:

- *We eat in their (the Marathas') homes and they eat in our homes. When there are festivals or weddings we are invited and eat with them. Times have changed. We have learned a lot from people like Mahatma Gandhi and Dr. Ambedkar. People are now more aware that caste differences are not good. We must treat each other equally.*[4]

When was the last time a Maratha ate in your home?

- *Oh, no Maratha has ever come to my home to eat.* (one of the men interjects saying) *People in Panchgani mix much more than in Raj Puri.*

What about inter-caste marriages?

- *Oh yes, there are many inter-caste marriages. Marathas are now marrying Dhangars and sometimes even Buddhists* (they no longer refer to themselves anymore as Mahars).

Who in Raj Puri, has married outside their caste?

- *Oh no, not here but in Panchgani there are many.*[5]

Can you name someone?

- *No I don't know anyone personally, but I have heard. Sometimes, people get married and no one knows their caste.*

One of the younger men present who also had a college degree, who had remained silent up until now joins the conversation:

- *Things have changed a lot in the past ten or twenty years. Before, Buddhists were not respected at all in the village. We had no say in public matters, and were treated as untouchables. We could not use the village wells and were looked down upon by everyone. We kept to ourselves and lived out our lives the best we could. But times have changed. People are more educated now. The higher castes treat us as equals like you people from Europe and America. We are not Mahars any more, we used to be but that is a bad word now. We are Buddhists. We converted many years ago and now worship Bhagwan Buddha.*

Then, as diplomatically as possible, I asked the group about the dirt road leading to their wadi from the village center they use to go into town everyday which is heavily littered with human excrement. The moment I brought it up the group fell silent. It was obvious that they were very embarrassed that I had noticed. Then, almost all at once, they began blaming each other for not bringing that up with the Sarpanch. I had obviously struck a sensitive chord. They claimed that the Marathas treated them well, but this chosen site of defecation was indicative of the true state of their relations. Through my observations I noticed many inconsistencies with what people told me and how they behaved. I never once observed friendly relations between the two groups. The interactions that I did notice occurred out of need and were brief and not overly friendly. Interactions were either business, political, or out of necessity. I never once observed social interactions between Marathas and people of lower castes in the village.

My observations of interactions and relationships between castes did not match what the villagers described. It soon became clear that there was a politically correct way to talk about caste relations. The traditional beliefs and values about caste hierarchy are very much alive in rural India. Of all the people I talked to about this subject, however, only two outwardly acknowledged that the caste system was indeed beneficial for society. One was of higher caste, and the other was an untouchable. They both rationalized that the caste system maintains societal equilibrium and provides a position for everyone in society, both socially and economically. However, the vast majority of the people interviewed spoke of the caste system in negative terms. There has been a lot of government propaganda over the years to abolish the system of caste, since it has been outlawed in the Constitution. People attempt to put their best foot forward when asked about controversial subjects such as caste relations. Therefore, observations and interactions with people were crucial.

The concept of the 'dominant caste' first introduced by Srinivas in 1955, is useful to our discussion of caste at the village level. In Srinivas' (1994: 79) words:

> A caste may be said to be 'dominant' when it preponderates numerically over the other castes, and when it also wields preponderant economic and political power. A large and powerful caste group can more easily be dominant if its position in the local caste hierarchy is not too low.

In most of these mountain villages and rural Maharashtra, the Marathas are considered the 'dominant caste.' They are numerically greater than other castes and are the traditional landholding élite. And though they do not rank at the top of the caste hierarchy, they are considered the 'dominant caste' in Danawli and in Raj Puri.

Srinivas (1994: 79) further argues that 'The essence of hierarchy is the absence of equality among the units which form the whole.' This unequal system within village communities might at first appear to be one of separation and distinction. Castes are distinct and segregated both socially and otherwise. Certain occupations are reserved for certain castes, and marriage between castes is rare. Many features of 'village life tend to insulate castes from each other: endogamy, the ban on commensality, the existence of occupational specialization, distinctive cultural traditions, separate caste courts, and the concepts of pollution, karma and dharma' (Srinivas, 1994: 94).

Yet, it is the very nature of these differences and segregating forces which make castes in multi-caste villages highly dependent on each other. Occupational specialization requires interdependence among castes. This specialization gives each group a 'vested interest in the system as a whole, because under it each group enjoys security in its monopoly. Monopolies are jealously safeguarded by various means. But the families enjoying a monopoly are also competitors, which means that kinship tensions and economic rivalries may drive each family to seek friends outside the caste' (Srinivas, 1994: 94).

Today, the system of occupational specialization is much less pronounced than before. The availability of occupations other than those specified by one's caste, allow villagers to move out of their hereditary occupation and pursue new forms of work and employment. Education, migration to towns and cities, and an increasingly diversified economy all serve to undermine the traditional occupational structure. Yet, caste remains an important variable at least at the village level prohibiting inter-caste marriage and thus insulating the hierarchy. But to regard caste as the sole determinant of power relations is to overlook other variables which affect position and influence.

The view that caste has a complete and firm grip on rural life is an oversimplification of a complex socio-political phenomenon. On the other hand, it is even more difficult to accept the even more simplistic view that caste has lost its preeminence in the social hierarchy, and that other variables like class, education, and family have become more dominant. The truth lies somewhere in between. In a rapidly changing society, caste is an important factor in rural communities.

Class

Class is another area of village life which requires analysis. This section deals principally with the organization of production in

Danawli. Though it is important to understand what is produced and the details of how goods are produced, I am more interested in looking at the class system as a system of social relations. Traditionally, class refers to the owners and non-owners of the means of production. And within an agrarian system, the means of production generally refers to land and its ownership.

Most villages in Maharashtra are agrarian, and the class structure has historically been conditioned by this fact. In recent years other factors such as income from off-farm employment and working conditions are important contributory variables within the class structure. In addition, modern material possessions resulting from the spirit of consumerism within rural communities, is another important variable that must be considered when analyzing class and class relations.

What follows is a discussion of the traditional agrarian class structure in India, distinguishing regional characteristics, and evolution of this system. Relations between landowners, tenants, and agricultural laborers have defined the class structure. It is therefore the relationships between these categories of people who are involved in the process of production that are most interesting. Within each village, production is

> socially organized to the extent that it involves relations between persons having more or less specific rights, duties, and obligations with regard to one another. The relations of production tend to create cleavages as well as bonds between classes or persons. These cleavages partly coincide with other cleavages in the social structure, such as those of caste, and partly cut across them (Beteille, 1996: 110–111).

Unlike the traditional caste system, classes are, in principle, open. People can move up or down within the class structure. A tenant can become a small landowner and vice versa. Vertical movement within the caste system is generally inadmissible, although it has been documented that there is some movement in practice (Srinivas, 1966a). Whereas in the class system individuals move up or down, in the caste system 'entire communities [can occasionally] change their position' (Beteille, 1996: 190). Mobility in the caste system is, however, a much slower process than in the class system. 'The style of life of a community has a complex and pervasive character, and it takes a long time to bring about a change in it' (Beteille, 1996: 190).

Due to the fact that in an agrarian system the class structure is, to a large extent, based on the ownership or non-ownership of land, mobility is much easier. Property can be acquired or lost very easily and over short periods of time as was discovered in the study villages (also see Attwood, 1992). Historically, the only way to acquire land was by inheritance, so land did not exchange hands very often. Once every generation there was a transfer of land from the old to the young. Landowners in the past were a much more homogeneous group. Due to a variety of variables, among which has been a move toward a cash-based economy, land is now being bought and sold by villagers from all strata of communities (Beteille, 1996: 112). This is dramatically altering the hierarchical structure of rural society.

Today people from a variety of social backgrounds are able to invest in land to which they previously had no access, and there is a great deal of buying and selling of land. Legislative changes have also contributed to this shift from a more homogeneous class of landowners to a more diversified group.[6] Particularly since the 1980s, village society has become much more egalitarian regarding the distribution of land. This is not to say however, that all people own land. In Danawli, out of the 104 households, twenty-three are still landless. Danawli has a total of 854 acres of farmland. Of these, on average only 781 acres approximately are cultivated annually.[7] Within the agrarian class system there are two major classes at the village level, the landed and the landless. A variety of classes, some more homogeneous than others, make up these two broad categories.

The absentee landlords constitute an important though increasingly diminishing social class who typically live and work in Mumbai and visit the village once or twice a year. They lease their land out to a variety of farmers and collect a nominal fee in addition to the farmer paying the annual revenue tax. Most absentee landlords try to maintain economic ties with the village but are more interested in their social ties. A marriage that occurred during this research illustrates this point. A family originally from Danawli that still owned land in the village but had been living in Mumbai for the past nineteen years arranged a marriage for their daughter to a man from Danawli. This girl who had grown up her entire life in the city was now expected to live the life of a village wife. And it soon became obvious to many people that this girl was going to have serious difficulty adjusting to her new life.

Some absentee landlords find it difficult and financially unwise to hold on to their land. More villagers are selling their land today because of the numerous opportunities a cash economy offers them. These villagers are finding better ways in which to invest their capital. They are selling their land and reinvesting. What is unique about this region of the state is that land prices have skyrocketed, because it has become a popular tourist destination,[8] and villagers want to sell their land to city folk for an astronomical profit. Villagers are often faced with a dilemma: hold on to the land until a city buyer comes along or sell to a fellow villager for much less.[9]

Another category within this dynamic class structure, which remains homogeneous, includes the resident non-cultivating landlords. Within Danawli there are only three families in this category, and each wields great power within the village. This land is leased to tenants who pay the tax on the land and an annual fee in cash, and are required to give a certain amount of their harvest to the landlord. The landlords claim that rice is usually the only crop offered; however, on several occasions I observed wheat, tomatoes, cabbage, or potatoes being given. The few people who belong to this category hold full and part-time jobs in Panchgani and Bhilar and return to Danawli at night. When asked why they do not cultivate their own land, one man told me:

- *I have a job in Panchgani in the bakery that pays good money. If I were to give up that job and only grow rice then I would be in much worse shape than I am. And now with the road it is very easy to go to Panchgani every morning and return every night. I used to only come back to visit my family on Sundays, but now I come home almost every night.*

Other categories within this class structure include the growing number of small landowners who cultivate their own land and others' land as well. There are those who lease land in addition to owning their own, and others who labor in return for cash. A few landless families lease a small plot of land to grow rice for subsistence, and hold full time jobs in Panchgani as *ayahs*, *malis*, and construction workers.[10] This village class structure is not rigidly fixed. People move in and out of the various categories and belong to more than one at the same time. As Beteille (1996: 119) contends, the structure of the class system is such that it:

> tends to impede the development of a consciousness of class, although the conflict of interest between classes is often acute and does sometimes come to the surface. More frequently this conflict tends to be posed in terms other than those of class and to run along cleavages which are more sharply defined in the social structure, such as those of caste.

In Danawli I found the class structure to be very complex. Land and its ownership or non-ownership is no more the sole determining variable of class. Other factors like off-farm income, material possessions, and working conditions were important. Over the past two decades more and more villagers have found employment in towns and cities to supplement their family income.

Migrating to Mumbai to work is very popular among the young male population. The income of these men is crucial for the sustenance of the family. According to one mother:

- *My son is only 19 years old, and he works in Mumbai as a truck driver. You have not met him yet because it has been six months since he returned. He will be coming in two weeks and then you will see him. If he did not work in Mumbai we could not live... We do not have much land and my Ganesh goes to school in Bhilar. My husband and I work in the fields and try to survive... Sometimes I work for other people in Bhilar during harvest and we make some money that way. But it is Sampat who makes life for us possible. I hope that he will marry soon and find a job in Panchgani, but that is also difficult. Mumbai is where all the work is.*

Those who work in Mumbai are valued not only for their income-generating abilities but because living and working in the city helps build status. These men, and it was solely men who migrated to Mumbai for work from Danawli and Raj Puri, return from the big metropolis wearing urban clothes, sporting sun glasses and baseball hats. Many villagers look up to these 'city' men with their modern ideas and values and regard them as worldly men who know a great deal about life in general. According to one prospective migrant:

- *Those who go to Mumbai to work are much better than us. They know much more and they get a lot of respect. If I go next year then I will get that type of respect when I come back and that is why I want to go.*

However, generally the elder more conservative members of the community, look down on these new clothes and ideas and regard these modern men as hopeless and corrupt who only know how to boast. And the villagers who understand the living conditions of those who work in Mumbai pity them. Migrants themselves acknowledge the poor quality of life in the city and agree that life in the village is better.

- *The way we live in Mumbai is very poor. We make good money to send back to our families, but we have a hard life. Everyone thinks that we have the good life in Mumbai because that is all they see on TV. But I sometimes would rather live in Raj Puri and not in Mumbai. (Then why don't you?) Oh no! I could never live here. What is there to do here? Sure my family is here and I miss them sometimes, but I have got used to the city life. I might return in ten years or so, but not now. Also my family relies on my work in Mumbai.*

Not only is income an important determining factor of class, but living and working conditions are as well. Suresh, a member of the Mahar caste in Raj Puri owned only one acre of land. He had a good job in Panchgani as a general store assistant and had built an extension on his house in the village. His moderate income enabled him to buy a color TV set, an electric fan, a steel bed, a small sofa, and a dining table. Suresh's job and material possessions more than his income and ownership of land contributed to his family holding a very high social status within the community. He was highly respected even in Maratha circles, and people came to him for help and advice. He was only a man of 34 years, but he held a position of respect in the village community.

The spirit of consumerism is rapidly taking over village life and is probably the most significant change one notices upon entering the village. Within the past seven years, there has been a marked increase in material possessions in village homes. Television is the most obvious addition. But electric fans, steel cupboards, water heaters, modern blankets, and urban clothing and styles were equally intriguing since growing up around these villages I rarely observed any of these material objects. The most surprising addition was finding a latrine in a village. For thirteen years growing up in this region I never once saw a latrine in the villages. This was seen as an urban luxury. Today, these modern appliances and conveniences are viewed by most as essential necessities of life. Basic needs are constantly changing. Fifteen years ago, a development organization tried to introduce latrines into villages around Panchgani. Villagers simply laughed at the idea and told these development practitioners that if they were going to spend money in the village they should give them something they really needed like wells or a school or a road.

Material possessions are becoming such an important variable within the class structure of village communities that an increasing number of villagers are opting to buy 'things' rather than invest in their land or in their children's education. Daily conversations often centered on who had what and how much it cost. When a villager acquires something new he goes to great efforts to make sure that the neighbors and others know about it.

In sum, the mountain villages of western Maharashtra are characterized by a complex class system. Today, access to capital is altering the traditional class and power structure of these village communities. Working and living conditions, and material possessions, are also important determinants of class. This power structure is closely tied to the economic system of the region and beyond. Whereas the power of the state is backed by physical force, power within the village community is backed by various other means: economic, ritual, social, and physical. The question is then: how is power distributed in the village and how is it supported?

Power Relations

Power is an important variable that runs through all types of relationships within the village community. Whether it is age, gender, educational status, class, or caste, it is power which rests at the foundation of all social relationships, and thus it is power which is most interesting. Beteille (1996: 144) distinguishes between power and authority, the latter being more narrow in scope: 'Authority is power which is legitimized; it necessarily operates within an institutional framework.' For example, the village Sarpanch has a certain amount of authority which the people of the village have invested in him. Likewise, the village Patil wields authority over conflicts within the community. A large landowner on the other hand, may have a certain amount of power, which he might use to influence individuals or groups, but he has no legal authority.

Weber's (1958: 180) use of the term power is useful within the rural context: 'In general, we understand by "power" the chance of a man or of a number of men to realize their own will in a communal action even against the resistance of others who are participating in the action.' In contrast to the idealized view of the village community, power struggles are a common characteristic of rural life. Traditionally, power resided with the higher castes and was synonymous with caste.

Over the last several decades, there have been shifts in the bases of power within village India. These shifts have greatly influenced the means by which power is achieved and maintained. Some of the old bases of power, such as birth and ritual status, have been supplanted by new ones. The mobilization and support of numerically preponderant groups is an avenue in achieving power. Attwood (1992) contends that new bases of power have emerged which are, to some extent, independent of both caste and class. Perhaps most important among these according to him is the strength of numerical power. The Maratha caste of Maharashtra enjoys strong popular support. The Mahars also, due to their large numbers mainly in the cities, represent a strong social, economic, and political force.

Other integral components of power at the village level include the ownership or non-ownership of land. Today, due to a variety of factors such as land reform, which Maharashtra has made great strides in, as well as a move into a cash-based economy with a growing off-farm employment sector, many traditional 'landless' castes are acquiring land and flourishing in occupations that give them more economic power in the rural community. Several

Mahar families in Raj Puri, a village just outside Panchgani, have in the past twenty years substantially increased their land holdings. They have gained access to credit and resources, which they traditionally did not have. Historically, familiarity with government officials and alignment with influential personages was a crucial avenue in obtaining and maintaining power. And though this is still an important force today, people are advancing through independent knowledge and information as well as through entrepreneurship. It is no longer a prerequisite to obtain approval from village leaders or seek their advice. Television is a factor that has leveled the playing ground, and now people from all strata of the community receive the same information. Yet whom you know remains very important. A villager in Raj Puri belonging to the Mahar caste was related to an influential official in Panchgani. The relationship helped this villager secure several strategic acres of land just outside the village with access to two wells. This acquisition elevated this individual to a very high status in the village, and soon he became one of the individuals people, both Mahar and Maratha, came to for advice and support in conflicts.

Beteille (1996) analyzes the political aspects of power, particularly in its relation to social stratification. He looks at the dynamics of power within the Panchayat, the political parties, and the local elites and argues that though a separate analysis of each is important, the real importance lies in the 'social networks [that] play an important part in the inter-linkage of these different structures of power' (Beteille, 1996:, 182). The ethnographic research conducted in Danawli paints a picture of power in constant flux.

A few men had monopolized political power within Danawli. These men were constantly being challenged, and they worked very hard at defending their power. The source of this power was based on two fronts. Ownership of land was an important factor, but one's popular support in the village outweighed any other factor. The methods of obtaining and maintaining this popular support often involve external political alliances. Political activism within the Shiv Sena political party was a major avenue in obtaining political leverage within the village community. The three men who were the most active in the party were also the village Sarpanch, the Patil, and the *Up-Sarpanch*. These three men were

continually challenged by a younger generation that, due to their
urban employment and modern ideas, a knowledge base, and
comparatively large capital reserves, acted as a powerful threat.
The younger generation continually attacked and lobbied against
the political power that resided in the hands of the older landed
élite.

Unlike some other Third World countries whose rural leaders'
main objective is to enter the urban élite, the rural leaders of
Maharashtra tend to identify with their village roots and work on
solutions to problems within that context. Attwood (1992: 293)
argues that:

> In many regions (in Africa, Latin America, and parts of India),
> this trend is encouraged by the failure of governments to invest
> in the countryside—that is, to invest in transportation, electrifi-
> cation, irrigation, education, public health, and other infra-
> structure which would provide the base for local entrepreneurs
> to build new institutions. Much has been written on how and
> why governments neglect the rural poor.... It is perhaps more
> difficult to explain why Maharashtra fails to fit the common
> pattern. It seems to me that some of the reasons go back to the
> region's distinctive geographic and historical roots.

Though it is not my intention to delve into an analysis of the
region's political history or to explore in detail the relationship
between the village and the state,[11] it is important to point out
that Maharashtra has a very strong sense of regional identity.
This identity 'binds people of different statuses and localities
together. Semi-isolation, due to mountain ranges separating the
Deccan plateau from Gujarat, Malwa, and the coast, is partly
responsible for this distinctive identity. In addition there is Maratha history' (Attwood, 1992: 294).

Maratha political activism, especially in Satara district, demonstrated the ability to carry nationalist issues into the countryside.
In opposition to the urban, high-caste leaders, the Maratha leaders
articulated a distinct set of interests supporting village development and gained popular support. Today, politics in Maharashtra
is not ideological but competitive, pragmatic, and dominated by
leaders from the countryside (Attwood, 1992: 295). It is therefore
the close association and active participation within this political
structure, which ensures village improvements. Power within the

village is closely linked with the political system outside the village. Those who are the most politically active in and out of the village are also those who wield the most power in the village.

The household unit is another level at which power should be analyzed. Gender and age relations have traditionally been clear and rigid. Women had a certain role, as did men. The young were supposed to respect and revere the old. Today, the lines which demarcate these relationships are blurring. On several occasions villagers commented that no one knew their role anymore. As we sat on the front step of her house one early afternoon, while the rest of her family rested inside, an elderly woman quietly confided:

- *You hear the way Luxmi bai (her daughter-in-law) talks to my son. She makes him do so much work. She is so lazy. She is like a queen. Women don't know their role any more. They talk back to their husbands. Times have really changed… Even these children never listen anymore. I don't know what is happening. See how these young girls and boys sit and talk and laugh during TV. When I was young we were not allowed to talk to boys. Nowadays men are doing women's work and women are doing men's work. You know Tara Bai (a neighbor) has learned to work the bullocks because her husband is in Mumbai for so many months.*

Power relations within the family are changing. Teenagers, both boys and girls, talk back to their parents and assert themselves. Television is a contributory factor. Due to its presence male and female, young and old, spend more time together in close proximity for extended periods of time. This, in addition to the modernizing influence of the content of many of the programs, has created a new dynamic within the household. Traditional power structures and relations are evolving not only within the village context but within the household as well.

Conclusion

The purpose in this chapter has been to analyze social change within the village community by focusing on three aspects of

1. A typical interview situation. It was difficult for villagers to take 2 or 3 hours off from their work to talk to me so we often talked while they worked.

2. A home in Danawli with gobar-gas technology which produces methane gas for cooking

3. A village boy dressed for school. This is the traditional attire for boys which is slowly changing.

4. Villagers gather every morning to take advantage of this new luxury—pumped water throughout the village.

5. The weekly market in Panchgani where villagers bring their produce for sale.

6. Women who cannot afford transportation walk great distances into town to sell milk every morning.

7. This is Dillip in his western clothing; rarely seen without a baseball cap (turned backwards).

8. The older generation maintains their traditional dress.

9. Women at a wedding in Danawli.

10. Men at a wedding in Danawli. Men and women are often segregated in public, but with the introduction of television into the home, there is much more gender mixing.

village life: marriage and the family, caste, and class relations. A broader look at the power relations which lie at the foundations of all these relationships has also been taken. All these areas of the social structure of village life are closely interwoven. Each inter-penetrates the other, though an attempt has been made to analyze each individually to provide an insight into their relationships with one another.

Economic change, political pragmatism, competitiveness, restructuring of ritual status and mobility, and the spirit of consumerism has created a new social environment within the village. If one is to understand village society, one must understand these political processes, power relationships, and the multitude of other forces within the village.

Notes

1. According to Attwood's (1992: 318) footnotes, 'A former Chief Minister of Maharashtra (Vasantdada Patil) once commented that 'Bombay is in Maharashtra, but Maharashtra is not in Bombay.' During my research the political party Shiv Sena, which appeals to the sentiments of migrant workers from the interior and rural Maharashtra who feel dispossessed in their 'own city,' was very active in and around Panchgani. They even put up banners along the roadside leading to Danawli. In fact, there was a belief that as Shiv Sena became more powerful, non-Maharashtrians would be less welcome in Maharashtra.
2. People are often treated as cash crops. Cheap labor exported from Mozambique, Botswana, and Lesotho is just one example where not only are wheat and vegetables exported as cash crops but people as well.
3. In Caldwell's study a broken couple in all cases represented death which is not true in this case. Many young married men traveled to Mumbai to work most of the year and only returned home occasionally.
4. In later chapters I will come back to this very conversation and highlight a few comments made about television and its role in changing people's attitudes.
5. The only case of a Maratha marrying a Mahar that I was able to find were two young people who had met in school in Panchgani and

fallen in love. They had eloped and now live in Pune. He works in a factory and she in a hospital.

6. In Maharashtra, there are laws which make the relationship between the tenant and the landowner important. Tenants who have labored continuously for several years on the same plot of land have the legal authority to claim it from the owner as their own. There are two sides to this type of legislation. It is beneficial to the tenant in that he has the opportunity to become a landowner and move up in the class structure. But at the same time it has kept landowners from renting their land thus leaving it fallow and unproductive, but more importantly it has compelled landowners to lease their land for short periods of time thereby not allowing the tenant the ability to claim ownership of the land. This consequence does not make it cost effective for the tenant to make any long-term investments in the land causing a gradual deterioration in the rented farmland.

7. These uncultivated acres of land fall under various categories. A large percentage is owned by absentee landlords, several acres have been untended for many years, and the terraced walls supporting those fields have eroded. In addition, there are a few acres that were disputed in the courts as to their proper ownership and therefore were left fallow.

8. This mountain region of the State is the most popular tourist attraction due not only to its cool weather but its breathtaking scenery. Other than during the heavy monsoons, the areas around Panchgani and Mahabaleshwar are year round tourist destinations.

9. Many villagers own land in areas on top of the mountain that are rapidly becoming targets for tourist housing. People from Mumbai buy an acre or two and build their summer homes on the land. Danawli is still not considered close enough to the areas that are prime real estate, but at the rate of growth of the tourist industry, it is only a matter of time before Danawli is directly affected by it.

10. This is an example of how certain castes are engaging in non-traditional occupations to maintain a livelihood. One mother takes her son into Panchgani with her every day to attend the school where she is employed as a kitchen worker. In return the child receives a free education.

11. Attwood (1992) has an entire chapter on this subject which does a superb job taking the reader through the political developments of the region.

6

Television in India

Setting the Stage

Just hours after my arrival in Mumbai International airport, I rode in a taxi on my way to Pune. As we crossed over the long toll bridge leading out of the city I observed a man on an elephant on the side of the road. The man looked as if he was a *sadhu*, because he had long hair and a beard and was dressed in only a loincloth. As we drove up next to him I could see that he had three ash lines on his forehead which confirmed that he was on a religious journey. As we got closer I noticed something that I will never forget. This man, who typified the romantic view of traditional India, was wearing a Walkman. And what appeared to be the elephant rocking him back and forth was actually him moving to the sounds of the music in his head set. This was my first introduction to modernizing India.

Not a day went by that I did not observe the stark contrast between traditional and modern India. These instances have increased dramatically since the mid-1980s. On another occasion while visiting Pune I observed a family of rope makers sitting on the side of the road engaged in their age-old occupation while next to them stood a business woman, dressed in a suit and high heels, hailing a taxi and talking on her cellular phone. It is scenes such as this which have become a common sight not only in urban environments but in rural India as well. Television is the most obvious reminder of this contrast between the haves and the have nots, between modern and traditional, and of the impact of Western cultures on Indians.

This chapter provides an overview of the place of television in India today. Three basic questions lie at the heart of the subsequent discussion. All concern television: What is the status of television in India? What is its role in the lives of villagers and how are they using it? And finally, what part is television playing in the ever-changing social fabric of rural India?

While sitting in a small teashop in Pune just days after my arrival in India, an old newspaper caught my eye. One headline read: 'Television: Satan's tool?' (*The Pioneer*, 26 December 1994). The article discussed the pros and cons of television in 'traditional' India. It cited an instance in which high rise dwellers in Mumbai, after hearing a sermon on the evils of television by a religious leader, threw their TV sets out of their windows. Quoting one housewife, 'our children were being corrupted. They would not study, instead of going to *namaz* they were interested in watching Hindi film songs.' Those who could not bear 'to reduce their substantial investment in color TV sets to smithereens gave away their sets or sold them until in a matter of weeks their high rise society of 300-odd flats had not a set left. They were doing away, they said, with Satan's tool' (ibid.). During this same time newspapers reported that the 'Ahmediya sect had launched a satellite TV channel to carry their message via satellite and cable to Ahmediyas worldwide, with Ahmediyas in Bombay tuning in as well' (Ninan, 1995: 1). While television is Satan's medium to some, it is God's tool to others.

On my way to visit my mentor, Dr. Baviskar, at Delhi University one morning, I passed by a building, which looked like the student center. On one of its newly white-washed walls was some graffiti, which read:

We don't want Coke and MTV, we want jobs.

This made me wonder what television was doing to India. Was it a powerful agent of social change, or was it simply the most visible symbol of modernizing India? And if it was influencing change, was it all negative or was this modern medium of mass communication having a positive impact on rural India?

Introduction

Today, Indian television has grown into one of the largest networks in the world (Malik, 1989: 459). Though introduced in 1959 and used as an educational and developmental tool by government agencies, television in India today is primarily a medium of entertainment. From films to music, and soap operas to game shows, Indian television has made the transition from an educational medium to one that is almost exclusively entertainment based. The lifeblood of this new entertainment medium is advertising.

Television networks are selling the Indian public *en masse* to advertising companies for a lot of money. The bigger the audience the better. The more detailed the demographic data about an audience, the higher the price. Advertisers want detailed information about whom they are targeting and want that target audience to be as large as possible. Television networks understand that engaging entertainment programs are the key to capturing that large audience, so that is what they are turning to.

When television was first introduced in India, the government stated that the purpose of this medium was to educate, inform, and entertain. Today however, audiences use the medium mostly for entertainment, but this does not mean that education and the transfer of information is not taking place. In fact, Indian villagers have never been more informed about news and current events and have never been more knowledgeable about the system in which they live. Villagers are now more than ever cognizant of their rights, choices, and responsibilities as citizens of the Indian Union. Villagers have entered the electronic information age and are taking full advantage of it. The down side to this development has been the emergence of an information underclass. This leap into the electronic age has resulted in the emergence of a group of people who cannot afford to purchase television sets and who have no access to it through friends or neighbors. This information underclass which used to comprise the majority of villagers has now diminished in size which has resulted in a more disadvantageous position for those excluded than before.

Today many villagers are aspiring to heights never dreamed of before. To quote a young man from Danawli whose family now lives in Mumbai:

- *I want things that my parents never had. I want to some day own a car and a better house in the city. I want my children to be able to go to the good schools in Panchgani and to eat with the rich children in the restaurants. I want to be able to visit different places in India and maybe even go to Dubai. Last year I finished my electrical degree from Wai College, and have already started to get business from people in Panchgani.... See, I even made my parents' home better with a doorbell and a stereo system (speakers throughout the house).... Life is different today. My parents had no idea about what they could do. They were satisfied with farming our 7 acres. See how those people are dressed* (pointing to some men on the television) *I have pants just like that. See how nice their house is, and they drive a nice car and have a lot of time to relax. I don't want to grow rice the rest of my life. I want to live in the city and go to movies and eat at restaurants.*

Dilip, sporting a baseball cap and tennis shoes, said these words as we sat in his small house in Danawli watching television and eating rice and dal. I noticed that on one wall was a shrine with several gods surrounded by oil lamps and *agarbati* (incense). In contrast, on the opposite wall above the television, were two posters. One was of a popular Hindi film star and the other of a sports car. Dilip, an unmarried man of twenty-four, represented this new generation of villagers. His aspirations, values, and ideas about life though not entirely different from his parents, were shared by many. And though it was difficult at first to determine the degree to which television was influencing the social fabric of village life, one could not miss its transforming influence in the way people structured their daily lives. The next chapter is devoted to an analysis of the role of television in the daily life of the villager.

What constitutes television in India varies according to who you are, what you can afford, and where you are located. The

majority of television audiences receive only the government network called Doordarshan. The other type of television, which is
growing at a rapid rate, is cable or satellite television.

Doordarshan

As a first step it is useful to briefly survey some of the important
milestones in the development of Doordarshan and relate them
to the socio-political context of the time. At India's independence
Nehru recognized the importance of television and called for it to
be put on the national agenda. From that point forward we can
trace the growth of television along two paths: the development
of both hardware (technology that includes high and low power
antennas, and satellites) and software (programming). The former made experimental television possible and enabled network
broadcasts to reach all corners of the country. The latter began to
shift the original mandate of television from educational purposes to one that is now primarily entertainment based. Within
this process of the development of Doordarshan I focus on two
issues. The first concerns advertising, and the second relates to
the ongoing tension between autonomy and government control
of the network.

It is not my purpose to attempt a detailed chronological
account of the development of television in India, or analyze the
events which led to the present state of television in the country.
However, certain key elements are essential for understanding
the position of television in India today.

The government owned and operated network is called Doordarshan, which means 'distant vision.' This national network, a
branch of All India Radio until 1976, had difficulty emerging as
an independent organization with its own mandate and funding.
It was not until Indira Gandhi, then Minister of Information and
Broadcasting, became Prime Minister that television began to
take hold in India. There is an old saying about the first three
Prime Ministers of India: Nehru was a visionary, Lal Bahadur
Shastri was a revisionary, and Indira Gandhi a televisionary. She,
more than any of her political contemporaries, understood the
great potential of television.

1982 was an important year in the development of Indian television. It was in this year that color TV was introduced, and advertisers began to realize the commercial potential of the medium. It was also in this year that low power transmitters initiated national transmission, and the first Indian domestic communications satellite was launched.[1] It was also during this period there was:

> a proliferation of both transmission and receiving technology in India. The key developments followed the ASIAD games, which were broadcast in color using a variety of microwave and satellite links to reach a large part of the nation. This was the beginning of the expansion of television's coverage, and most of the country was soon brought under the umbrella of the National Network that carried the bulk of television programs in India (Mitra, 1993: 21).[2]

Installing both high-powered and low-powered transmitters became priority throughout the country. Politicians began to realize the benefits of having transmitters in their constituencies, and between July and October of 1984 an average of one transmitter was installed in India every day (Ninan, 1995: 30). By the time I arrived in India in 1995 the drive to cover the entire country with television transmitters was in full swing.

Doordarshan has been used as a propaganda tool of the ruling party. However, in the late 1980s and early 1990s, efforts by the government resulted in a gradual move toward increased autonomy for Doordarshan. It was hoped that in giving the network its own sphere of independence within the government framework of the ministry of information, it would attain more credibility among the public. But for every two steps the organization made toward this goal, an election or the passage of a new bill pulled it back down a step. And though the government has worked hard at elevating the network's credibility, it was not until the early 1990s, fighting for its survival against newly-born cable companies, that Doordarshan emerged as a powerful competitive national network.

The 1980s also witnessed the development of what has become the single most popular genre on Indian television after films: the soap operas or what are referred to as serials in India. For almost a decade between 1976 and 1985 Indian television was dominated by Hindi films and film-based programs. The only sit-coms, soap operas, or other shows aired on Doordarshan were borrowed from foreign television—American shows like *I Love Lucy* and *Star Trek* or British shows like *To the Manor Born* or *Sorry* (both of which were regional in their humor and accent). British television did, however, provide Indian viewers with some of its foremost productions such as Bronowski's *Ascent of Man*, Kenneth Clark's *Civilization*, and various nature documentaries. But it was not until the mid-1980s that domestically-produced Indian language television serials came into their own.

These serials were directly inspired not by American daytime soap operas but by the success of Mexico's Televisa, a private commercial network, in producing popular melodramatic series. These series in Mexico promoted adult literacy, family planning, health, and sanitation. In 1983, David Poindexter, President of the Center for Population Communications International in New York, who had played a key role in popularizing development-oriented soap operas in Mexico, arranged for a delegation from India, Egypt, Nigeria, Kenya, and Brazil to visit Mexico City and confer with Miguel Sabido, the producer. S.S. Gill, Secretary of the Ministry of Information and Broadcasting, led the Indian delegation.

On his return, Gill handpicked a few individuals who worked to produce India's first indigenous soap opera called *Hum Log*. One hundred and six episodes of the serial were telecast twice a week from July 1984 through December 1985. This was a milestone in Doordarshan's history. It was the first serious attempt to combine entertainment with the promotion of ideas of social development. The central theme of this seventeen month long drama was family planning, but by the time it was over it was felt that the central message had been effectively drowned in an ocean of melodrama (Singhal and Rogers, 1989).

It was at this time that advertisers began to realize the power of television. Maggi 2-minute Noodles, a product of a Nestle subsidiary sponsored *Hum Log*. The success of this advertising campaign resulted in other advertisers jumping on the Doordarshan bandwagon, enabling the network to raise its advertising rates 150 per cent in three years. By 1987 there were forty domestically-produced programs on the air, from soap operas to detective serials, and documentaries to sporting events. The Mumbai film industry (commonly referred to as Bollywood), recognizing the potential revenue in this new medium, quickly moved in. Low budget film directors and producers made great inroads into television. But it was the big commercial box-office filmmakers who succeeded in taking over television by storm. Productions such as *Ramayan* and *Mahabharat* established themselves as religious soap operas bringing the mythology and the magic of early Indian cinema to TV. Mitra (1993) engages in a contextual analysis of how the *Mahabharat* fits into Indian popular culture. This particular program ran for ninety-three weeks, and when it concluded in July of 1990 a newspaper poll reported that nearly 92 per cent of the total television audience watched the serial (ibid.: 90). This was the greatest audience rating that any Indian television program had received. Even though Doordarshan had grown into a powerful network by the 1990s, it still faced a major problem with the lack of program development.

Programming was still primarily in Hindi with much of the news and current affairs focused on Delhi. Even today much of the country receives television in Hindi as opposed to regional native languages. Villagers in Danawli and Raj Puri receive only two hours of Marathi television a day, even though very few of them speak anything but Marathi. Many criticized Doordarshan for not making enough headway in establishing regionally based programming. In 1985 a working group on programming for Doordarshan was set up and headed by Professor P.C. Joshi an economist and sociologist and president of the Indian Sociological Society from 1989–91. The report the Joshi Committee published in 1985 made several recommendations to create the appropriate environment for the development of creative programming by Doordarshan.

The two-volume report recounted the vision of Vikram Sarabhai that television must be used to reach the most backward first. The effort of SITE in the mid-1970s was a great step toward the realization of this dream. This rural development initiative is now a distant memory as Doordarshan has steadily moved toward being a medium of mass entertainment and advertising. With overwhelming faith in the power of television to bring

about social and economic development, family planning,) and
nation-building, the Committee argued that:

> The audiovisual mode of communication has the potential of
> serving as the most powerful promoter of growth with equity
> in an illiteracy- and inequality-stricken society if this mode is
> consciously utilized for communicating information to the tar-
> get groups and for awakening and activising them in defense
> of their rights. The true communicator is transformed into
> a communication activist in an in-egalitarian society (Joshi,
> 1985: 38).

It questioned the centralized manner in which programming was
being produced in Delhi and called for a more participatory,
decentralized, and regionally-run network.

The committee believed that an integrative, interactive, and
participatory model of communication was imperative. It stressed
the urgency of setting up decentralized district-level television
stations based on low-cost production equipment and area-
specific, people-centered, problem-oriented program production
and community viewing. The report argued that developing
countries like India are exposed to the dangers of erosion of their
national cultural identity and that domestically produced programs were extremely important in resisting the cultural invasion
from outside. The committee warned against India's population
becoming addicted to films, cautioned the urban middle class not
to monopolize the medium which was originally meant for the
illiterate, underdeveloped rural people, and projected the possibilities of the medium becoming a propaganda tool for the short-
term gains of politicians. All of the committee's concerns have
come to pass. Though several recommendations were useful, the
vast majority were never fully implemented.

Rajiv Gandhi was the first Indian Prime Minister to recognize
the poor quality of programming on India's national network.
He decided that the entire media system, especially television,
needed overhauling. He wanted Doordarshan to acquire a for-
ward-looking image that matched his own. He hired a whole new
staff, and for the first time the network began to attain a certain
amount of autonomy. In fact, opposition parties began to get airtime, which strengthened its credibility. Doordarshan hired a

cadre of journalists to upgrade its news bulletins that had been produced since 1965, but by the elections of 1988 the ruling party had monopolized the network for their own gains. Doordarshan was again a victim of politics, and Indians gave little credibility to their national television.

During a visit to India in 1988–89, I witnessed the elections once again. Television was a key tool of the ruling party in its campaigning. The Janata Dal party pulled off a victory in spite of all the bad publicity that V.P. Singh had received on Doordarshan.[3] And soon after his election Singh, keeping to one of his campaign promises, began to prepare the legislation to create an autonomous corporation called Prasar Bharati that would incorporate Akashvani—or All India Radio—and Doordarshan. This would have created the world's first TV and radio network which was overseen by a Parliament. But shortly after the passing of this Bill, the government changed hands and the implementation of the Bill was shelved. And though ruling parties have promised to work on privatizing television ever since, Doordarshan remains state-owned and state-run.[4]

A villager who lives within range of a low- or high-powered transmitter needs only a television and an antenna propped on top of his roof to receive Doordarshan's transmissions. Both Raj Puri and Danawli are situated on mountaintops and receive a fairly clear picture most of the time. Other villages situated too far from a transmitter or hidden in a deep river valley are unable to receive transmission. And though Doordarshan has added three channels to its network (DD1, DD2 and DD3) the Ghat villages around Panchgani still receive only DD1. DD2 and DD3 are geared more to urban audiences. DD2 is referred to as the Metro channel airing primarily English programs and is solely entertainment based. DD3, the newest of Doordarshan's channels, began airing in mid 1996.

Today, primarily due to the efforts of the former director-general Ratikant Basu, Doordarshan has made great strides in improving its public image. He understood that to become a winner in the race for advertising, the network had to gain popular support. It has revamped its programming in an effort to compete with other cable networks. An illustration of this move can be seen when MTV, which had entered India via a satellite network beamed out of Hong Kong, appeared on Doordarshan just months after parting company with the satellite network. In another attempt to stay competitive, Doordarshan in April of 1996 began a movie channel just months ahead of another satellite network. And by 1995 it had already launched its third channel, DD3.

Doordarshan has positioned itself to take on any rival network. India's national television network has emerged after decades of trial and error as a viable network for the subcontinent. Its program quality, diversity, and attitude is competitive. Yet, by being swept up in the tumult of competition for survival, Doordarshan has lost sight of its original mandate for the development of India's poor. This country is still waiting for 'development communication' to take place.

Satellite Television

The arrival of satellite television in India has had a dramatic impact on the country as a whole. According to Ninan (1995: 154):

> No country, no industry, and no state owned television network have been as radically changed over a short period of three years on account of a single technological innovation the way that India, the media industry here, and Doordarshan have been. All three have been affected substantially by the invasion, if you will, of a country and society by foreign satellite channels. The fact that this invasion coincided with the opening up of the Indian economy during the same period has triggered enormous interest in the Indian market from foreign investors.

This single technological innovation has had its most striking impact transforming television from a state-run and operated organization to one of the largest competitive new businesses in the country. The television industry, as a result of the satellite, has grown into a vast industrial complex. It has generated more money than ever dreamed of before. It has revolutionized the advertising industry and wooed journalists away from print media with promises of high salaries.

Satellite TV began as most new industries do—it started small. At first 'Satellite TV' was limited to closed circuit television. Flats in high rises were wired up to central control rooms where video players transmitted Indian films, foreign films, and television programs taped abroad. In the early eighties it was estimated that only a few hundred such skyscrapers were hooked up in this way. But by 1991 cable companies were sufficiently equipped to offer their viewers CNN coverage of the Gulf War.

Access to current world news quickly captured urban audiences, and when the war ended this middle class group was fairly hooked. In the fall of that same year satellite viewers were introduced to Star TV, based in Hong Kong, which beamed transmissions into India from five transponders on Asiasat I. With one channel at first and then four soon after, viewers began watching MTV, BBC documentaries, entertainment programs, and sporting events. Before long Indians tuned in to the BBC World Service Television for updates on domestic news, because they did not trust the state-owned and operated Doordarshan for honest reporting.[5]

By early 1995, in addition to the six satellite channels on Asiasat and CNN, there were five other channels being beamed into India: Jain TV, Sun TV, Asianet, EL TV, and ATN. Doordarshan had increased its own transmissions to three terrestrial channels and ten satellite channels, which offer some regional programs as well.[6] This television explosion was the backdrop for the scene that I found myself entering. Since 1993, the boom in hardware development expanded the programming industry and dramatically increased the earnings and output of the advertising world of television. Today, Indians watch a variety of programs which include sports, news and current affairs, serials, soap operas, sitcoms, talk shows, game shows, films, music videos, and some development-oriented fare.

Because of its simplicity and low cost, satellite television is accessible to an increasing number of rural Indians. There are two options for villagers wanting to receive satellite television in their homes. The first is to buy a small satellite dish for Rs. 5,000 (approximately $150), install it next to one's house and hook it up to the television set. This limits the cost to a one-time fee for the purchase of the dish. The second option is to pay a neighbor who owns a dish to connect one's own television. This requires an installation fee and monthly payments for the duration of the hook-up. Most villagers cannot afford to purchase a satellite dish themselves, so they opt for the monthly fee of Rs. 28 (approximately 80 cents). In 1996, no one in Danawli owned a dish, but a few individuals in Raj Puri and several in Panchgani did. Many villagers in Raj Puri had been receiving satellite television for two years and were not about to give it up. The villagers in Raj Puri complained about the monthly service charge paid to one of three individuals in the village, but none were willing to disconnect from the service. They were hooked.

Video

A discussion of the television revolution in India would be incomplete without referring to the video industry. I visited a few remote villages which were hidden in deep valleys and therefore were unable to receive television transmissions. This did not deter the villagers from gaining access to their favorite television shows and films through video. In one village several families pooled their money and bought a VCR. Every week one of them traveled to a neighboring village where they would rent video cassettes of their favorite programs. The following week, they would return the tapes and rent new ones. This benefited them and created a small business for those villagers who were able to tape television programs.

To estimate the number of VCRs and VCPs would be impossible since most are imported or smuggled into the country. Recently however, domestic VCR production has grown rapidly, which has dramatically reduced imports. During the late 1980s the estimated rate of growth of VCRs was put at 20,000 per month. Today some estimates are as high as 80,000 per month. Video ownership is not only a means of access to video but also a source of extra income. Video has taken over the function of cinema theaters. Whether it is video parlors, video restaurants, video clubs, or video buses, Indians have ample access to televised media wherever they go. In Panchgani itself there were between thirty-five and forty-five video parlors or home theaters.

These establishments charged an average of Rs. 5 per person. Films ran all day and night, and people who rented out rooms of their homes were making a bundle.

While strolling through the streets of Panchgani one afternoon, I decided to visit one such parlor. I did not know what was playing, but my intention was to see for myself what it was like to visit one of these establishments. As I parked my motorcycle outside this particular parlor and made my way to the entrance, I felt as though everyone in the street was watching me. This was not uncommon since I stood out as a 6 foot 2 inch blonde American, but I experienced this feeling only outside of Panchgani, since most people in town knew me. But on this particular Tuesday afternoon I was certain people were staring. I decided to ignore it, and I pulled the curtain covering the door and entered the dark room. A man whom I did not recognize came up and greeted me, saying, *Namaste* Johnson *Saheb*. My eyes had not adjusted to the darkness of the room, so I could not tell whom he was, but I handed him my money, and he showed me to my seat. The movie had already begun. As I looked around the room I heard a strange moaning sound. I could not tell where it was coming from and then all of a sudden everything made sense. I became fully aware of the reason why people were staring at me outside on the street. I had just entered a video parlor which showed blue movies. There in front of me on the screen were two naked blonde women kissing. I had never been more embarrassed in my life. Everyone in this town knew me, but more importantly, knew my parents, who were highly respected. Without trying to hide the fact that I was visiting this parlor I walked in under broad daylight. No wonder people were staring at me outside. I immediately stood up and walked out. The entire episode, which seemed like an eternity must have only lasted a minute and a half.

The subject of soft pornography came up more than once during the course of my research. People of all strata were curious to know about the women and men portrayed in these films. One evening on a bus returning from a three-hour trip to Pune, I sat near a group of railroad workers traveling to Mahabaleshwar for a holiday. There must have been ten or fifteen of these men, and most of them were fairly drunk. I made the mistake of starting up a conversation with one of them, which turned into a three hour long interrogation of life in America. These men specifically wanted to know about the women in the West and if they really acted like what they had seen on television and in blue movies. Sex is something one does not discuss in public in India, and this made me very uncomfortable. What surprised me even more, however, was the detailed information these men had about breast implants, various sex toys, and the practice of swinging. And during the research, several village men also asked similar questions about sex and Western living. Video parlors provided these rural men and young boys easy access to blue movies and other films which portrayed a lifestyle very different from their own.

I later learnt that most of these parlors are illegal but are allowed to flourish with police and municipal officials cashing in on large bribes. Video piracy is big business in India. Most of the tapes I saw during my research were not originals and were of very poor quality. But one of the adjustments the video parlor industry has had to make due to the popularity of satellite television is to open its doors to advertising. Videos contain advertising along with the movies listed on the cover. There are regular interruptions during the films as well as a logo or two on the screen at all times reminding the viewer what soap to buy or what liquor to drink.

Conclusion

Television in India today has little if any resemblance to television thirty years ago. Television was brought to India for the purpose of development. In a country of close to a billion people with a literacy rate under 50 per cent, television was seen as a possible answer to the country's many social and economic problems. The SITE experiment in 1975 which used this medium is still regarded as one of the hallmark initiatives in development communications. Today, however, the television industry is criticized by some for being wooed away from its humanitarian goals and becoming a medium for the urban middle class. It is this class which owns and operates most of the television industry in India.

And it is also this class which is transmitting its own values, principles, and opinions to the rest of India. And though Doordarshan has attempted to stay true to its original goals it has had to succumb to market forces to survive.

This is the television landscape I observed upon entering the field to conduct my research. And after coming to some understanding of the present state of television in India, I ventured to ascertain its role in village life.

Notes

1. This satellite subsequently failed, but the leasing of foreign satellites soon after enabled India to enter the era of satellite broadcasting.
2. I clearly recall these events as a teenager in school in India. This was the first time that television had made an appearance in Panchgani. The ASIAD games were incredibly popular, and the school set up a TV set in the main auditorium. Between classes, after school and on weekends hundreds of children flocked to the auditorium and watched in rapt attention the various athletic events of the games. Even back then I realized that this would soon change our lives in a big way.
3. Rajiv Gandhi was under attack by both the print media and the opposition for allegedly being connected with the Bofors gun deal, which had produced very large commissions.
4. The ruling party monopolized Doordarshan for its own gain. A case in point was reported in *India Today* (15 March 1996: 164): 'It was prime time, and viewers were sitting expectantly for more information on the Jain hawala case on a news program. Suddenly the audio went on the blink. Reason: some non-Congress (I) politicians were referring to Prime Minister P.V. Narasimha Rao's alleged involvement in the case. Though Doordarshan blamed it on technical failure, the producers of the program felt it was deliberate.'
5. The director-general of Doordarshan, forecasting the future of the network, stated to a journalist in July 1990, 'How far does the government think it can use Doordarshan to fight its battles? If Doordarshan was the panacea, Rajiv Gandhi would still be prime minister. They don't realize that Asiasat is coming next year. They won't learn until they wake up one morning and discover that Doordarshan is irrelevant' (Ninan, 1995: 155).

6. And though the prediction of the director-general was bleak, Door-darshan survived and has triumphed. As Ninan states, 'Doordarshan bestirred itself to respond and did not become irrelevant. But it did in the post cable and satellite phase often seem unrecognizable as the timid state broadcaster of yore. The competition from abroad had the most impact on Doordarshan, changing its agenda irrevocably' (1995: 155–56). Apart from its efforts at national integration propaganda and slanted political coverage, Doordarshan is not very different from any of the other commercial cable companies. They have forced Doordarshan into the position it finds itself in today, which is not a tool of development anymore, but primarily one of entertainment, which depends on advertising.

7

Television and Village Life

This chapter provides an overview of television in the village. It describes the television audience and programming. It compares programming which villagers in Danawli receive with those in Raj Puri and focuses on some of the implications of television since its arrival in the village.

Television in the Village

Television came to Danawli in 1985, and there are now twenty-five television sets. The village had only twenty-three television sets when I arrived, but two families acquired sets during the course of my field work. About half of these sets were acquired as part of a dowry, and the rest were purchased. TV sets are now thought to be part of any dowry settlement, and of the eight weddings which occurred during my research all but one included a television with the dowry.

In the past ownership of media was limited to the higher status members of the community (Hartmann et al., 1989: 195), but today television ownership spans all strata of the society. Though eighteen of the televisions in Danawli were owned by wealthier families, three landless families, two small holding families, and two Dhangar families owned TV sets. Of the forty-three Mahar homes in Raj Puri, twenty-one owned TV sets. In Panchgani television ownership is no longer a status symbol. People of all strata own televisions.

At present in Danawli Doordarshan is the only television network received through the antennas that sit high on top of the mud, stone, and straw huts. Doordarshan is aimed at a diverse society characterized by eighteen national languages and a multiplicity of dialects. In an effort to address this pluralistic landscape, the national network has three types of service on offer. National Programming, which is beamed to the entire nation from Delhi, airs the bulk of entertainment fare. National programming also attempts to foster social, economic, and cultural awareness and to promote a spirit of national integration. These programs demonstrate the progress India has made in industrial, cultural, and technological fields.

Regional Programming is produced in Mumbai primarily in Marathi. These programs address both general and specific audiences such as farmers, women, children, and small entrepreneurs. The programs run for a few hours in the late afternoon and early evening Monday through Friday. The third kind of service provided by Doordarshan involves developmental and educational fare. After the success of SITE in 1975, Doordarshan continued to produce and broadcast development-oriented programs. According to an official at Doordarshan, this service is 'designed to sensitize the target audience on various issues to do with agriculture, health and hygiene, besides social issues of various kinds' (Malik, 1989: 460). Programs which are geared toward improving teaching standards and targeting undergraduates are poorly utilized. One reason for this is that 'the transmissions do not fit in with the daily timetables of schools, and consequently students and children find the timings inconvenient' (ibid.).

An important component of the research was to observe viewing behavior and to identify discernible patterns and preferences. Past research has documented the popularity of entertainment media, especially television (Mitra, 1993; Kottak, 1990; Hartmann et al., 1989). People are more interested in watching entertainment during their leisure time than watching educational programs. Though news and current affairs programs have been reported to be popular, they do not compete with entertainment programs. It was important to discover whether this was true in

Danawli and whether this influenced the programming on Doordarshan, whose mandate is first to educate, second to inform, and finally to entertain.

Doordarshan begins airing at 5:55 A.M. with *Vande Mataram* and the *Thought for the Day*. The network goes off the air about nineteen hours later at 1:00 A.M. The regional programming, some of which is in Marathi, airs between 4:35 in the afternoon and 8:30 at night. These four hours are generally the only programming that villagers can really understand, since most of them speak only Marathi. The Hindi programs that were most understood by villagers tended to be films. Hindi films are structured in such a way that it is possible to follow the plot of the movie without knowing the language, which is one reason they are so popular throughout India.

Educational and developmental programs are aired during the day usually in the morning before 8:00 A.M. Occasionally, such programs are broadcast in the early afternoon between 1:00 and 2:00 P.M.

Power outages are common occurrences in this region of western Maharashtra. Electrical power is prioritized to ensure that industries and irrigation schemes receive a continuous supply during the day. A factor in the frequent power outages is the poorly maintained infrastructure. This posed a problem in determining patterns of television viewing. Did villagers find certain programs uninteresting, or were they not watching because the power was shut off? During the World Cup cricket tournament of 1996, not one power outage occurred for three entire weeks. This was due to the fact that the local and regional officials in charge of the power station recognized how dangerous it would have been for them to shut off power during any of these matches. I decided to report television viewing as it occurred, whether there was a power outage or not, since that was the natural environment.

Programming on Doordarshan

Doordarshan programming was, for analytic purposes, divided into four major thematic categories: (*a*) Informational; (*b*) developmental; (c) art and culture; and (d) entertainment (which includes sports), as shown in Table 7.1. Advertising, though not considered programming in itself, is included as a separate thematic category in the table. The percentage of advertising reported here is limited to those segments which are solely dedicated to that purpose, since during some programs on Doordarshan such as Hindi films, advertising logos are present on the screen throughout the length of the program. These findings are compared with a survey conducted in March 1988 in two villages on the outskirts of Delhi (Malik, 1989).

Table 7.1: Thematic Contents of Doordarshan Programming

Theme	Percentage of total output	
	*March 1988**	*March 1996*
Informative	21	23
Development orientation	24.5	14
Art and Culture	23	12
Entertainment	24.5	40
Advertising	7	11
Total output	100	100

* These figures are totaled from two separate tables in Malik's (1989) article.

The following operational definitions were used. Informative programs were defined as news, current events, and parliamentary debates. Development fare centered on social, economic, or educational programs. Art and culture was defined as programming that reflected traditional Indian culture; therefore pop music was not included. Entertainment was defined as any program which did not have a developmental or informative message and that was watched purely for relaxation. This included game shows, serials, films, and pop music programs.

As the number of networks increased in the 1990s, resulting in a more competitive television industry, the scope of Doordarshan's programming has changed dramatically. Entertainment fare now dominates. In 1988 the total proportion of Doordarshan's entertainment fare was 24.5 per cent (see Table 4.3), and by 1996 it had jumped to 40 per cent. This is due in part to the large increase in program development which took place in the early nineties. The number of private and government sponsored program companies increased in order to fill the vacuum provided by the increase in the number of networks. Executives were also turning to data obtained from audience research, which showed entertainment fare was the most popular programming. The major reason for this shift in programming was the acknowledgment by Doordarshan and the government that if the national network was to remain a viable component of modern India it had to compete with the other satellite networks which are primarily entertainment based. This was true on several occasions when informants confided that they did not see the need to purchase or become cable receivers, because they did not see enough difference between Doordarshan and the other cable networks. According to one man:

- *When I first bought my TV there were not many good programs. Most were very boring, and sometimes I regretted spending so much money on something that I did not enjoy that much. But now my family watches movies several times a week, and we also watch many serials like* Chandrakanta. *Some of the Marathi programs and movies are also very good, so I am satisfied.*

A drastic drop in the total percentage of developmental programs from 24.5 per cent in 1988 to 14 per cent in 1996 accompanied the rise in entertainment shows. This trend demonstrates the move away from Doordarshan's original mandate to an increasingly entertainment based focus. The rise in advertising also demonstrates how commercial this branch of the government has become. To stay competitive it offers more frequent spots to advertisers in the hope that they will not take their money elsewhere. The most commercials were aired during entertainment programs, which reflected the recognition, by advertisers, of the popularity of entertainment fare. Advertisers are unwilling to put their commercials on the air for developmental programs or other less popular segments.

The Audience

This section takes a closer look at the television audience. It is important to note that even if 50 per cent of the programming on Doordarshan is developmental, what really matters is whether villagers are watching it. What follows is a presentation of the data on the viewing audience.

In Danawli, a sample was taken of fifty children, fifty men and fifty women who lived in homes that did not own TV sets. A profile of this sample is presented in Figure 7.1. An attempt was made to cover all strata of caste, class, and educational status in the village. The number of persons in each category was representative of the village as a whole. The data in Table 7.2, reflects

Figure 7.1: Profile of Sampled Television Audience in Homes Without TV Sets

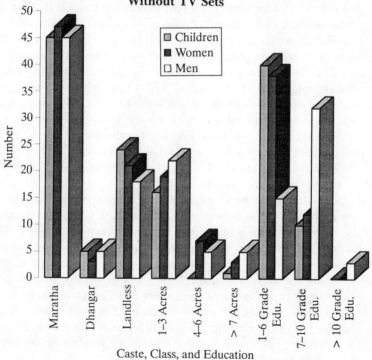

Table 7.2: Percentage of Villagers without TV Sets who have Access to Television

Days	Percentage		
	Children	*Men*	*Women*
Saturday–Sunday	89	68	59
Wednesday–Friday	71	57	46
Monday–Tuesday	63	42	31

the percentage of villagers without television sets who had access to television.

It should be noted that not all those interviewed had access to television. Some informed me that they had not seen television in months. However, of those who did manage to go to a neighbor's house the children were by far the most numerous. Eighty-nine per cent of children surveyed had watched television that week-end, while only 59 per cent of women without TV sets were able to watch their favorite programs. Men are more mobile in the village, and therefore more men than women have access to TV sets. It is the women who must stay home and prepare the elaborate evening meal while the man might wash his hands and face and go to his friend's house to watch the news or a popular serial. It is only after dinner that women get the chance to wash and go to the neighbors to watch the evening Hindi film. The early afternoons however, are a time when women are fairly free of their duties and are able to watch a popular serial called *Shanti* without having to worry about other chores.

Table 7.3 shows the number of hours that the segment of villagers without TV sets watched Doordarshan. Children watched the most out of this group with a total of twenty hours per week. Most of the television viewing occurred on the weekends when popular serials and Hindi films are aired.

During the course of the research I selected five households that were representative of the twenty-five that owned television sets. I spent a week at a time in each of these households to observe television viewing habits. Each home had had a TV set for over five years and had become comfortable with its presence.[1] The quantitative data gathered on the number of viewing

**Table 7.3: Viewing Hours of those without TV
Sets who have Access**

Days	Number of hours		
	Children	Men	Women
Saturday–Sunday	12	8	7
Wednesday–Friday	5	5	5
Monday–Tuesday	3	2	1
Total hours per week	20	15	13

hours by category and types of programs watched are presented
below along with selected qualitative data.

As Table 7.3 shows, children watched the most television followed by women and then men. It should be pointed out that
though women watched more than men, their viewing habits
were different. Women were often seen doing other work and
watching television at the same time, while men and children
were much more tuned in to the television programs. Household
duties needed to be carried out even if a favorite serial or a popular Hindi film was on. On more than one occasion women confided that they were not pleased with this arrangement. According
to one mother of four:

- *Do you see how much work I have to do, and I am the only one who
  does work. I used to help my mother all the time when I was a child
  but now my two daughters are only interested in watching TV. The
  work needs to get done, and so I am the one who does it. Yesterday
  you saw how Sunita answered back to me? Children behave much
  more differently today than we used to.*

And according to another woman in her mid-forties:

- *I love to watch TV, but someone has to cook and make sure everything
  is ready and all the small chores are done. I manage to follow the
  programs most of the time by just listening from the other room and
  coming in when there is a song or dance.*

Most of the popular shows are aired on Saturdays and Sundays
thus drawing a much higher viewing audience on the weekend.

Table 7.4: Number of Viewing Hours for those with TV Sets

Days	Number of hours		
	Children	Men	Women
Saturday–Sunday	18	10	13
Wednesday–Friday	8	6	7
Monday–Tuesday	5	3	5
Total hours per week	31	19	25

Ever since the unrivaled success of serials like *Ramayan* and *Mahabharat* in the late 1980s, Sunday morning has become a valued spot, and advertising slots are in high demand. Friday and Saturday nights are also popular times to watch television, since Hindi films are aired from 9:20 P.M. to 1:00 A.M. It is also on these two nights that women are freer to engage in viewing. On more than one occasion chores traditionally completed at night were left for the next morning, so women would be able to watch the evening movie. On one early Saturday morning I had risen to find the mother of the house washing the dishes. I asked her about this, since I had always seen her doing it at night, and she explained that she had not finished in time for the movie, so she just left it. When I mentioned this to her husband later that day he said:

- *Because of this TV we are working less than before. My wife begins the evening meal earlier so she can begin watching TV in the evening. This makes me upset since she sometimes leaves me in the fields in the afternoon alone to work.*

The least popular shows, aired on Monday and Tuesday, draw much less of the viewing audience. Comparing the data in Tables 7.3 and 7.4, it becomes clear that ownership of a TV set increases the time spent viewing. The most dramatic rise in viewing time was among women. Women who had access to television but who did not have one in their homes watched an average of thirteen hours of television per week. Women who lived in a household where a TV set was present spent an average of twenty-five hours a week watching programs. This sharp rise can be explained by the fact that the woman turns on the TV while she carries out household chores alone. There is not a major difference in viewing behavior among men in households with or without a TV. I often observed men returning from the fields after a long day of work and soon after dinner gathered together in a home with a TV set to relax and watch the evening shows together.

Table 7.5 supports conclusions of earlier research (Hartmann et al., 1989; Mitra, 1993; Kottak, 1990), that entertainment media, in this case television, are by far the most watched programs. Children spend the most time watching entertainment, and when asked why they were watching programs on development they said that there was nothing else to do. They often watched programs which their parents were watching, not because they enjoyed the programs, but because the television was on. The only programming they enjoyed watching was entertainment: serials, cartoons, films, and popular music programs, which have become one of the most popular genres on television in India. The music programs are the easiest to produce and command some of the largest audiences. They are based on Hindi film songs, interviews and other popular music. In contrast to traditional mores of gender interaction, men and women are less inhibited on these shows. It is not uncommon to see scantily dressed women seducing men they had just met.

Table 7.5: Most Popular Programs

Program	Average number of viewing hours per week spent watching particular program themes[2]		
	Children	*Men*	*Women*
Informative	1	4	2
Developmental	2	1.5	2
Art and culture	7	2.5	7
Entertainment	21	11	14
Total number of hours	31	19	25

For all three categories of the population, entertainment fare was the most popular. For women and children, art and culture came in second. Men seemed to enjoy the informative programs but watched news and current affairs more for the weather forecasts, state, and national political news.

Table 7.6 shows that children watched entertainment programs 64.5 per cent of the time while men and women watch entertainment programs 57 per cent and 56 per cent of the time, respectively.

Table 7.6: Entertainment Television

Entertainment Fare	Percentage of total viewing hours spent watching entertainment fare		
	Children	*Men*	*Women*
Viewing hours	21	11	14
Percentage	64.5	57	56
Total viewing hours	31	19	25

This is particularly true for those without a TV set who visit friends and neighbors to watch television. The vast majority of men, women, and children without TV sets acknowledged that they made the effort to visit a friend's home in order to watch entertainment television. Owning a television increases the likelihood that the members of the household would be exposed to programs on art and culture, news, or programs on development. Those without TV sets find it not worth their while to make the effort to go and watch other programs. As one woman stated:

- *It is not our home, and therefore I feel bad letting my children go and watch television throughout the day and night. I only let them go when there is a movie or serial, and I go myself also. But sometimes we are not treated very well. They look at us badly if we are always going over to their house. Someday my husband will buy a TV for us, and we will not have to go to other people's homes to watch. Then I can watch whenever I want.*

More and more families are beginning to budget for the purchase of a television set. Some families with sons that are coming
of age opt not to buy a set but instead wait for the wedding and
demand one as part of the dowry.

In conclusion, the data presented here demonstrate the role
television plays in the lives of the villagers. In the 1990s, the
introduction of this medium has completely reordered the daily
routines of these people thereby adding a new dimension to village life. People with television in their homes spend many hours
a week watching it. As the data show, lack of ownership does not
mean lack of access. Only 11 per cent of children, 32 per cent of
men, and 41 per cent of women who did not own TV sets did not
have access to television. Television has touched the lives of most
people in Danawli, and at the same time has created an information underclass among those without access to this medium. The
programs on television are part of everyday conversation in the
village. Those without access are automatically left out of these
conversations.

Television in Raj Puri

What follows is a description of television in Raj Puri. There is a
stark contrast between television reception in Raj Puri with that
in Danawli. Not only are there differences in the number of channels, length of airtime, and type of programming, but satellite
television has created a very different social environment as well.
Raj Puri represents a direction in which Danawli and most other
villages in this region are heading.

Raj Puri is a large village on the outskirts of Panchgani, and
therefore has many of the amenities that are available in the
larger town. One of these amenities is satellite television. The
television landscape in Raj Puri is very different from Danawli
not only in the programming received but in the various social
categories created as a result of satellite television with certain
rights, privileges, responsibilities, and status. In Danawli, there
are three such categories: those who own a TV set, those who
have access to television, and those who have no access. The

social dynamic created by satellite television is much more complex. The categories of people in Raj Puri include: (*a*) those who own a Satellite dish; (*b*) those who pay to receive satellite television; (*c*) those who do not have a television but who have access to satellite television; (*d*) those who receive only Doordarshan; (*e*) those who do not have a television but have access to homes with Doordarshan; (*f*) those who have access to both Doordarshan and satellite television; and (*g*) those who have no access to TV at all. The arrival of television has created a new social dynamic within village life, but satellite television has made that dynamic more complex.

A certain status is assigned to each of these categories of television access. Unlike Raj Puri, in Danawli there are only three such status levels. A decade ago, caste, class, education, and political awareness contributed significantly to one's status in the community. Today, television, and more specifically satellite television, is an important variable that contributes to one's status in the community. The case of two individuals will further illustrate this argument.

Shinde and Mohan are two men in their forties who live in Raj Puri. They both belong to the Maratha caste, own similar amounts of land, both have a tenth grade education, and until two years ago maintained a similar status in the community (both were members of the Gram Panchayat). Today, however, Shinde's status in the village is much higher than Mohan. In 1993 Shinde decided to invest in a satellite dish. He spent Rs. 10,000 (it now only costs between Rs. 4,000 to 5,000) and purchased a dish. Within six months his dish was hooked up to eighteen homes which paid him Rs. 28 a month. Many people now depend on Shinde to satisfy their viewing needs. Through his satellite dish people watch television shows from around the world and can no longer imagine their lives without it. The obvious question that arises from this is: what is different about satellite television that makes it so popular?

In Raj Puri satellite television consists of ten channels including Doordarshan. The TV network called Star (Satellite Television Asia Region) began operating out of Hong Kong in 1991 and has several channels including Star Plus, BBC, Star Sports, Channel V, and Star Movies. Other networks like Zee TV, EL TV, TVI Network, and Sony Entertainment Television are also very popular. Most of these channels are on the air twenty-four hours a day offering sports, movies, and music videos. While villagers in Danawli can stay up as late as 1:00 A.M. watching their favorite movies, on several occasions I observed people in Raj Puri watching television past 3:00 A.M. On two occasions I fell asleep watching television and awoke several hours later with people sitting all around me still engrossed in the little black box in the corner.

Star Plus is primarily an English channel that airs everything from American soap operas like *The Bold and the Beautiful* and *Santa Barbara* to the *Oprah Winfrey Show*. This channel also airs *Baywatch*, which is very popular. Channel V is the Asian version of MTV with music videos and films songs as well as concerts and provocative interviews. Zee TV made its debut in October of 1992 with primarily Hindi programming. Satellite television consists of an array of programming which caters to all people both young and old, modern and traditional, women and men. Villagers in Raj Puri thought life could not get any better when they received Doordarshan in the late eighties. Today with the multitude of channels offered on satellite television, a large part of their days and nights are spent watching television.

An analysis follows of the implications of television since its arrival in Danawli. The household is the unit of analysis organized through a system of statuses and roles (Sháh, 1974; Srivastava, 1979). Maharashtrian village society is characterized by families that are patrilineal and virilocal (Mandelbaum, 1970; Sháh, 1974). Although the typical family in Danawli and Raj Puri is predominantly agnatic, if observed over a long period of time, it is not uncommon to find non-agnatic relatives living as members of the same household. These relatives might include, a widowed daughter (and in some cases her children), a son-in-law, a wife's brothers, and her parents. Thus, the family type which is commonly seen in Maharashtra and which I found in the research villages is not a purely agnatic family. Each member of the family whether agnate or not, holds a certain status. These statuses are traditionally based on age, sex, and relative closeness of one's hereditary link to the male head of the household.

The most effective way to demonstrate how television has influenced the daily activities and social relations within the household unit is to allow the data to flow undisturbed in the natural setting through time. The data presented here reflect the typical household and as such have been compiled from various homes. These data have been integrated to see culture in process (Beals, 1967). The data presented in this section are from my own research in both Danawli and Raj Puri as well as from the information from pre-television ethnographies of the region (Dandekar, 1986b; Kamble, 1979; Karve, 1968; Kulkarni, 1967).

A Day in the Household Prior to Television

Seven family members sleep next to each other in neat bundles on the floor. There are no separate bedrooms. Next to this room is the kitchen with a smaller room next to it which is used for storage. Just outside this bedroom is the verandah, which during the day, is the central gathering place of the household. The livestock are kept just a few feet below the verandah. On many occasions when the group was large, meals were served on this verandah. I soon got used to a cow's nose or a goat's whiskers nudging my back as I sat eating in this part of the house. It is usually fairly dark with only one 40 or 60 Watt bulb to light the room. And though the floor is plastered with manure, and the livestock essentially live in the house, there is little smell other than fresh spices and rice being cooked in the kitchen.

The average day begins at approximately 5:00 A.M. when the grandmother awakes. It is still dark, and she turns on the light in the kitchen so as to not wake anyone still asleep in the adjacent room. She fills a small pot of water from the bucket in the corner and steps outside the front door to wash her face and blow her nose. She then brushes her teeth. After brushing she spends what seems like a long time, cleaning her tongue. This is done quite forcefully and when observed by a foreigner can seem as if serious damage is being done as it sounds as if she is vomiting profusely, and blowing her nose sounds like she is hurting her sinuses. She goes back inside to fetch another pot of water and makes her way to a nearby field to defecate. Upon returning she washes her hands, which is the common practice. While doing so, she awakes her daughter-in-law and eldest granddaughter. It is now approximately 5:30. The first thing the mother does is put some water on the stove for tea. She too engages in the same rituals as the grandmother, washing, brushing, and defecating. The granddaughter has trouble getting up and grumbles that it is still dark outside. As the mother walks out of the house on her way to defecate she yells at the daughter to get up and prepare the water for tea. She obeys reluctantly and begins to groom herself as well. By 6:00 A.M. the rest of the household is up and about.

It is usually the women who get up first and make their way to the fields to defecate. This is done in order to avoid coming in contact with the men of the village engaging in the same morning ritual. The mother or grandmother heats a bucket of water for the man of the house to bathe. This water is warmed with an electric heater, which takes fifteen or twenty minutes. The members of the household do not all sit down to eat together. The mother is busy preparing breakfast in the kitchen, and whenever anyone has finished their morning grooming they venture into the kitchen and are fed breakfast. Breakfast can include simple tea and *bhakri* (a thick tortilla styled bread that is typically found in villages) or left over rice from the night before with some curry that is heated for the meal. Breakfast is usually the simplest meal of the day and always includes several cups of sweet milk tea. In poorer families without any cows, tea is prepared black because they cannot afford milk on a daily basis.

After breakfast the eldest son and sometimes the father milk the family cows.[3] This is done by hand and can take up to thirty minutes depending on the number of cows. The son helps the father in almost everything he does. He is preparing his son for his future duties as head of the household. The daughters are given much less attention because they are seen as a liability. They will leave the household upon marriage, and any investment the parents have made in the daughter is gone. According to one mother:

- *Why should I send my daughter to Bhilar for school?[4] What good is that going to do me? She will not take care of me when I am old, my son will. I love my daughters but they are a big headache. I try to make them good enough that they will get a good husband and that we might not pay too much dowry. But if my sons are educated and make money, they will get good hard working wives from well off*

families. Also my husband and I need help in the fields. If all my
children were in school we would have to hire more than one laborer
to help us and we don't have money to pay for more than one.

Those families who own a motorcycle transport their milk to
Panchgani. This is usually the job of the eldest son or the father.
They return home by 9:30 or 10:00 A.M. and go to the fields to
work. Those families who do not own a motorcycle transport
their milk to Bhilar on foot and receive a much lower price than
those who sell the milk in Panchgani, but under the circumstances this is their best alternative. They return home by 11:00
AM and rush to the fields to work.

Depending on the season, how much work there is in the
fields, and how far the fields are from the house, farmers might
eat a lunch in the fields which has been prepared by the wife that
morning. The daughters might need to go home and fetch the
lunch for the men. After breakfast the mother usually begins
cooking lunch and finishes by 10:30 A.M. During this time she
also folds all of the bedding and cleans the house. She sweeps all
the rooms which creates a lot of dust in the air, and also cleans
out the animal stalls. The grandfather and sometimes a young
son who does not attend school take the animals out to graze.
After their morning grooming and breakfast the children going
to school get dressed in their uniforms and make their way to the
village school by 8:00 A.M. They return home for an hour lunch
break and are in school until 3:30 P.M.

Young boys do not have much responsibility and are, in a way,
freeloaders. They rarely clean up after themselves and are given
preference in almost all matters. They are the members of the
household with the least responsibility and the most free time to
play and frolic. Daughters as young as 5 years old have several
responsibilities, from cooking and cleaning to caring for younger
siblings to feeding the livestock. The younger daughters have
the responsibility of caring for the baby while the mother cooks
and cleans. Older daughters are given much more responsibility
and are essential contributors to the daily operations of the
household. The elderly are seen as non-contributors and non-
productive members of the household. For this reason they have
lost status within the family, but have gained in that they are
older and therefore command more respect. Young men, though

lower than their fathers and grandfathers in status, are pampered more than the daughters are. Other than their work in the fields and delivery of milk, older sons are given little work to do around the house. Older daughters are constantly seen working throughout the day, cleaning, cooking, doing laundry, and fetching water.

There is approximately a two hour break in the afternoon when the working members of the household rest either under a tree in the fields or in the house, sometimes listening to the radio or napping. There is little interaction among boys and girls or between men and women throughout the day. They may be in the same room or working together in the field, but not much verbal interaction takes place. When asked about this, a man replied:

- *What is there to say. We have work to do, and we do it. When there is time to relax I want to relax and not be nagged by my wife or mother. I work hard and need time to relax. Women like to talk about things that do not interest me. I like to discuss politics and economics. Women are always grumbling about how hard their life is and are never grateful for what they have.*

Whereas a woman once told me:

- *I talk to my husband all the time, but he never listens. Really, there is not much to talk about. We get up every morning, work hard all day and go to sleep. At least the men have time to relax. I work from morning till I go to sleep. Not only do I cook all day long and clean, but I also work in the fields. My life is very difficult, and you could never understand. I often go to sleep with my whole body aching and wake up with it still aching. And on top of all this I gave birth to four children and have to raise them. Life is hard... That is all I can say.*

After school the children return home for tea and a small snack. They change their clothes and go out to play. The young girls are often given some chores to do in preparation for dinner. The men arrive from the fields at about 4:30 or 5:00 P.M. They drink their tea and sit down in the verandah and visit with each other. They sometimes read the newspaper or listen to the radio.

Occasionally they will nap waiting for dinner to get ready. The women are busy in the kitchen preparing dinner that usually consists of rice and dal. Before dinner the mother milks the cows and stores the milk in a container to be transported to town the next day. Dinner is served at about 7:30 P.M. with the men eating first while the women serve them, and if there is no serving to be done the women and older daughters sit there and watch the men eat. They continuously refill the men's water glass and offer more rice or dal or *bhaji* (vegetables). After completely filling their stomachs the men wash their hands over their plates using the water in their glass and go out into the verandah to relax. It is then the women's turn to eat what is left. After they are done they clean the *thalis* (plates) and cooking pots and prepare for the night. The mother unfolds all the bedding and places them next to each other on the floor in the central room of the house. She prepares some more tea for everyone and sometimes warms up some sweet milk. By 9:00 P.M. she finally sits down to relax for the first time in the day. By 9:30 the lights are turned off and everyone is sound asleep. Seven hours later the process begins all over again.

The Arrival of Television into the Household

According to one author, 'Television... is making inroads into the life and psyche of the villages. The social ethos that has reigned for millennia is experiencing a slow, but steady, change. The communal, religious, and sex barriers that permeate the traditional lifestyle are perceptibly breaking down' (Malik, 1989). Is there any truth to this statement, or does it bestow unwarranted power on television? This conclusion is true when analyzing the household structures and activities. The arrival of television has dramatically altered the structure of daily life in the village household.

One of the most obvious impacts of television is that time is now defined by the television programs and not the position of the sun in the sky. The day begins with the mother of the household waking up at 6:00 A.M. and turning on the television. By the time she has completed her morning cleansing rituals, and returns to the family sleeping quarters, she finds everyone still curled up in their blankets but all awake watching television. She no longer has to yell at her children to get up but now has to yell at them to stop watching TV and get on with their morning chores. At times her yelling turns to beatings even though several young children still did not take their eyes off the television set during the ordeal. Time is structured according to television. People wake up and go to sleep depending on when the television begins airing and goes off the air. Since satellite television in Raj Puri does not go off the air but is on twenty-four hours a day, villagers often get little sleep and are visibly exhausted during the day. While growing up in Panchgani I remember the town shutting down at 8:30 or 9:00 P.M. But in 1996, while riding my motorcycle through town at 2:00 A.M., I could see the flicker of the television light on the windows of many homes. People are sleeping much less today than ten years ago. And their daily schedule is organized around their favorite programs. Instead of playing the traditional village games like *viti dandoo, kabaddi,* or *hadhki,* children now run home during their lunch break from school to watch their favorite soap operas.

Another stark contrast between those homes with and without TV sets is that there is much less noise in the latter. The television is kept so loud most of the time that even if someone wanted to talk they probably would not be heard. The members of the household go about their morning activity in silence with one eye on their chores and another on the television. Even in rooms without television one can still hear programs clearly, and people are ready to run into the TV room if something interests them. Conversations within the household often center on television programs. While evenings were once spent conversing with friends, family and neighbors, now they are spent watching television. Though it may seem discouraging at first, television has created a new social environment that many believe to be positive.

Women and men interact with each other more due to the presence of television. Instead of a man going out to visit with his friends he is spending time in the home with his wife and children. Excerpts from a few interviews confirm this:

- *My husband used to never spend time with us in the evenings. He is a nice man, and I like him very much. Ever since we bought this television he spends more time in the house. He even helps Suresh with his homework.*
- *Television has been good for my family. I only tell you this because you are my good friend. But since we got television, my wife and I have become interested in each other. We see how some married people behave on television, and we act like that. My wife wants more attention now and I think that is good.*
- *Before television we used to not have any possibility of seeing girls. But now we go to our friend's house to watch television, and there are girls there, and we have become friends. You know Mahendra and Tara got married last year. It was an arranged marriage, but they were also in love. And it is because they spent much time visiting each other to watch television.*

The arrival of television presents opportunities for young people to get to know each other and spend time with each other in a controlled environment. Growing up in Panchgani I was unfamiliar with the term dating. There was no such thing. If you were seen talking to a girl you were immediately labeled a couple, and people ridiculed you so you would never do it again. In the village it is even stricter. Young men and women do not interact under any circumstances. However, the arrival of television has created a forum for this interaction to take place under the supervision of elders, and both the adults and the teenagers seem to like it. On numerous occasions while watching television I witnessed unrelated men and women looking at each other and laughing or smiling; a man might even pat a woman on the shoulder and make a comment about a particular scene or character. Without the presence of television, this behavior would seem totally foreign and out of place. In addition, there is a breakdown in the sex-role differentiation of work. Traditionally it is the woman's job to put out all the blankets and quilts for sleeping. I often observed men helping the women clean up after dinner and preparing the room with pillows and blankets in preparation for a movie or serial. There is such great anticipation for these programs that dinner is prepared earlier so women do not have to be bothered with cleaning during the program. And often dishes and pots and pans are cleaned the following morning because there is just not enough time at night due to television.

Many people without television complain that since its arrival in the village there have been more arguments and beatings in their own homes. Husbands and wives are fighting because one wants to go see a movie at a neighbor's house and the other does not. Children are constantly sneaking out of the house even missing their dinners, so they can watch television at a friend's house. Parents in Raj Puri complained that their children were watching too much Channel V and getting bad ideas and morals from that type of programming. One parent had given up on his son and had stopped trying to regulate his television viewing. He said that it was too much trouble, and now the child does not go to school but instead sits at home all day watching television.

The television is kept in the central room of the house. It is mounted on top of a table or cabinet in the most prominent corner. This room is kept especially clean compared to the other rooms in the house. On the walls next to the TV set are hung decorative items like a battery operated clock and family pictures. A nice expensive cloth is bought from town to cover the television when it is not in use. Children are not allowed to play in this room. More light is brought into this central room to show off how well it is kept and how nice the decorations are. Grain that was sometimes stored in the back of this room in large containers has been moved to make the TV room more spacious and bright. This room is usually rearranged several times for the best fit. Expensive cabinets and cupboards are brought out from interior rooms and arranged neatly in this room. In several homes the traditional wooden loft used for storage was removed to give the appearance of a more airy and spacious feeling.

Similar to reports of television first entering American homes in the 1940s and 1950s, villagers dressed up for the evening news and serials for the first several weeks upon acquiring a TV set. According to one lady:

• *I want to make a good impression, I don't want to be seen in my old sari.*

This changed once the novelty wore off and people became comfortable with having 'strangers' entering their home every evening through the television set. Children were scolded for making too much noise or fidgeting. At first women tended to sit on one side of the room and in the back while the men occupied the center of the floor. After time, this segregation began to change, and there was more mixture in seating arrangements between men and women and different age groups. It was interesting to see at times during a late night movie, unrelated men and women sprawled out on the floor next to each other watching television.

Many elders are not very open to purchasing a television set, arguing that it is better to spend the money on something productive instead of something vain and useless. An old farmer told me:

• *My son wants to buy a TV but I won't let him. His wife is always pressuring him to buy one, even his children. But what is the use? Our neighbor has a TV and we go to their house all the time to watch. Why should we spend so much money to buy something that we already have next to our house?*

Yet, another elderly man, after having a television for five years, cannot imagine life without it:

• *Television has changed my life completely. I cannot do much work anymore, and I used to sit around the house doing nothing all day. But now that my son bought a TV, I can watch different programs all day long. I don't feel bored anymore.*

Sunday has become an agricultural holiday for villagers. Ever since serials like *Ramayan* and *Mahabharat* aired in the late 1980s, Sundays have become 'television day' for many village families, during which, especially before noon, the village is a ghost town. My first visit to Danawli was on a Sunday morning, and I thought something was terribly wrong. I was so used to the hustle and bustle of village life that to see a village with absolutely no one in the streets and no children coming up to me was very strange. I soon realized that the village and the household activity was structured according to television. The streets might be deserted for several hours, and then all of a sudden women came running out of their huts carrying empty pots on their way to the water pump. Just as quickly as they appeared they all disappeared back into their huts for the next captivating program.

Conclusion

Today, the dynamics within the village household are different from what they were only ten years ago. Children are being born into television families, and they regard television as a permanent fixture in their lives. Villagers spend many hours every week watching this new medium, and this is reflected in the change in household activity and relationships. Traditional village life comprises four major divisions of the day. The morning is a time to prepare for the day ahead, to organize materials, and plan work. The day is a time of work and not leisure. Dusk is a time to settle one's affairs and prepare for the evening. Night is a time to relax and recuperate from a long day's work and prepare for the day ahead. Night is also when transactions take place and relationships are nurtured. Television has dramatically changed these divisions, especially the last period. Night begins at a much earlier time, and people watch television into the early hours of the morning. The time once used for important transactions and networking is now spent moving between houses to watch television.

What are people watching? Entertainment television in both Raj Puri and Danawli is the most popular of all types of programming. My own and other data support this conclusion.[5] To satisfy this need for entertainment and to stay competitive with other satellite networks which offer entertainment fare, programming on Doordarshan has consistently moved away from developmental and educational fare to entertainment based programs.

Entertainment shows are seen as attractive if not addictive. The influences of this type of entertainment programming can be seen in several areas of household life. Villagers spend a large part of their week watching television, which has resulted in a restructuring of their daily lives. People are going to sleep much later than before and waking up at approximately the same time, allowing for less sleep and therefore less motivation for work. Villagers complain about being tired but do not turn off the television at an early hour in the evening. Children are playing less than before and watching more television. They are also not spending as much time on their schoolwork.

This chapter offered a picture of the role of television at the level of the household. Television viewing is a priority for villagers, and the time spent in front of the box is influencing their lives and relationships. Though not the only contributory factor, television is an important variable in the changing landscape of household life in rural India. As villages move toward the adoption of satellite television, exposure to television increases, as does the rate of change of that landscape.

Notes

1. This is in contrast to a family who acquired a TV set during this research and was much more enamored by it than other households. This family watched much more television than the other families observed. As time went on the novelty began to wear off, and their viewing habits, though still not representative, were beginning to mirror those of other households.
2. Figures are for those who own television sets. Five homes were observed for a week at a time over the course of the research.
3. The indigenous dairy cows are water buffalo, but in the past fifteen years other breeds have been introduced into these villages. The jersey cow is the most popular of these new breeds and if healthy produces five times as much milk as the water buffalo. However, these jersey cows are prone to sickness and disease and are hence not very reliable. I met three individuals who had invested in the jersey cow when it was first introduced, and all three cows died within two years of purchase. Farmers are becoming more educated as to the maintenance of these non-indigenous animals and more are opting to invest in them.
4. As mentioned earlier, Danawli has a school that offers education only up to fifth grade, after that the children must go to Bhilar or Panchgani for school. Bhilar has a school up to eighth grade, so a child must commute into Panchgani if he wants a tenth grade education. Few go for further education after tenth grade. Those who do pursue specific diplomas in electrical engineering, plumbing, and accounting if they are men while women usually get a seamstress diploma or a secretarial degree. Most however, opt to stay in the

village after eighth grade and engage in agricultural labor or travel to Mumbai in search of work.

5. Ninan (1995: 68) suggests that the 'highest viewership in India's villages is unambiguously for entertainment, films and film-based entertainment, not for development-oriented programs. The latter often go un-comprehended by their target audience because they are not in the regional language, particularly the prime time family planning literacy and girl child spots.' Doordarshan's first rural sample survey of fifteen states (which accounted for 97 per cent of the population of the country) reflected these same findings (ibid.). Malik's (1989: 482) survey of two villages in northern India 'clearly shows that it is the entertainment quality of the programs, with an element of story, engrossing format and technical finesse, which has enraptured large audiences.... Television is a good source of relaxation and diversion was the view of most people.... By contrast the viewing of informational and instructional programs was low and to a great extent either incidental or forced. Inconvenient times, unpopular formats and a heavy information content were some of the reasons for their unpopularity.'

8

The Dynamics of Social Change:
The Role of Television

Introduction

While the preceding discussion focused on the role of television
within the household, I now look at the role of television in the
changing social landscape of village life. And though it is not easy
to determine the influence of mass communication in general
(Hartmann et al., 1989) and television in particular, the analysis
now attempts to locate the influences of television in the context
of village dynamics. Television can alter knowledge, attitudes,
opinions, and behavior in a village. Its influence can be immediate or delayed, long-lasting or short-lived. The effect of television
on villagers might be translated into institutional changes, or it
might not. Knowledge might change without a corresponding
change in behavior and attitude. Determining the role of television in the process of social change therefore, is no easy task.
Keeping these complexities in mind, I venture to explain change
within village culture and the role television plays in that process.
The analysis is limited to certain features of village life which
were more influenced by television than others.

India, a country which occupies only 2.4 per cent of the world's
landmass, is extremely diverse. With close to a billion people, 75

per cent of whom live in villages, India is one of the most varied nations on the planet. Differences exist between villages in various parts of the country, and any generalizations should be made with caution. There are enough similarities though, that some attempt at generalization is warranted. It is necessary to note that not all social change, even if it represents development, is necessarily positive for all villagers. Change can benefit one section of the community, damage another, and remain insignificant to yet another. Therefore, it must be recognized that social change in the rural context is not a simple process; it involves the interaction of a great many factors. And what makes the present village studies even more complicated is that these remote villages have jumped in just a few years into the electronic information age through television.

Oral to Electronic

Harold Innis (1972) claimed that societies generally move along a linear path from oral to literate to electronic forms of communication. He argued that oral communication set basic parameters to the functioning of those societies in which it was predominant. Whereas literate societies are governed by written law and by the principles and statements of a constitution, oral societies are governed by knowledge preserved by certain speakers. According to Innis, oral societies become literate, and literate societies move toward electronic forms of communication. Thus societies are structured according to the type of communication used.

Maharashtrian villages have leaped from the stage of oral communication into the electronic age of mass communication. This jump, at first a result of radio, is primarily due to the influx of television and its unrivaled popularity. A society that was defined and organized by its oral traditions and stories is now more than ever being structured and reorganized by a foreign source through television. Today illiteracy does not stand in the way of information. The majority of villagers, literate or not, have access to knowledge and information unobtainable twenty years ago.

Traditionally, villagers spent their leisure time engaged in activities like singing *bhajans* (religious and folk songs), playing *kabaddi, kusti,* or *lejhim* or watching the *Tamasha* (annual play). Men were the only ones allowed to watch the *Tamasha* which was considered lewd and inappropriate for female eyes. Women's leisure activities were generally more limited. During certain festivals women did, however, sing and dance but this activity occurred only once or twice a year. Women would also often visit the temple, cook festive dishes, and engage in the traditional art of *rangoli* (floor painting). Today, participation in these activities has decreased substantially. According to a few elders interviewed:

- *These young people today.... They are hopeless. They watch television all the time and do not understand their history.*
- *Children used to come to me to hear the stories of olden days. Everyone used to listen to me. When I was a child I listened to the stories of my father and grandfather. The young people today only want to watch television and movies and go to Panchgani until late at night. They even sometimes go to Wai on motorcycles.*
- *Television is ruining our culture.... People no longer speak like they used to. They all, especially the young people, talk about the life in the cities or in England or America.... They don't know anything about our own history or traditions. I have heard some even talk about love marriage.*
- *Do you ever see any young people during the bhajans? No. They are all either watching TV or in Bhilar or Panchgani. The bhajans are very important for us. When I was young my father forced me to go sit during the bhajans. But now my grandchildren do not listen, and all they want is jeans, sunglasses, motorcycles and movie songs.*

According to these village elders, television is turning their culture into something which mirrors Mumbai more than Danawli. In addition to its cultural impact, television's influence is also seen at the individual level. It effects people's perceptions of themselves, their society, and the world at large.

Television, though significant, is only one variable in the complex dynamics of social change. Referring to the impact of television in Brazil, Kottak (1990: 193) states:

...TV impact is one highly significant part of a more general process of urbanism, nationalism, and state solidification, with many mutually reinforcing aspects. [Television] characters tend to belong to the national elite, enjoying the good life of wealth, power, and leisure, encourages local-level acceptance of the external messages. Townspeople mine the world of [television programs] for patterns and values that eventually influence local prestige norms. More and more people emulate them. Over time... TV gradually aids a national process of social liberalization.

The key phrase here is 'over time.' Kottak views the impact of television as a process; this process will be discussed further in the next chapter.

Television and Social Processes

Some scholars argue that television significantly contributes to the introduction of new ideas into traditional societies and in many cases initiates and reinforces modernizing processes. Salzman (1993: 1) points out that:

while the world may never quite become the 'global village' rhapsodized by Marshall McLuhan, each village, whether rustic or urban, pre- or post-industrial ... is becoming more and more global, as, electronically, the world increasingly comes to each village and neighborhood, hamlet and settlement, quarter and suburb.

In surveying ethnographic literature Salzman highlights the increasing role television and the media in general, are playing in the modernizing processes of rural life. In particular he points to four processes—democratization, consumerism, urban modeling, and linguistic hegemony—that are 'presently widespread and each has major ramifications for cultural life locally and beyond, and they all deserve close and detailed attention by anyone trying to understand contemporary life' (Salzman, 1993: 7). These and other processes are at work in rural Maharashtra. Some are more influenced by television than others, yet each of the following processes illustrates the role television is playing in the social evolution of family life.

Consumerism

The process of consumerism defined by Salzman (1993: 7) as 'the cathecting of consumption as an appropriate orientation' is rapidly becoming an accepted part of the culture of rural Maharashtra. As the village moves toward a more cash based economy, things that were once thought to be a luxury are now seen as a necessity. Television is a good example of this. Fifteen years ago villagers would never have dreamed of owning a television set. Today, people feel deprived and even embarrassed if they do not own one. I once asked a villager in Danawli if I could visit him in his home. He thought for awhile and then said he would prefer to visit me in his neighbor's house. After several minutes of probing, it became clear that he wanted to meet in his neighbor's house because he did not have a TV set in his own home.

Eleven per cent of Doordarshan's output comprises advertising, which is aired mostly during entertainment programming, since these shows command the largest and most attentive audiences. Therefore, a child who watches thirty-one hours of entertainment television a week is exposed to almost three-and-a-half hours of commercials. From toys to hand cream, from liquor to blue jeans, the products advertised are now perceived as necessities. According to a pharmacist in Mahabaleshwar:

- *Villagers come to me all the time and tell me they need medicine for their back or cold or what ever it is. I give them some medicine and they tell me, 'No, I want that medicine they advertised on TV last night'. I tell them that this one is better and even cheaper, but they don't want it. They want what they see on TV.*

I often heard young women comment on an actress' dress or how beautiful a sari was on TV. One girl yelled out to her mother while pointing at the TV:

- *That is the sari I want to wear for my marriage. Do you think it is too expensive?*

A widowed mother once confided in me that her children were demanding things she could not afford:

• *My children see things on television and they think they can have them. What can I tell them. We can't even afford a television, but they go to other people's homes and see things on television. They are always talking about coke. Do you know how much one coke costs in Panchgani?*

Though all members of village families are influenced by the advertisements they see on television, my observations indicate that children and teenagers are more swayed than others. Chapter 9 examines this subject in greater depth.

Linguistic Hegemony

India is considered one of the most diverse nations in the world. It has more than eighteen official languages and a multitude of dialects. One would think that television programming would cater to this diversity, but just as the film industry is based primarily in Hindi, television has made Hindi the dominant language as well.[1] And with the onslaught of satellite television, Hindi and English are the predominant languages on air. Although efforts at decentralizing program production have resulted in more Marathi programming in the past five years, most of these shows are of little interest to villagers. What little Marathi entertainment programming exists airs before 8:30 P.M. when most villagers are still settling down for the evening. The Hindi serials and movies along with the multitude of English programs on satellite television are most popular in Raj Puri.

This 'privileging of certain languages, dialects, concepts and terms' (Salzman, 1993: 7) is resulting in an increased use of both Hindi and English by Marathi-speaking villagers. For example, the English phrase 'love marriage' is now part of village vocabulary. This phrase is foreign both in language and meaning; the very concept of marrying for love is out of the question. One of the basic and fundamental principles in traditional village society is the concept of 'arranged marriage.' A girl is raised with the hope that if she is beautiful, strong, healthy, fair, and educated enough, her family will not have to pay a huge dowry. A boy is raised with the hope that one day the parents might secure a nice girl from a wealthy family with a hefty dowry which will add to the family wealth. It is part of the psyche of every villager and is the norm in village culture. As a result of television this new concept of love marriage has become part of village culture and a realistic alternative for a few. When I arrived for this research the biggest blockbuster film in India was about the evils of arranged marriage and the beauty and innocence of love marriage. Millions flocked to the cinema to see this film and cheered when the two lovers ended up together forever. This is a recurring theme not only in the movie theaters but now also on television. And though I did not find any villagers in love marriages, more and more people are willing to talk about it and claim they know people who are together through love marriage.

As Salzman (1993: 7) points out 'television programs which express and illustrate dynamics and discourses in one society become challenges and alternatives when aired in other cultural contexts.' The introduction of a new language that carries with it new ideas, concepts, and values has an undeniable impact on village culture. By continuously airing certain themes, television legitimizes certain processes which were hitherto foreign to village society. This is not to say that television is the direct cause of certain changes in the village household, but that it acts as a legitimizing agent displaying certain ideas or practices to be congruent with accepted norms.

Urban Modeling

Increasingly village society today mirrors cosmopolitan models of life. It is not uncommon to see motorcycles and cars beeping their horns while driving through village streets, or modern appliances like electric fans, boom boxes, hot plates, and steel cupboards decorating village huts. More people build latrines next to their homes instead of defecating in nearby fields. Instead of traditional village attire, teenagers today wear blue jeans and T-shirts and wear baseball caps instead of *topis*. Girls are copying the hairstyles they see on television instead of pulling their hair back in a single braid.

Throughout village society one witnesses the reflections of urban styles of life and work. Villagers take Sundays off from work to relax and watch television. Parents are spending more time with their children, and there are beginning to be examples of affection between fathers and teenage sons. Over time villagers begin to imbibe many of the ideas, images, principles, and values they see on television, and the evidence suggests that their behavior begins to reflect some of those values and images. While it is clear that economic factors are important contributors, many television programs legitimize urban lifestyles and depict images that villagers begin to accept as norms.

Dilip, a 24-year-old man living alone and working in Danawli for the past five years, is a classic example of modeling urban life. Dilip has never been to the city but knows it well by what he sees on television. He wants to be married someday and work in the city. He wants his wife to be educated and modern looking. Yet, though he understands how attractive love marriage might be to some people, he prefers the traditional path and wants an arranged marriage. He watches a great deal of television and continually looks to the images displayed there: modern clothing, sports cars, good jobs, tiled floors, running water, indoor toilets, air-conditioning, and attractive men and women. He would repeat English phrases from television and ask what they meant. He would ask if girls in America really wore bathing suits like that or engage in pre-marital sex. Dilip went so far as to install a doorbell in his hut and a wooden front door with a lock. He could not imagine life without television. He was never without a baseball cap and tennis shoes. This young man represents a villager who has never visited the city but who learns, through television, new ways of living. And though on the surface he seems modern in every respect, he values arranged marriage over love marriage and works his family's land in the village, as is the tradition.

Changing Gender Relations

The process of changing gender relations and how it relates to the presence of television in the household is a central theme of this research. There are two aspects which need to be analyzed when focusing on television in the home. The first relates to the simple presence of television, while the second concerns the content of television programming, and both facets are intimately tied to the changing gender relations within the household.

Men in homes with television tended to do more household chores than those without it. Shahir confided that his wife used to milk the cows in the evening but now he has taken over that chore. He said that since they like to watch television after dinner, there is no time for her to milk. So while she prepares dinner he milks the cows and also arranges the TV room for the evening. Shanta bai, his wife, explained that she does not like to take lunch to him in the fields because she would miss her favorite serial in the afternoon, so she sends her daughter Sungeeta who is not at all pleased at going. When Sangeeta is not home, Shahir has to walk a great distance back for lunch. Shahir has argued with his wife about this to no avail. He is not pleased with the situation but admits that he too has started watching the soap opera with his wife and likes it. The simple presence of television in the home is influencing certain gender roles.

Cooking habits and menus are also changing as a result of television. Women understand that if they are to watch television in the evening they must begin cooking earlier in the afternoon. They stop their work and leave the men in the fields earlier in the afternoon in order to begin cooking. Dinner preparation which used to begin at 4:30 or 5:00 P.M. now starts as early as 3:00 P.M. Women have also incorporated various non-traditional foods such as noodles and sliced bread in their family's diet.

The types of television programs and the values and ideas they convey are an important aspect in determining the influence of television. Several scholars have analyzed the role of television in relation to gender roles in the home (Rao, 1992; Ninan, 1995; Mitra, 1993; Unnikrishnan and Bajpai, 1996; Khrishnan and Dighe, 1990). My own evidence on this subject is primarily from the male's perspective due to the fact that my access to the females of the household was limited.

There were many men who said that they were open to the idea of female empowerment. Many had chosen to educate their girls as well as their boys. Several men agreed that women do much of the work in the household. But when asked about the way women were portrayed on television, few men liked what they saw. During television programs men often commented: 'look how that woman is dressed, she has no shame' and 'these women don't do any work.' There was constant reference to how times were changing, and men grumbled about the changing roles of women. A newly married man said:

- *I have no control over my wife. She never does any work. She sits watching TV all day long, and I have to do all the work. If my mother was here she would show her how to work. Girls nowadays are lazy, and watch too much television. They all dream that they can become like those rich Bombay women they see on TV, and they are fooling themselves. Women are supposed to take care of their husbands and the house. But they don't want to do that any more.*

While certain gender roles within the household might be changing, it is still very clear that many roles remain rigid. Women are lower than men in all aspects of household life. It is the man who makes every financial decision. He decides which children to educate and what crops to grow. Men eat while the women serve and watch. What is changing is that both men and women are more open to ideas of change than before.

With the arrival of television in the home, men and women are spending much more time together and in closer proximity. This increase in physical proximity increases the interpersonal interactions among the sexes. Unrelated men and women interact more, and most seem to like it. Women have shifted their orientation from the demands of their husbands and fathers to the demands of TV.

The Role of Television in the Process of Social Change

What follows is a more detailed analysis of the role of television in the process of social change. A variety of propositions are made which illustrate the influences of television on various aspects of village life. It is necessary to reiterate the findings of Hartmann et al. (1989) and Rao (1966) who engaged in similar village studies on the role of the media in the process of social change. They both concluded that the mass media are far less important sources of information and influence than interpersonal communication.

However, Hartmann et al. (1989: 260) also state that, 'This is not a particularly surprising finding since the exposure of most villagers to mass communications is fairly low: many people have barely any media exposure which is highest among the young, the male, the better educated, and the better off.' This is no longer the case. People from all sections of the community are increasingly gaining access to media through television. In homes with television women watched more TV than men. The present data suggest that the level of education, income, and status of villagers is much less a factor in determining media exposure than it was in the 1980s.

Both studies (Hartmann et al., 1989; Rao, 1966) occurred at a time when television was still a novelty in India, and none of the villages being researched possessed a single television set. Today, with mass access to television, the landscape of village India has changed quickly and dramatically. A discussion follows of television's role in the process of social change of three broad areas of rural society: economic, social, and political spheres.

The Economic Sphere

1. *Television contributes to a spirit of consumerism.*

> The sovereign nations shall cross the great mountain range
> With offerings of tooth cleaners and colored water
> And of all the native merchants peddling their 200 decade
> secrets
> Of clove oil and colored water
> None but a few shining stars will last. (Nostradamus)[2]

The presence of television influences people's lives as does the content of the medium. Consumer goods and modern ideas about life and work are introduced indirectly as part of regular programming and directly in commercials. Leading characters discuss their wish to buy a new car or new clothes, or they may display alternate ways of earning a living. What villagers see on their favorite programs is often reflected in the advertisements on television. Sponsored television programs prominently reflect the product throughout the duration of the program. During a cricket match players drink from Coke glasses, and characters in a serial may brush their teeth with toothpaste whose brand name is clearly visible. It was surprising to see so many villagers using toothbrushes and toothpaste to brush their teeth. The traditional way of brushing one's teeth in these villages was to use a twig of the neem tree, which has certain medicinal properties and has in recent years become very popular in the West. It is also a norm to rinse one's mouth with water after a meal or snack. I observed two young men in Danawli rinsing with mouthwash which is advertised a great deal on television.

When directly probed about this spirit of consumerism in the village, many young people strongly denied that television was a contributory factor.

- *No, TV has nothing to do with why I want tennis shoes.*
- *Yes, we see many advertisements on TV, but I don't think that they affect my decisions about what to buy. I buy what I need.*
- *TV is only for entertainment. We like to watch because it is relaxing, and we sometimes learn about other places. But TV has not influenced my life at all. My father is a farmer, and I will be a farmer, what has changed? Nothing.*

Yet, others acknowledged that television did create a desire for things.

- *I want many things that my parents never had. I want a motorcycle and a nice color TV. I want to eat mutton (goat meat) once a week instead of three times a year.*
- *TV shows us what is good to buy.*
- *People in the village today are very greedy. I even want many things that I can't have. We see many things on TV that we would like to have, and therefore we become greedy.*

The older generation has a different view of television as it relates to consumerism in the village. Almost all the older people, above forty-five years of age, stated that television is having a negative impact on the young people. According to them, it creates desires which cannot be satisfied due to their economic position.

- *People must learn to be satisfied with what they have and not want everything they see on TV. I have always been happy with what God*

> *has given me. I have worked hard and tried to provide for my family. TV is ruining these young people... they all want to have what they see in the advertisements, but that is for rich people and we are not rich.*

> • *People were more satisfied before television. Now these young people, all they do is watch TV, and they want everything they see on TV. No one is satisfied any more. Everyone is greedy.*

While sitting outside on the front step of a house talking with two men in their late fifties, one of them pointed at Dilip who had just passed by and said:

> • *See Dilip, he wears those clothes trying to act like Amit (Amitabh a movie star), but he will never be able to do anything with his life. He is fooling himself. Poor chap, he thinks he can have everything he sees on TV.*

This spirit of consumerism coupled with a move into a cash-based economy has created a new atmosphere in the village. Villagers are increasingly looking outward. The need to satisfy this new-found appetite for consumer goods requires new forms of employment and lifestyle. Whereas traditionally the family was the unit of production and consumption, today this is changing. The idea of sharing within the family is being challenged, and many villagers relate this to the influence of television advertising. According to one young man who dreams of the city life:

> • *I want to move to Pune, but my father won't let me. I have no future here in Danawli. I want to have the good life. I see many things on TV that I want and I cannot have. I want to go to movies and ride a motorcycle. So since I cannot go to Pune I try to make a small business here in Bhilar with some friends, and I don't tell my father about the money I make.*

Television has its greatest influence on children and youth. Forty per cent of Indians are younger than fifteen years of age. This group watches the most television and is most influenced by television advertising. The most dramatic changes in their way of thinking are reflected in their approach to clothes, to concepts of beauty, to their commitment to certain lifestyle images which are constantly impressed upon their minds through television.

Television reinforces certain patterns of consumption, which create a new dynamic within the village community that can create a strain in certain relationships.

2. *While television has devalued traditional village life for some, it has for others reinforced traditional agrarian culture.*

There are two sides to the messages portrayed on television. On the one hand, urban, modernized styles of living and consumption are valued. Programs depict the 'high life' in a positive light, and some villagers identify with this and restructure their lives accordingly. At the same time, television often romanticizes the agrarian lifestyle, which reinforces the views of others. It is generally the younger generation which identifies more with the modern messages on television while older people seem to seek out those programs which elevate farming and traditional life. According to some young people:

- *I don't want to be a farmer like my father. I want to live in the city, maybe Pune. I know someone in Panchgani who went to Dubai to work. I hate sitting here in Danawli in a broken house watching TV every night about people living the rich life in the city. I want to be like them.*
- *There is nothing for me in Danawli. My family has only 2 acres of land, and half will go to my brother. They show us on TV how to work and earn a living that is better than farming. I will leave here some day.*

Older people gain a different sense of satisfaction and fulfillment in village life from television:

- *These young people nowadays have no commitment to our traditional way of life. They do not realize how good farming is. God has given us this land, and we must be thankful. Last week on TV they showed a program about different villages, I think in Gujarat and Maharashtra. They showed how honorable this life style is and I felt very good.*

According to Babu, the resident historian and ex-Sarpanch:

- *TV is good because it shows some of our traditions and history. Maharashtra has a great history, and we are all Marathas. The*

Marathas took control of politics from the Brahmins many years ago. It is the farmers in all the villages that are behind the Shiv Sena (political party). Farmers keep the country running. If it was not for us everyone would starve.

3. *Television reinforces the pull of the city.*

The first thing I noticed when entering the villages was the multitude of television antennas. The second was that there were very few young men in the village. A large percentage of men between eighteen and thirty migrate to Mumbai, and some to Pune, in search of work and a better life. Dandekar (1986) studied the impact of this migration on a village 50 miles from Danawli. She documents this migration trend dating back to the 1800s. Migration in Danawli is a much more recent phenomenon. It began about twenty years ago, and today, most young people speak of moving to Mumbai for work. Though most return every six months for harvest, there are a few who have become permanent residents of the city. Television reinforces the pull of the city. It glamorizes urban life and work. Many young men said they yearned for the time when they could move out of the village. Though not directly admitting that television influenced this desire, many spoke of the urban lifestyle portrayed on the TV set.

Mohan, a newly married man in his mid twenties, commented during a television program:

- *I would love to move to Mumbai or Pune. This life in the village is hopeless. I can find work in the city. Here there is only so much I can do. But in Mumbai there are many possibilities. See that man (pointing to the TV set); he has a job that I would like. I could move my wife there as well and she could become a maid for a rich family. My children could go to good schools.*

According to another young man who dreams of the day when he will leave the village:

- *People in Mumbai have much more opportunity than we do. That is why so many villagers go there to work. I am convinced that my destiny is in Mumbai. Every time I watch TV I get more excited about going to Mumbai. I can't wait for that day.*

4. *Television broadens the entrepreneurial base.*

Traditional village society was characterized by the wealthy land-lords cornering the business activities of the community. Today, the village economy is much more diversified allowing people from all segments of the community to take part in the buying and selling of land. Television has contributed to expanding the entrepreneurial class. By equally informing all viewers about markets and methods it helps villagers of all castes and classes take advantage of growing opportunities. According to Pradeep, a Mahar farmer in his early forties who owns three and a half acres of land:

• *You know I sometimes watch the farm programs that inform me of good fertilizers I can use on my fields. I also find out about medicine for my jersey cow. TV is good. I used to have to rely on the develop-ment officer for information about improving my crops and my cows, and he was never very helpful. He used to only talk to certain people in the village who had power and influence. We had to sometimes bribe him for information... now I can turn on the TV and I learn a lot of good information from the local programs in Marathi about how to get loans, who is eligible to get loans, and many other things. Now these few people* (referring to the influential villagers) *are not the only ones who can buy land. I can go to the bank any time I want and get a small loan for whatever I want. I have bought 2 acres of land in the past five years.*

This illustrates how television broadens the entrepreneurial base and acts as an democratizing agent by breaking the monopoly on information previously held by the rich and politically connected.

The Social Sphere

1. *Television is an important factor in the restructuring of human rela-tionships.*

Research on the impact of media on village life has concluded that face-to-face interaction is a more important source of influ-ence than any other type of communication. According to Hart-mann et al. (1989: 262–263), 'In general, where there is evidence that mass communication is a factor in change, it is normally subsidiary to other factors: word-of-mouth communication is usually a more important source of information and influence.' Face-to-face communication is a crucial component of village relationships. However, with the arrival of television into the village, the role of face-to-face communication has changed on two levels. First, television directly contributes to a new social order within the village. Information is no longer filtered down through the elite to the poorer segments of the village. Almost all people have access to television. Therefore, one's knowledge of the world is no longer dependent on relationships but on individual access to television and the information and images it conveys. Second, television allows interaction between individuals that normally would not have taken place, thus restructuring the social dynamic within village life. Villagers are interacting more with one another and are meeting on common ground. Shinde, for example, never had a chance to talk to the Sarpanch, but since the arrival of television they see each other more often at friends' and neighbors' homes and have developed a friendship that has been an advantage to Shinde. According to him:

- *Suresh (the Sarpanch) never used to speak to me. I don't know why. I think because we had a misunderstanding once about something. But now we are friends. We see each other very often while watching TV, and he has helped me many times with the bank and other things. He and his family are very powerful in the village, and also in Bhilar they are recognized. So it is good I became his friend. (How did you become friends?) I told you, because I go to Sampat's house to watch TV, and Suresh is usually there. So we talk, and after some time we become friends.*

In the past if an individual wanted to meet with an important person in the village he would have to go to his house and meet on his turf. Today, because of television, people are meeting more often on common ground. Instead of Suresh going to Shahir's (the Patil) house to talk about a problem, they happen to meet at a neighbor's house while watching television. With the presence of television in the room Suresh feels more like Shahir's equal since the TV set is the focal point of everyone's attention. No longer does he have to sit at Shahir's feet and humble himself. They sit together side by side watching television, and they discuss the matter which is bothering Suresh.

2. *During the initial phase when ownership of TV sets has not yet become universal, television contributes to an expansion in the number and type of relationships.*

People who would normally not be in the same networking circle come together as a result of television. With the arrival of television in the village, people who see each other only in passing spend more time together watching television at a mutual friend's home. For many, this has increased their level of influence and standing within the village. Ajeet, a 40-year-old man, explained:

- *Before television came, I did not talk much to those people* (referring to some of his neighbors). *We had nothing to talk about. I used to stick to my family and not interact much. But now I go to [their] house to watch TV at night and we see each other there. We have become close friends now, and they even sometimes come to my house for tea. My son is still quite young but I have been discussing it with Sanjay, and we might arrange for him to marry his daughter.* (So, do you think television is good?) *Oh yes. I have many friends now, and sometimes when I need help they help me. Once I needed someone respected from Danawli to come to Bhilar and help me with my loan. Sanjay came and helped me. Before TV we never talked to each other. But now we see each other every night and have become good friends.*

At another time, while taking a break from working in the fields a woman told me:

- *You know us women we have a lot of work to do. Not much time to visit with friends. I work all day in the fields and then cook and clean all night. But now that we have bought a TV... now five years we have it.... Many of my friends come to my house. So I get to talk to a lot of people. Before TV came our house was very quiet.*

According to Sakharam television has been life changing:

- *Oh Kirk Baba, you don't know how much things have changed. Before I was a very poor man. No one talked to me. Even within my own group I was not popular* (referring to the Kasurde group).

But one day Shahir invited me to his house to see TV. I started going all the time. Now Suresh and others know me and many of these people (referring to the Kasurde group) *try to be friends with me.*

Pradeep thanks television for his daughter's wedding:

• *In a way I must thank the TV because it is the TV that helped me manage to arrange my daughter to marry. I knew Prakash, but we were never good friends. But before I got TV I used to go to Baboo's house to watch TV. Prakash used to go there as well, and we used to talk a lot. Then over time the topic of marriage came up, and we felt like they might be a good match (my daughter and Prakash's son). He is a good man and did not ask too much dowry. Now I am a happy man.*

This may change over time as more people buy TV sets for their own homes. Once that happens, the opposite might occur: since people have no incentive to visit other people's homes the number of relationships and influence one has within the village might decrease as people become more isolated from each other. This is a question for future research.

3. *Television reinforces the trend in delayed marriage and the desire for fewer children.*

In rural south India Caldwell et al. (1988), identified three broadly classified areas which most influence demographic change. These include education, penetration of villages by politicians, and contact with urban life and the media. In Caldwell's study the 'media' included only the cinema. He argued that an important element in village society was the cinema, yet the 'nearest cinema was 6 or 7 miles away' (ibid.: 23). It is important to keep in mind the differences between the cinema and television. Going to the cinema costs money for tickets and travel, and attending a picture once a month is considered expensive. Even so, in Caldwell's research, the elders of the study village gave this as the 'reason for social and demographic change more than any other factor' (ibid.: 23).

If the cinema, access to which is extremely limited in villages, was such an important factor influencing demographic change, then there was a good possibility that television would have a much greater influence due to its potentially ever-present influence. The evidence overwhelmingly supported this speculation.

All the young people interviewed in this research said that they did not want to marry young like their parents. They wanted to *enjoy life a little*. Many of those interviewed wanted to postpone marriage, and several men expressed a desire for a more educated and mature woman:

- *I don't want to marry a girl, I want to marry a woman. In the old days they used to marry very young girls. Do you ever see young girls on TV that are married? All the women that get married on TV are older. I don't mind marrying now (21 years old), but I told my father that I will not marry a young girl; who wants to marry a child?*

- *I think that one reason we girls do not like to marry very young anymore is because we want to live a little. My parents also want me to be mature. Last year there was a girl from our village who got married, and she was 17 years old. That is not too young, but still there was a lot of talk in the village about how young she was. I think the parents did not have to pay much dowry; that is why they married her off. TV has taught us that marrying young is not so good. TV tells us that we should get married older and have fewer children. Many times I see on the TV women getting married and they are 21 or 22 years old. I think I would like to get married at that age as well. That is a good age don't you think?*

Other villagers explained that it was more advantageous to have fewer children than before. Economic and social factors played a part in this rationalization. Villagers also pointed to television as a contributory factor in this demographic shift.

- *You know people used to have many children. Not anymore. It is difficult to find many couples in Danawli who have had more than four children. Most people have only two or three children. Times have changed. We don't need many children. It is too costly to have many children. Also there are many programs on TV that explain to us that fewer children are better. We do need two or three children especially boys. We need help in the fields and someone to take care of us when we grow old. But we are satisfied with only two children now.*

4. *Television aids in the process of status change from heredity to achievement.*

Information has always been a source of power and influence within village culture. This is reflected in the status of the teacher or the priest or scholar. Traditionally, a few powerful individuals in the community monopolized information, and these people were the only ones to initiate change. It was this educated minority in the community which was aware of new ideas and opportunities. Television has changed this. Even today only a few can afford a higher education, but television has taken previously monopolized information and disseminated it throughout village society.

Though hereditary status is still an important force in village life, knowledge and its use has become an essential measuring device. Knowledge and information are no longer in the hands of a small élite. Most people attempt to use this newfound knowledge to better their lives. Some are more successful than others are; these achievers command great respect and hold high status within the community.

Entertainment television is an important source of new ideas and values. Television programs continually portray characters who begin with little and end up with everything. And though television is not the only contributory factor, it is nonetheless an important source of information and ideas. My field notes from 1 May, 1996 demonstrate television's role in changing a person's status based on achievement as opposed to heredity:

Sitting on the front step of Prakash's home today I visited with Lina Bai, Shanta Bai and Sangeeta. We were very much alone since all the men were in the fields or in town and the children were in school. As we drank some tea we laughed and talked about everyday things. The women were concerned about the monsoons. They wondered if it would be a good year or would it be like last year with little rain. They also wondered how I was doing with my work. The villagers are always very concerned with how I am doing and always willing to lend a hand if I need anything. I assured them that I was doing well (since I was ill the previous week) and my work was progressing. As we chatted, Ashok, a man of about 42 years of age, walked by. We greeted each other and he continued on to his house. The conversation that followed was very interesting.

The women said that Ashok had become very respected in just a few years. He used to be a man like any other. He owns 3 acres of land and two cows. According to Shanta Bai,

- *Ashok first became popular when he bought a TV about five years ago. Back then there were just a few TVs in the village and so many people wanted to go to his house to watch. He broke one wall of his house and made it bigger. He even has tiles in the TV room.*

Lina Bai replied,

- *Yes, my husband used to go to his house to watch TV before we had one. He is very much liked in the village. His family did not have much but he has made a good life for them. When his daughter got married two years ago, it was a big event. He even served mutton. People do not usually serve mutton for so many people. He made a very good wedding. People say that he might be the first in Danawli to get satellite TV. I would not be surprised. Many people go to him for advice and to talk about things. I know that sometimes the Sarpanch goes to him for advice. His wife told me about Ajeet Saheb from Bhilar* (an important political figure) *who came to his house for tea. Ashok is so respected that sometimes my husband goes to his house to watch TV even though we have one in our house.*

Ashok was elected to the village Panchayat for the first time two years ago soon after his daughter's wedding. Many villagers think of Ashok as an informed person with many new ideas about how the village can improve itself. He was instrumental in securing a grant from the government for a water project. Television has contributed significantly to Ashok's new status within the community. He is one of the few in the village who speaks some English as a result of watching English television, and the villagers were proud of him for knowing a little of my language. Both Shanta Bai and Lina Bai mentioned television when speaking about Ashok's new found status and respect within the community.

5. *Television influences change in traditional age and gender relations.*

Television is generally thought of as an isolating technology. It is believed that television tends to make people to stay home and not visit with friends and relatives. However, television in both Danawli and Raj Puri was a catalyst which regularly brought together men and women of all ages in close contact for extended periods of time. This has created new types of relationships among people of different ages and genders. In addition to bringing about daily physical proximity of people, television informs and imparts messages and images to every viewer equally. One does not have to be literate, knowledgeable, or educated to watch television. Children and youth are often equally informed and knowledgeable as adults and sometimes more so. Family members' desire to watch television initiates a breakdown in the sex-role differentiation of work toward sharing certain responsibilities in order that everyone is able to watch television. Women were observed eating at the same time as the men, so they would be able to watch their favorite program.

Not everyone in the village is happy about this status change. The advancement of one is seen as a loss by another. When a woman asserts her rights within the family the husband views this as a loss of his own position and influence. According to one husband:

- *Since TV has come to our village women are doing less work than before. They only want to watch TV. So we men have to do more work. Many times I help my wife clean the house.*
- (Field notes 16 June, 1996): Tonight while walking through the village I noticed someone at the water pump. I approached the figure and realized that it was Shankar. He was filling a bucket with water (this is traditionally a woman's job). He was very uneasy as I approached and asked him what he was doing. He tried to ignore me but could not. He acknowledged to me that his wife was preparing dinner and had run out of water, but did not want to come get water herself since that would delay dinner and her favorite TV program was coming on. He also said that his two children were very lazy and only watched TV. *They never listen to me anymore, times are really changing. I like TV very much, but it is changing many things in the village.* He ended the conversation abruptly and walked away.

6. *Television helps promote a greater receptiveness to new values and norms and an openness to change.*

Many value that television exposes them to foreign cultures and ways of living. Villagers in both Raj Puri and Danawli view television as providing alternative ways of organizing themselves and their relationships.

- *Because of TV I know many things about how people live in Mumbai and other places. I know a lot about rich people now and about people from many places.*

According to a villager who prided himself on being a modern man and whose clothes reflected the fashions on television:

- *When I was young I only knew Danawli and this region. I seldom went to Panchgani and almost never went to Wai. But now every day I learn about how people all over India and many other places live. People talk very differently from us and live very differently from us. We learn about politics in other countries and about life. We still do not understand many of the things we see on the TV, but we know much more than we used to. Today, these young children know much more about the world than I knew at their age. Many are picking up English and Hindi by just watching TV.*

Many villagers view television as an agent of change which encourages alternative lifestyles. One Sunday morning I noticed an older man sitting outside a house packed with people watching the very popular weekly serial *Chandrakanta*. As we began to talk the frustration in his voice was evident. After several minutes he said:

- *There is no doubt about it. You can ask anyone. TV is the one thing that has most changed the way people live. You see how people watch TV. They are all so into the TV that nothing else matters. The house could be burning and no one would realize it. TV is very powerful. Our young people see things on the TV that we never saw, and this has changed the way they behave. They want everything they see. They are not satisfied any more with working in the fields and providing for the family.*

According to another man in his late fifties:

• *I am old now and probably will not live much longer. I have seen many things in my life, but this TV is the most significant thing that has happened to our village ever. Our whole day is now organized around the TV. At first I did not want my son to get one, but now even I watch many hours of TV. Even though I am old I am learning every day about many things. I hope that one day my son can have some of the things that we see on TV. We bought a fan last year for when it is very hot. All the people in the city have fans so we bought one too. (how do you know all the people in the city have fans?) Oh! I see it on TV. We learn many things from TV.*

Television programs, which most often portray urban rather than rural ways of living that glamorize consumerism and paint a picture of social mobility and achievement, have influenced many villagers, especially the young, into rejecting rural and agricultural life for alternative ways of living. Therefore, while television supports change, in doing so it has devalued traditional rural life in the eyes of many villagers. Few young people today hope to do what their fathers and grandfathers did for a living.

The Political Sphere

1. *Television influences a change in the political landscape of the village.*

Television is so popular among villagers that its ownership or non-ownership is a crucial factor in determining one's social standing and influence. Television ownership is not limited to the higher status members of the community any longer. Though the ownership of land is still an important variable in determining one's standing and influence, the ownership of a television and more importantly access to satellite television has also become a determining factor.

The village élite no longer has sole control of information, which is no longer filtered through them to the poorest of the poor. Some poor people have access to the same information that higher status members of the village do, and this has created friction. Though it is still too early to understand the full impact of television on the changing political relationships within the village, there is evidence to suggest that the power of the traditional élite is beginning to be threatened. Villagers who had little influence within the community five years ago are beginning to assert themselves. According to one man in his early thirties:

- *My family did not have much influence in the village. My father did not have much respect, but I do. Last time I almost beat the Sarpanch in the elections. Maybe next time I will win the elections, and that will be the first time that one of us Kasurdes holds such high office in the village. Times are changing. It does not matter as much any more that you belong to the older powerful families in the village.... (Why?) Because they are not the only ones who know how the system works. We all watch the same programs on the TV, and we all know what our rights are. We are not satisfied anymore to sit back and be treated unfairly. My father bought a TV when I was 22 years old. I have watched TV for many years and know everything about the world that those people know. They cannot bully us anymore.*

2. *Television has created a more disadvantaged information underclass.*

Traditionally, there existed a small section of the village population which had access to information. Today, television has resulted in more people having access to what had been privileged information. At the same time it is the arrival of television that has introduced a new set of relationships and restructured what I will term the *information underclass*. While television appears to benefit some villagers, it has at the same time made the lives of others worse. In the village there exists an information underclass that is today more disadvantaged than before. People who have *no access* to television are no longer able to converse on the same level with those with whom they used to associate. One woman does not speak to her neighbor, who owns a TV, because of an incident at the water pump over a year ago, and another has a friend with a TV but lives so far away that she is afraid to go there at night. While television has made a significant contribution to breaking down the informational barriers between the higher and lower status members of the community, it has also damaged the standing of a small segment of the lower class. The group which has no access to television is now much smaller and therefore less powerful than before. Members of the group rely solely on face-to-face communication. According to two villagers who belong to this information underclass:

- *You know these people* (referring to neighbors), *we used to be close friends. Somehow they managed to become friends with the up-Sarpanch and now go to his house to watch TV every Sunday. We don't go because we are not welcome there. All they talk about now is what they see on TV, and we are not very good friends now. I think they learn a lot from TV, and I wish we could go and watch. Also they meet many people at the up-Sarpanch's house and make good connections. It's all because of TV that they have improved their lives. They get more jobs now because of all the people they talk to.*
- *TV is the devil. Why are you interested in TV? It has only caused us pain and is very bad for us. We never get to see the TV. We are now like outcastes in our own village. Many people get to watch TV, and they are all good friends. They learn a lot from TV, see new places and all that. But we are nothing now. Only very few of us cannot watch TV. We are not welcome to those people's houses. My son once went to watch with his friends. He was thrown out. So now I never let him go to see TV. He begs me but I won't let him. All his friends are learning much more than he is, and I don't know what to do. We are too poor to buy our own TV.*

3. *Television initially influences a change in perception regarding caste relations if not actual practice.*

Upon entering the field it became clear that villagers' words and behavior did not always match; political correctness was common. For example, people seemed to be aware of the 'appropriate' number of children a family should have regardless of the number they actually had. And it also became clear that these politically correct responses were a result of television viewing. When I questioned people about caste relations within the village I was assured that relations were good and that times had changed. Villagers explained that relations over the past fifteen years had improved markedly. Without participant observation I would have left the village with an impression of the village as a peaceful place without problems related to caste relations. But if villagers of different castes got along well why were they segregated? Why were there no inter-caste marriages in the study villages? Why did I not observe a Mahar and a Maratha engaging in friendly conversation or visiting each other's homes? Why were Mahars not allowed to draw water from the main wells in the village?

While television was influencing a status change in relation to age, gender, economic and class relations, it was influencing people's perceptions of each other in relation to caste and not necessarily their actions. According to one Mahar woman, *TV has taught us that we should live together equally.* While a Maratha said:

- *There used to be a different feeling toward the Buddhists in the village. This was many years ago. They were not treated very well. But now what we have learned from TV is that we are all Indians. And people like Mahatma Gandhi have told us to live together without putting any one down. The Buddhists live in that wadi because that is where they have always lived. If they want they can come and live here if they had land to build their house. But we are all living here in Raj Puri, and we all have the same rights and responsibilities.*

Seldom did villagers outwardly acknowledge any problems with caste relations. They had learned the accepted way of living from television and did not want to appear backward. However, reality rarely corresponded with the information presented by villagers. There had never been an inter-caste marriage in either village. The Mahar representative on the village Panchayat in Raj Puri seldom participated due to pressure from the Marathas. No one could ever give an instance of a Maratha or Mahar visiting each other's homes. The only conversations I ever witnessed between Mahars and Marathas were business related and were never friendly. Mahars never used the main village wells and were never seen walking through the village center. Marathas continued to defecate on the road leading to the Mahar wadi for the duration of the research yet no one ever admitted to doing so. Television has influenced what people say about caste relations but not yet how they behave. This may change over time, as television remains an important influence.

4. *Television threatens the position of traditional leaders.*

Traditional leaders are being challenged from younger, more informed members of the community. The incumbents actively search for new ways of maintaining their power and seek out advantages over the younger challengers. Villagers are discovering new ways of dealing with their problems and this threatens the legitimacy of the village leaders. An example that illustrates this point concerns disputes within the village. Traditionally, differences among villagers were settled within the confines of the village with the help of leaders like the village police Patil. Today more and more villagers are taking their cases to be settled by the courts. According to one man:

- *We have learned that our leaders are corrupt. Even the national leaders are very corrupt. On TV they show us about how corrupt parliament members are and even Prime Minister Rao. If the leaders of this country are so corrupt how can we expect our local leaders to be just? TV has taught us about our rights, and we have learned about the court system. Now when someone has a problem they do not automatically go to Shahir. Sampat went to court about his land, and he won the case. Now people are not afraid to go to court. TV is good in that way. It has taught us many things. Our elected officials are hopeless. Every one is corrupt.*

On the morning of Gudhi Padva, the first day of the Hindu calendar, the men of the village come together to discuss the affairs of the community. The most vocal participants in this gathering were the younger men.

- *You say you are our leaders but none of you really know what you are doing.*
- *Why has nothing been done about the water scheme? Why are the pipes still sitting in the center of the village? If you can't get the job done we should elect someone else who can.*

This questioning of authority by the younger generation was unheard of twenty years ago. According to one of the elders in attendance at that meeting:

- *When I was young I would have never spoken like that to my elders. Dilip has no shame. He thinks he knows everything now that he bought a TV and visits Mumbai. He thinks he knows better than us. He shows us no respect. The Sarpanch is the man in charge of these meetings but you tell me who did more talking.*

Conclusion

An attempt has been made in this chapter to illustrate the role of television in the process of social change at the village level. Many remote villages in India have leaped from a society governed by oral traditions to one that is based primarily on electronic media conveyed through the medium of television. Most have arrived at this stage very suddenly and are still attempting to adjust to this new way of life.

Television has in the past seven to ten years transformed village culture in many ways. It has emerged as a new focal center of village life adding to traditional institutions such as the family, religion, agriculture, and traditional leadership. Its influence reaches into almost every corner of the community. Yet, though the data suggest that television is influencing numerous aspects of village life, the magnitude and long lasting structural influence of television remains to be determined.

Notes

1. The South Indian film industry is the exception. Hindi is not as commonly spoken or accepted in the South as it is elsewhere in India. Films in Telugu, Malayalam, Kannada, and Tamil are much more popular in the South than Hindi films.
2. Quoted by Brand Equity. *The Economic Times*, 5 January 1994.

9

In Conclusion

While sitting under the shade of a large mango tree, I noticed a shadow out of the corner of my eye. I looked up from my laptop computer to find a young village boy gazing intently at my computer screen. I invited him to sit down beside me and began to show him the different things the computer could do. After several minutes he said that he had seen a laptop just like mine in one of the Rambo movies he had watched on television. Time and again the villagers of Danawli and Raj Puri displayed knowledge of things not found in villages and showed greater levels of understanding of world events and the happenings around them.

The central question explored in this research involved the role of television in rural India. To do this it was necessary to understand the social processes of village life and locate television within that context. The question throughout focused on the relationship between television and social change within the village community. Through numerous in-depth interviews and months of participant observation the elements of this relationship began to emerge.

In the preceding chapters I have outlined the importance and rationale for the specific focus and methods of this study, surveyed the literature in this field, and presented the contending approaches and theories to the study of television. I have delineated the parameters of the methods used and the reasons for their use, examined television from the national perspective, and established the context, both physical and socio-economic, for an analysis of the role of television in rural life. In this book I have presented the salient features of village life which are most influenced by television.

Television Influence as a Process

According to Kottak (1990: 139) 'TV impact should be interpreted as a phenomenon that occurs in stages.' He has developed four stages which societies go through. In the initial stage television is a novelty, and its strangeness captures the wholehearted attention of the audience. It is in this stage that the medium rather than the message is the mesmerizer. When people become more comfortable with television and accustomed to its everpresent nature they enter stage two. Viewers become more selective about what they watch, and there begins a process of 'rejection, interpretation and reworking of TV messages' (ibid.). This second stage according to Kottak can last anywhere from ten to fifteen years.

During the third stage television has reached most homes in a locale, and the fourth stage is represented by 'the continuing and lifelong impact of tele-viewing on full-grown natives who have spent their entire lives in a national culture pervaded by television and the mass phenomena it spawns. During this fourth phase the more profound and long-term sociocultural effects of television become discernible' (Kottak, 1990: 143). Meyrowitz (1986) has related this process to television in the United States. He (ibid., 1992: 218) says that

in 1950, only 9 per cent of U.S. homes owned television sets. Little more than twenty-five years later, only 2 per cent of households were without one. In a remarkably short time, television has taken a central place in our living rooms and in our cultural and political lives. On average, a U.S. household can receive thirty channels; only 7 per cent of homes receive six or fewer stations. Some 95 per cent of homes own a color TV, 63 per cent own two or more sets, and 64 per cent own a video cassette recorder.

Television is the most popular of the popular media. Indeed... there are fewer things that Americans do more than they watch television. On average, each household has a TV on almost fifty hours a week. Forty per cent of households eat dinner with the set on. Individually, Americans watch an average of thirty hours a week. We begin peering at TV through the bars of cribs and continue looking at it through the cataracts of old age.

The study villages of Danawli and Raj Puri were both in stage two. Television arrived in these villages approximately ten years ago, and its initial novelty has worn off. People are beginning to selectively choose what programs to watch. They organize their work in order to be free to watch their favorite shows in the afternoons and evenings. It is only a matter of time before television sets begin to saturate these villages catapulting them into stages three and four. Most young children today have no knowledge of what life was like before television. I once asked an 8-year-old boy in Raj Puri who received satellite television in his home, 'Would you agree to never watch TV again if I gave you anything you wanted in return?' I got the idea for this question from a Bill Moyer special on PBS in the United States. The response from this village boy was exactly the same as the response Bill Moyer got from an American kid living in a little town in the Midwest. The village boy said:

- *You mean that I should give up TV, and you will give me anything I want. (Yes). I can never watch it again as long as I live? (Yes). Then I must say no. I would love to have nice toys and nice clothes and for my mother not to work so hard, but without TV what would I do.*

The young boy was unable to comprehend life without the presence of television. Children spend so much time in front of the little black box that for them life without it is not possible.

It is these early stages of television exposure that have the most influence on social change both individually and collectively. Contrary to popular belief that television is an isolating and alienating device, the initial stages of exposure promote social contact. Television brings people from different households, classes, ages, and genders into close proximity on a regular basis for an extended period of time. These people are in a relaxed atmosphere with the sole purpose of enjoying the television programs and each other's company. This spirit of fellowship is conducive to fostering new-found relationships which would not have occurred were it not for television. Kottak (1990: 146) found that as Brazilian villages moved into stages three and four television appeared to be 'strengthening the nuclear family and the household at the expense of general community life.' This is yet to be seen in the villages of Maharashtra where television ownership is not as widespread. People in these villages are still drawn together every evening to watch TV.

Structural vs. Psychological

The study of Danawli and Raj Puri was useful in documenting and illustrating the role of television in the process of social change in rural India today. Change occurred on both a structural level and a psychological level. The former centers on variables such as marriage, religion, and relationships between people of different ages, castes, and genders, while the latter focuses on changes in attitudes, fears, values, images, opinions, and needs. These are no doubt important variables in the process of social change. To limit the analysis of the impact of television to psychological variables, when attempting to understand social change would fall short of what is often the most significant aspect of change. An important element in any discussion of development communication is the social structure and the analysis of structural conflict. Too often such 'discussions view the people as an amorphous mass; where distinction is evident between social-strata, is it usually between the city-based élite and the rural masses. This leads to the assumption of a harmony of interests among the rural population' (Hartmann et al., 1989: 256). These village studies show that there is little warrant for such an assumption. Village society is highly differentiated by

class, caste, access to resources, and other divisions. It is characterized by competition between various groups for scarce resources.

Television influences certain psychological variables. For
instance, though caste prejudice still exists, and lower castes are
still often treated unfairly by higher castes, television has, in part,
contributed to a change in the way people voice their prejudice.
Television has made it clear to people that caste prejudice is unac-
ceptable, and therefore few villagers acknowledged their views
openly to me. Another example involves villager's basic needs
which have changed dramatically in the past ten years as a result
of television exposure. The accumulation of modern material
things is at the forefront of people's minds.

Most of the obstacles to change are structural rather than cultural; changing attitudes and ideas are important but insufficient
on their own to make any real progress in toppling the prevailing
structures of inequality within village culture. The arrival of television into the village has influenced certain structural barriers.
For instance, access to information has been an important avenue
by which the village élite has traditionally maintained its position
in the community. By monopolizing the information, whether it
is political, economic, or social, the élite has been able to manipulate the masses. With the arrival of television, this long-standing
strategy has been removed. Now people from all sections of the
community, without regard to class, caste, gender, age, or educational status, have equal access to the same information. The
exception to this is the emergence of a severely disadvantaged
information underclass which now relies on the élite and also
their peers for information. The élite has been forced to scramble
to find new ways of maintaining their position and influence. A
related structural influence of television has been its role in the
changing judicial system. Through television villagers are gaining
a deeper appreciation of their rights and are less often relying on
the traditional village Patil to solve their disputes. Villagers are
much less trusting of their own community leaders after seeing
negative stories about them on television.

Another area in which the traditional structural barriers to
change are being broken down relates to social contact. Television has, within the span of only a few years, altered the way people have related to each other for centuries. People who would

normally not socialize with each other are now more than ever seeing each other regularly for long periods of time. People from different economic classes, genders, and age groups are spending more time together as a result of television.

Active vs. Passive

There is a tendency in communication theory and practice to regard the television audience as passive beings who are molded and manipulated by media messages. This attitude as it relates to communication and social change has a number of unfortunate consequences. For one thing, the SMCRE formula—source, message, channel, receiver, and effect—becomes the standard for any analysis of the communication process. Within this formulation the audience is analyzed without regard to the social context. The result of this is that 'the advertising campaign becomes the dominant model for development communication. There is talk of "injecting" the development "message" into communications directed at the "target audience," as though development were a commodity to be sold like soap powder... The underlying imagery is parallel to that of the physiological response to a stimulant or electric shock; the receiver is supposed to be prodded into action' (Hartmann et al., 1989: 257).

This mechanical model has resulted in research that focuses on the audience's response to deliberate 'campaign type' development messages. Most of the SITE research in India tended to follow this approach—focusing on short-term influence on attitudes and opinions after viewing certain development programs. As has already been mentioned the 'general run of mass communications—the music, drama, and news that most people with access to media attend to most of the time—has received little research attention, since this is not thought to have much relevance to development' (ibid.). Therefore, the present research study did not limit itself to the developmental fare on television but instead looked at the medium from a more holistic perspective. The vast majority of television programs aired and watched tended to fall into the entertainment category, and therefore special attention was given to it. Instead of attempting to determine the effects of the medium on specific attitudes and opinions I studied the role of television in the lives of villagers. Through this process attitudes and opinions became manifest, as did an understanding of the way in which television's presence was influencing relationships and the structure of the daily lives of villagers within the household and beyond.

In the study villages the television audience were active rather than passive participants in the communication process. Kottak (1990: 192) concludes that rather than being passive receptacles into which television messages are filled, viewers are:

> human beings who make discriminations about and use television in ways that make sense to them. They watch to validate beliefs, develop fantasies, and find answers to questions that the local setting discourages or condemns. People use TV to relieve frustrations, build or enhance images of self, chart social courses, and formulate daring life plans.

It is not sufficient anymore to limit the analysis of television to the 'informational' content. Though one of the most influential writers on development communication three decades ago, Schramm's (1964) arguments can no longer be justified. According to him (ibid., 1964: 231):

> It is hard to argue that these [entertainment programs] have much to do with economic development. On the other hand, in a given country it may be highly desirable, at a given point in development, to offer some of this relaxing program fare, and it may be that the bonus of news, public affairs, and instruction mixed with entertainment programs might be enough to justify expenditure for television in development terms as well as entertainment terms.

Though television began in India as a limited developmental tool with programming orchestrated by the government, the medium today has blossomed into one of the largest competitive entertainment industries in the world. Villagers are not simple peasants passively waiting to be manipulated and prodded into action by their government, but are active members of a vibrant society using the media for their own advantage.

Level of Influence

The evidence presented in the preceding chapters suggests that television is influencing the economic, social, and political land-scape, and relationships of village life. Whether it is the messages portrayed or the mere presence of television, villager's relation-ships, economic decisions, political awareness, participation, and worldview are being influenced by television. Yet, the words of a landless villager in Raj Puri still make me pause and think:

- *TV has not been here very long. We have lived like this for centuries. Our fathers and their fathers worked the fields and lived very much as we live today. We have had our traditions and way of life for as far back as any one can remember. All of a sudden TV came into our lives and now people think that everything is changing. Sure, TV is great. I personally watch every night. I love the movies and the sports. Many things might seem to be changing but is it really?*

Television is still very new in these mountain villages of western Maharashtra. Ten years is a blink of an eye when compared to the ancient history of this region. And though this new medium of mass communications has influenced village life at various lev-els, it remains to be determined whether the age-old traditions of rural culture will be influenced at all. There are certain areas of village life that will require further research as television contin-ues to be incorporated further into village culture. For instance, 'love marriage' is now part of the vocabulary of villagers, but arranged marriage is one of the fundamental traditions of these people. Whether this cultural tradition will change is still to be seen. Caste relations is another area that needs to be examined. It was determined that political correctness exists when discussing caste but that behavior had not changed much. People spoke of inter-caste marriage, but no instances were found to exist in the study villages.

There will always be a need for further research as television continues to saturate village communities. Of all the mass media, television has had the most influence on village life. Due to its unique character this medium of mass communication has a particularly effective cultural effect. Yet, further research is needed over time to determine the *depth* and *lasting influence* of television.

A Final Word

As I sit in the comfort of my home on this brisk autumn morning to pen the last few words of a manuscript that has taken me months to write I am moved with nostalgia to find myself at this point. My only thoughts are of my childhood. I moved to Panchgani, India, with my family as a young boy of only three years and spent the next thirteen developing a deep love and appreciation for the people with whom I grew up. And it was only when I returned after living and working in North America that I could more fully appreciate the life I had known.

The mountain villages of Western Maharashtra, while extremely beautiful, are not the easiest places in the world to live. Life is extremely difficult and in many ways it is only the fit who survive. The inequalities and harshness of village life turn many villagers into skeptical people, yet it is these same people who are some of the most hospitable, considerate, hardworking, ingenious, insightful and spiritual human beings I have ever known.

I went to India to research the role of television in village life. I gained much more than that. I gained an appreciation of the struggles and complexities of rural life. I have seen, even if just for a moment, what a villager thinks about himself and his world. And I have had an opportunity to learn from these villagers more than I ever thought possible. But most importantly I have gained the friendship of people who have forever made a lasting impression on my life. I hope that other researchers see the importance of this subject matter and endeavor to contribute to this field of knowledge. The role of television in rural life is no doubt an important element in the process of social change.

I feel honored and blessed to have lived and learned in both worlds.

Appendix A
Maharashtra

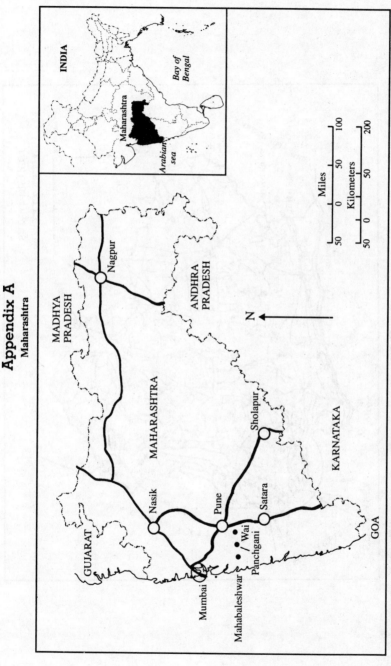

Source: Bartholomew World Travel Map – India: Subcontinent.

Appendix B
Satara District

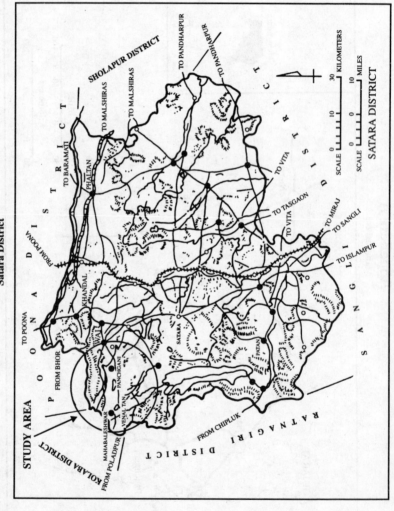

Source: Census of India 1996, District Census Handbook, Maharashtra Census Office, Bombay.

Appendix C
The Study Villages and their Immediate Region.

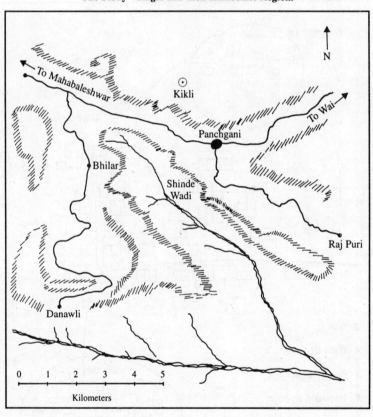

Appendix D
Village Settlement

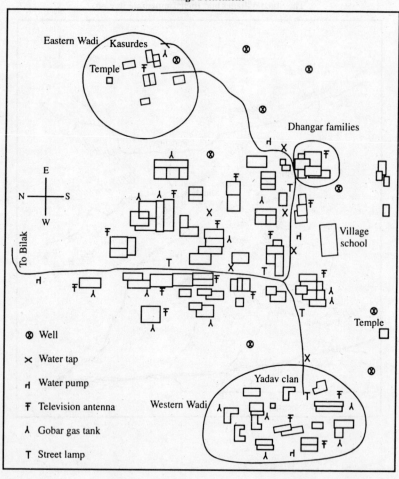

Eastern Wadi Kasurdes

Temple

Dhangar families

E
N — S
W

To Bilak

Village school

Temple

⊗ Well

✕ Water tap

⊣ Water pump

☤ Television antenna

⋏ Gobar gas tank

T Street lamp

Yadav clan

Western Wadi

References

Agrawal, Binod C. 1978. *Television Comes to the Village: An Evaluation of SITE*. Bangalore: Indian Space Research Organization.

———. 1980. *Women, Television, and Rural Development: An Evaluative Study of SITE in a Rajasthan Village*. Government of India, Space Applications Center: Ahmedabad.

———. 1985. *Communication—Anthropological Methods for Communication Research, Experiences and Encounter During SITE*. New Delhi: Concept Publishing Company.

———. 1986. *Communication Research for Development*. New Delhi: Concept Publishing Company.

Allen, Robert C. 1987. 'Reader Oriented Criticism and TV,' in Robert C. Allen (ed.) *Channels of Discourse*. Chapel Hill: University of North Carolina Press.

Ang, Ien. 1983. 'Feminist Desire and Female Pleasure.' *Camera Obscura* 16: 179–91.

———. 1985. *Watching 'Dallas': Soap Operas and the Melodramatic Imagination*. London: Methuen.

———. 1990. 'Melodramatic Identifications: Television Fiction and Women's Fantasy,' in Mary E. Brown (ed.) *Television and Women's Culture*, 74–88. Newbury Park: Sage Publications.

Attwood, Donald W. 1979. 'Why Some of the Poor Get Richer: Economic Change and Mobility in Rural Western India.' *Current Anthropology* 20: 495–508, 657–58.

———. 1984. 'Capital and the Transformation of Agrarian Class Systems: Sugar Production in Western and Northern India,' in M. Desai, S.H. Rudolph, and A. Rudra (eds.) *Agrarian Power and Agricultural Productivity in South Asia*. Berkeley: University of California Press.

Attwood, D.W., M. Israel and **N.K. Wagle.** 1988a. *City, Countryside and Society in Maharashtra*. Toronto: University of Toronto, Center for South Asian Studies.

Attwood, D.W., M. Israel and **N.K. Wagle.** 1988b. Risk, Mobility, and Cooperation in Maharashtrian Villages, in D.W. Attwood, M. Israel, and N.K. Wagle (eds.) *City, Countryside and Society in Maharashtra.* Toronto: University of Toronto, Center for South Asian Studies.

————. 1988c. 'Poverty, Inequality and Economic Growth in Rural India,' in D.W. Attwood, T.C. Bruneau, and J.G. Galaty (eds.) *Power and Poverty.* Boulder: Westview Press.

————. 1992. *Raising Cane: The Political Economy of Sugar in Western India.* Boulder: Westview Press.

Bandyopadhyay, S. and **D. Von Eschen.** 1982. The Conditions of Rural Progress in India: A Case Study of Bengal. *Report to the Canadian International Development Agency, Ottawa.*

————. 1988. 'Villager Failure to Cooperate: Does it Matter? What Accounts for it? Some Evidence from West Bengal, India,' in D.W. Attwood, and B.S. Baviskar (eds.) *Who Shares? Cooperatives and Rural Development.* Delhi: Oxford University Press.

Barrios, L. 1988. 'Television, Telenovelas, and Family Life in Venezuela,' in James Lull (ed.) *World Families Watch Television.* Newbury Park: Sage Publications.

Bauer, R.A and **A. Bauer.** 1960. 'America: Mass Society and Mass Media,' *Journal of Social Issues,* 10(3): 3–66.

Baviskar, B.S. 1980. *The Politics of Development: Sugar Co-operatives in Rural Maharashtra.* Delhi: Oxford University Press.

Beals, A.R. 1967. *Culture in Process.* New York: Holt, Rinehart, and Winston.

————. 1980. *Gopalpur: A South Indian Village (Fieldwork Edition).* New York: Holt, Rinehart, and Winston.

Beteille, André. 1996. *Caste, Class, and Power: Changing Patterns of Stratification in a Tanjore Village.* Berkeley: University of California Press.

Blumer, Herbert. 1933. *The Movies and Conduct.* New York: Macmillan.

Bordenave, Diaz. 1976. 'Communication and Agricultural Innovations in Latin America: The Need for New Models.' *Communication Research,* 3: 2.

Bogdan R.C. and **S.J. Taylor.** 1975. *Introduction to Qualitative Research Methods: A Phenomenological Approach to Social Sciences.* New York: John Wiley.

Canclini, Nestor. 1993. *Transforming Modernity: Popular Culture in Mexico.* Translated by Lidia Lozano. Austin: University of Texas Press.

Caldwell, Reddy, and **Caldwell.** 1988. *The Causes of Demographic Change: Experimental Research in South India.* Madison, Wisconsin: University of Wisconsin Press.

Carey, J. and **A. Kreiling.** 1974. 'Toward a Cultural Studies Approach for the Sociology of Popular Culture.' *Communication Research* 5(3): 240–63.

Carter, Anthony. 1974. *Elite Politics in Rural India: Political Stratification and Political Alliances in Western Maharashtra.* Cambridge: Cambridge University Press.

———. 1988. 'Land Transactions and Household Dynamics in Maharashtra,' in D.W. Attwood, M. Israel, and N.K. Wagle (eds.) *City, Countryside and Society in Maharashtra.* Toronto: University of Toronto, Center for South Asian Studies.

Chatterjee, P.C. 1987. *Broadcasting in India.* New Delhi: Sage Publications.

Chaudhuri, M.M. 1986. 'India: From SITE to INSAT.' *Media in Education and Development*, 19: 134–40.

Coldevin, G. and **C. Amundsen.** 1985. 'The Use of Communication Satellites for Distance Education: A World Perspective.' *Canadian Journal of Educational Communication*, 14: 4–5.

Collins, Richard. 1986. 'Seeing is Believing: The Ideology of Naturalism,' in John Corner (ed.) *Documentary and the Mass Media*, 125–38.

Comstock, G. and **Thomas Bowers.** 1978. *Television and Human Behavior.* New York: Columbia University Press.

Dandekar, Hemalata. 1980. 'Gobar-Gas Plants: How Appropriate Are They?' *Economic and Political Weekly* 15(20): 887–93.

———. 1983. 'The Impact of Bombay's Textile Industry on Work of Women From Sugao Village.' *Third World Planning Review* 5(4): 371–82.

———. 1986a. 'Rural Housing and Infrastructure: The Neglected Frontier in Developing Countries.' *Central Papers on Architecture* (Winter): 15–29.

———. 1986b. *Men to Bombay Women at Home: Urban Influence on Sugao Village, Deccan Maharashtra, India.* Ann Arbor: Center for South and Southeast Asian Studies, University of Michigan.

Dandekar, V.M. and **M.B. Jagtap.** 1959. *Maharashtrachi Grameen Samajrachana* [Social structure in Maharashtrian villages]. Pune: Gokhale Institute of Politics and Economics.

Dale, Edgar. 1970. *Children's Attendance at Motion Pictures.* New York: Arno (originally published in 1935).

DeFleur, M.L. 1970. *Theories of Mass Communication.* New York: David McKay.

DeFleur, M.L. and **Sandra Ball-Rokeach** 1976. 'A Dependency Model of Mass Media Effects.' *Communication Research*, 3: 3–21.

———. 1982. *Theories of Mass Communication*, 4th ed. New York: Longman.

Desai, Sudha V. 1980. *Social Life in Maharashtra under the Peshwas.* Bombay: Popular Prakashan

Dickey, Sara. 1993. *Cinema and the Urban Poor in South India.* Cambridge: Cambridge University Press.

Ellen, R.F. 1984. *Ethnographic Research: A Guide to General Conduct.* London: Academic Press.

Eppan, K.E. 1979. 'The Cultural Component of SITE.' *Journal of Communication* 29: 106–13.

Femia, Joseph. 1981. *Gramsci's Political Thought.* Oxford: Oxford University Press.

Fiske, John. 1982. *Introduction to Communication Studies.* London: Methuen.

———. 1987. 'British Cultural Studies and Television,' in Robert C. Allen (ed.) *Channels of Discourse*, 254–90. Chapel Hill: University of North Carolina.

Fowles, J. 1992. *Why Viewers Watch.* Newbury Park: Sage Publications.

Fuller, C.J. 1996. *Caste Today.* Delhi: Oxford University Press.

Kukazawa, Hiroshi. 1991. *The Medieval Deccan: Peasants, Social Systems and States, Sixteenth to Eighteenth Centuries.* Delhi: Oxford University Press.

Gadgil, D.R. 1948a. *The Industrial Evolution of India in Recent Times (1860–1939).* London: Oxford University Press.

———. 1948b. *Economic Effects of Irrigation: Report of a Survey of the Direct and Indirect Benefits of the Godavari and Pravara Canals.* Pune: Gokhale Institute of Politics and Economics, Publication No. 17.

———. 1955. *Economic Policy and Development.* Pune: Gokhale Institute of Politics and Economics, Publication No. 30.

Geertz, C. 1973. *The Interpretation of Cultures.* New York: Basic Books.

Glaser, Barney. 1978. *Theoretical Sensitivity.* Mill Valley, California: Sociology Press.

Glaser, Barney and **A. Strauss.** 1967. *The Discovery of Grounded Theory: Strategies for Qualitative Research.* Chicago: Aldine.

Grunig, J.E. 1971. 'Communication and Economic Decision-making Processes of Colombian Peasants.' *Economic Development and Cultural Change.* 18: 580–97.

Guba, E.G. and **Y.S. Lincoln** 1982. 'Epistemological and methodological bases of naturalistic inquiry.' *Educational Communication and Technology Journal*, 30: 233–52.

Gupta, A.R. 1984. *Caste Hierarchy and Social Change: A Study of Myth and Reality.* New Delhi: Jyotsna Prakashan.

Gupta, Giri Raj. 1974. *Marriage, Religion and Society: Pattern of Change in an Indian Village.* Bombay: Vikas Publishing House.

Harris, Marvin. 1968. *The Rise of Anthropological Theory.* New York: Crowell.

Hartmann, Paul, B.R. Patil and **Anita Dighe.** 1989. *The Mass Media and Village Life: An Indian Study.* New Delhi: Sage Publications.

Hedebro, Goran. 1982. *Communication and Social Change in Developing Nations: A Critical Review.* Ames: Iowa State University Press.

Hobson, Dorothy. 1981. 'Crossroads,' in Richard Dyer (ed.) *Coronation Street*, 9–26. London: British Film Institute.

Innis, Harold. 1972. *Empire and Communications.* Toronto: University of Toronto Press.

Jagtap, M.B. 1974. *Notes on the Mahars of Gulumb.* In Marathi. Unpublished. Copy at the Gokhale Institute of Politics and Economics, Pune.

Joshi, P.C. 1985. *Communications and Nation-Building: Perspectives and Policy.* New Delhi: Publications Division.

Kamble, N.D. 1979. *Poverty Within Poverty: A Study of the Weaker sections in a Deccan Village.* New Delhi: Sterling Publishers.

Kaplan, Ann. 1987. 'Feminist Criticism and Television,' in Robert C. Allen (ed.) *Channels of Discourse.* Chapel Hill: University of N. Carolina Press.

Karve, Irawati. 1961. *Hindu Society: An Interpretation.* Pune: Deshmukh Prakashan.

——— 1968. *Kinship Organization in India.* Bombay: Asia Publishing House.

Karve, Irawati and **J.S. Ranadive.** 1965. *The Social Dynamics of a Growing Town and its Surrounding Area.* Pune: Deccan College.

Karve, Irawati and **Y.B. Damle.** 1963. *Group Relations in Village Community.* Pune: Deccan College Monograph Series No. 24.

Katz, E., J. Blumler and **M. Gurevitch.** 1974. 'Utilization of Mass Communication by the Individual' in M. Blumer and E. Katz (eds.) *The Uses of Mass Communications.* Beverly Hills: Sage Publications.

Katz, E., M. Gurevitch and **H. Haas.** 1973. 'On the Use of the Mass Media for Important Things.' *American Sociology Review,* 38: 164–81.

Kent, Susan. (1985). 'The Effects of Television Viewing: A Cross-cultural ✓ Perspective.' *Current Anthropology* 26: 121–26.

Klapper, J. 1960. *The Effects of Mass Communication.* New York: Free Press.

Kolenda, Pauline. 1978. *Caste in Contemporary India: Beyond Organic Solidarity.* Prospect Heights: Waveland Press.

———. 1981. *Caste, Cult and Hierarchy: Essays on the Culture of India.* Delhi: Folklore Institute.

Kothari, Rajni. 1970. *Caste in Indian Politics.* Delhi: Orient Longman.

Kottak, Conrad. 1990. *Prime Time Society: An Anthropological Analysis of Television and Culture.* Wadsworth: Belmont.

Khrishnan, Prabha and **Anita Dighe.** 1990. *Affirmation and Denial: Construction of Femininity on Indian Television.* New Delhi: Sage Publications.

Kulkarni, A.R. 1967. 'Village Life in the Deccan in the Seventeenth Century.' *The Indian Economic and Social History Review* 4(1): 38–52.

———. 1973. 'The Marathas,' in H.K. Sharwani and P.M. Joshi (eds.), *History of Medieval Deccan, Vol. 1.* Hyderabad: Andhra Pradesh Government Textbook Press.

Kumar, Dharma. 1965. *Land and Caste in South India.* Cambridge: Cambridge University Press.

Kumar, Ravinder. 1965. 'Rural Life in Western Maharashtra India on the Eve of the British Conquest.' *The Indian Economic and Social History Review* 2: 201–220.

Lakshmanna, Chintamani. 1973. *Caste Dynamics in Village India.* Bombay: Nachiketa Publications.

Lasswell, H. 1948. 'The Structure and Function of Communication in Society,' in W. Schraam (ed.) *Mass Communication.* Illinois: University of Illinois Press.

Le Bon, Gustave. 1960. *The Crowd: A Study of the Popular Mind.* New York: Viking (first published in Paris 1895).

Lekshmi, T., 1987. A Study of TV Commercials Reaching Trivandrum Viewers Through Delhi Doordarshan. University of Kerala Masters Thesis.

Lele, Jayant. 1981. *Elite Pluralism and Class Rule: Political Development in Maharashtra, India.* Toronto: University of Toronto Press.

Lerner, Daniel. 1958. *The Passing of Traditional Society.* New York: Free Press.

Liebes, T. and **E. Katz.** 1989. 'On the Critical Abilities of Television Viewers,' in E. Seiter, et al. (eds.) *Remote Control: Television Audiences and Cultural Power,* 204–222. London: Routledge.

Lindlof. 1995. *Qualitative Communication Research Methods.* California: Sage Publications.

Lipton, Michael. 1977. *Why Poor People Stay Poor: A Study of Urban Bias in World Development.* London: Temple Smith.

Lofland, John. 1971. *Analyzing Social Settings: A Guide to Qualitative Observation and Analysis.* Belmont: Wadsworth Publications.

Lull, James. 1988. *World Families Watch Television.* Newbury Park: Sage Publications.

———. 1990. *Inside Family Viewing: Ethnographic Research on Television Viewing.* London: Routledge.

Madan, G.R. 1990. *India's Developing Villages.* Bombay: Allied Publishers.

Maharashtra Government. 1986, 1996. *Satara District Census Handbook.* Bombay: Maharashtra Census Office.

Malik, Saroj. 1989.'Television and Rural India.' *Media, Culture and Society* 11: 459–84.

Malinowski, Bronislaw. 1922. *Argonauts of the Western Pacific.* London: Routledge.

Mann, Harold H. 1917. *Land and Labor in a Deccan Village.* London and Bombay: Oxford University Press.

Mann, Harold H. and **N.V. Kanitkar.** 1921. *Land and Labour in a Deccan Village: Study No. 2.* London and Bombay: Oxford University Press.

Mandelbaum, David. 1970. *Society in India. Vols. 1 and 2.* Berkeley: University of California Press.

Marriott, McKim. 1955. *Village India: Studies in the Little Community.* Chicago: University of Chicago Press.

Mathur, K.S. 1964. *Caste and Ritual in a Malwa Village.* Bombay: Asia Publishing House.

McRobbie, Angela. 1984. 'Dance and Social Fantasy,' in A. McRobbie and M. Nava (eds.) *Gender and Generation,* 130–61. London: Macmillan.

McQuail, Dennis. 1972. *Sociology of Mass Communication.* Harmondsworth: Penguin Books.

————. 1983. *Mass Communication Theory.* London: Sage Publications.

————. 1984. *Theories of Mass Communication.* London: Sage Publications.

McQuail, D., J.G. Blumler and **J. Brown.** 1972. The Television Audience: A Revised Perspective in Denis McQuail (eds.) *Sociology of Mass Communication.* Harmondsworth: Penguin.

McQuail, Dennis and **S. Windahl.** 1981. *Communication Models.* London: Longman Press.

Meyrowitz, Joshua. 1986. *No Sense of Place: The Impact of Electronic Media on Social Behavior.* Oxford University Press: New York.

Miller, Cynthia. 1995. *Media, Audience, and Ethnography: Situating Mass Communication in Everyday Life.* Unpublished Manuscript: McGill University.

Mirchandani, G.C. 1976. *India Backgrounders—Television in India.* New Delhi: Vikrant Press.

Misra, B.B. 1983. *District Administration and Rural Development in India: Policy Objective and Administrative Change in Historical Perspective.* Delhi: Oxford University Press.

Mitra, Ananda. 1993. *Television and Popular Culture in India: A Study of the Mahabharat.* New Delhi: Sage Publications.

Moore, Erin. 1985. *Conflict and Compromise: Justice in an Indian Village.* Berkeley: University of California, Center for South and Southeast Asia Studies.

Moores, S. 1993. *Interpreting Audiences.* London: Sage Publications.

Morley, David. 1980a. 'Texts, Readers, Subjects,' in Stuart Hall (ed.) *Culture, Media, Language.* London: Hutchinson.

————. 1980b. *The 'Nationwide' Audience: Structure and Decoding.* London: British Film Institute.

————. 1986. *Family Television.* London: Comedia.

————. 1990. *Television Audiences and Cultural Studies.* London: Routledge.

Ninan, Sevanti. 1995. *Through the Magic Window: Television and Change in India.* New Delhi: Penguin Books.

Noelle-Neumann. 1973. 'Return to the Concept of Powerful Mass Media.' *Studies of Broadcasting,* 9: 66–112.

O'Hanlon, Rosalind. 1985. *Caste, Conflict and Ideology: Mahatma Jotirao Phule and Low Caste Protest in Nineteenth Century Western India.* Cambridge: Cambridge University Press.

Olson, Mancur. 1965. *The Logic of Collective Action: Public Goods and the Theory of Groups.* Cambridge: Harvard University Press.

Omvedt, Gail. 1976. *Cultural Revolt in a Colonial Society: The Non-Brahman Movement in Western India.* Bombay: Scientific Socialist Education Trust.

———. (ed.). 1982. *Land, Caste, and Politics in Indian States.* Delhi: Authors Guild Publications.

Orenstein, Henry. 1965. *Goan: Conflict and Cohesion in an Indian Village.* Princeton: Princeton University Press. .

Peterson, Ruth and **L. Thurstone.** 1933. *Motion Pictures and Social Attitudes of Children.* New York: Macmillan.

Poffenberger, Thomas. 1976. *The Socialization of Family Size Values: Youth and Family Planning in an Indian Village.* Ann Arbor: University of Michigan, Center for South and Southeast Asian Studies.

Poffenberger, Thomas, and **Shirley B. Poffenberger.** 1971. *Reaction to World News Events and the Influence of Mass Media in an Indian Village.* Ann Arbor: University of Michigan, Center for South and Southeast Asian Studies.

Pokharapurkar, Raja. 1993. *Rural Development Through Community Television.* New Delhi: Concept Publishing Company.

Pool, Ithiel de Sola. 1963. 'The Mass Media and Politics in the Modernization Process,' in Lucian W. Pye (ed.), *Communications and Political Development.* Princeton, N.J.: Princeton University Press.

Popkin, Samuel L. 1979. *The Rational Peasant: The Political Economy of Rural Society in Vietnam.* Berkeley: University of California Press.

Punekar, S.D. and **Alka R. Golwalkar.** 1973. *Rural Change in Maharashtra: An Analytical Study of Change in Six Villages in Konkan.* Bombay: Popular Prakashan.

Rao, B. 1992. *Television for Rural Development.* New Delhi: Concept Publishing Company.

Rao, K. Ranga. 1980. *Village Politics: A Longitudinal Study.* Bombay: Popular Prakashan.

Rao, Y.V. Lakshmana. 1966. *Communication and Development: A Study of Two Indian Villages.* Minneapolis: University of Minnesota Press.

Radway, Janice. 1984. *Reading the Romance: Women, Patriarchy, and Popular Literature.* Chapel Hill: University of North Carolina Press.

———. 'Where is the Field: Ethnography, Audiences and the Redesign of Research Practice.' Paper presented at the University of Pennsylvania.

———. 1988. 'Reception Study: Ethnography and the Problems of Dispersed Audiences and Nomadic Subjects.' *Cultural Studies* 2(3): 359–76.

Reddi, Usha. 1989. 'Media and Culture in Indian Society: Conflict or Co-operation?' *Media, Culture and Society,* 11: 395–413.

Rogers, Everet. 1962. *Diffusion of Innovations*. New York: Free Press. ✓
———. 1969. *Modernization Among Peasants: The Impact of Communication*. New York: Holt, Rinehart, and Winston.

Rosengren, Karl, and **Lawrence Palugreem** (eds.) 1985. *Media Gratifications Research: Current Perspectives*. Beverly Hills: Sage.

Salzman, Philip. 1993. 'The Electronic Trojan Horse: Television in the Globalization of Para-Modern Cultures.' Presented at the Plenary Session '*Societies, Evolution and Globalization*,' Thirteenth International Congress of Anthropological and Ethnological Sciences, Mexico City.

Schramm, Wilbur. 1964. *The Mass Media and National Development*. Palo Alto: Stanford University Press.

Schramm, W., Jack Lyle and **Edwin Parker.** 1961. *Television in the Lives of Our Children*. Palo Alto: Stanford University Press.

Schwartz, Howard and **Jerry Jacobs.** 1979. *Qualitative Sociology: A Method to the Madness*. New York: Free Press.

Sháh, A.M. 1974. *The Household Dimension of the Family in India*. Berkeley: University of California Press.

Sháh, A.M. and **I.P. Desai.** 1988. *Division and Hierarchy: An Overview of Caste in Gujarat*. Delhi: Hindustan Publishing Corporation.

Sháh, A.M., B.S. Baviskar and **E.A. Ramaswamy.** (eds.). 1996. *Social Structure and Change (Vols. 2): Women in Indian Society*. New Delhi: Sage Publications.

Shankar, Prem. 1988. *Indian Village Society in Transition*. New Delhi: Commonwealth Publishers.

Sharma, Miriam. 1978. *The Politics of Inequality: Competition and Control in an Indian Village*. Hawaii: University Press of Hawaii.

Shingi, P.M. and **B. Mody.** 1976. 'The Communication Effects Gap: A Field Experiment on Television and Agricultural Ignorance in India.' *Communication Research*, 3: 171–90.

Shukla, S. 1979. 'The Impact of SITE on Primary School Children.' *Journal of Communication* 29: 99–103.

Singh, V.P. 1992. *Caste System and Social Change*. New Delhi: Commonwealth Publishers.

Singhal, A. and **E. Rogers.** 1989. *India's Information Revolution*. New Delhi: Sage Publications.

Sirsikar, V.M. 1970. *The Rural Elite in a Development Society: A Study in Political Sociology*. Delhi: Orient Longman.

Spradley, James. 1979. *The Ethnographic Interview*. London: Holt, Rinehart, and Winston.

———. 1980. *Participant Observation*. London: Holt, Rinehart, and Winston.

Srinivas, M.N. 1966a. *Social Change in Modern India*. Cambridge: Cambridge University Press.

——— 1966b. *India's Villages*. Bombay: Asia Publishing House

Srinivas, M.N. 1976. *The Remembered Village*. Berkeley: University of California Press.

———. 1994. *The Dominant Caste and Other Essays*. Delhi: Oxford University Press.

Srinivas, M.N. and A.M. Sháh. 1960. 'Myth of the Self-Sufficiency of the Indian Village.' *Economic Weekly* 12: 37.

Srinivas, M.N., A.M. Sháh and E.A. Ramaswamy (eds.) 1979. *The Field Worker and the Field: Problems and Challenges in Sociological Investigation.* Delhi: Oxford University Press.

Srivastava, R. 1979. *The Developmental Dimension of Domestic Groups in India*. New Delhi: Books Today.

Streeton, Paul and Javed Burki. 1978. 'Basic Needs: Some Issues.' *World Development* 6 (3): 411–21.

Surgeon General's Scientific Advisory Committee on Television and Social Behavior. 1971. *Television and Growing Up: Report to the Surgeon General, U.S. Public Health Service*. Washington D.C.: U.S. Government Printing Office.

Trivedi, Harshad. 1991. *Mass Media and New Horizons: Impact of TV and Video on Urban Milieu*. New Delhi: Concept Publishing Company.

Unnikrishnan, Namita and Shailaja Bajpai. 1996. *The Impact of Television Advertising on Children*. New Delhi: Sage Publications.

Valunjkar, T.N. 1966. *Social Organization, Migration and Change in a Village Community*. Pune: Deccan College.

Vilanilam, John. 1989. 'Television advertising and the Indian Poor.' *Media Culture and Society* 11: 485–97.

Wade, Robert. 1988. *Village Republics: Economic Conditions for Collective Action in South India*. Cambridge: Cambridge University Press.

Walker, Thomas and James, G. Ryan. 1990. *Village and Household Economics in India's Semi-arid Tropics*. Baltimore: The John Hopkins University Press.

Weber, Max. 1958. *The Religion of India*. New York: Free Press.

Whyte, William. 1984. *Learning from the Field*. Newbury Park: Sage Publications.

Williams, Tannis. 1986. *The Impact of Television: A Natural Experiment in Three Communities*. Orlando: Academic Press.

Wiser, William and Charlotte Wiser. 1971. *Behind Mud Walls*. Berkeley: University of California Press.

Zelliot, Eleanor. 1970. 'Learning the Use of Political Means: The Mahars of Maharashtra,' in Kothari, R. (ed.) *Caste in Indian Politics*. New Delhi: Orient Longman.

Index

About the Author

A unique blend of east and west, Dr Kirk Johnson spent over thirteen years of his childhood in rural India. An Assistant Professor of Sociology at the Univerity of Guam in the Western Pacific, Dr Johnson received a master's degree in Sociology and another in International Studies from Ohio University in Athens, Ohio. He later traveled to Montreal, Canada where he received his Ph.D. in Sociology from McGill University. Dr Johnson's areas of research and interest include development and social change, globalization, mass media, culture and ethnic relations.